The Homocysteine REVOLUTION

MEDICINE FOR THE NEW MILLENNIUM

Kilmer S. McCully, M.D.

Foreword by Andrew T. Weil, M.D.
Introduction by Walter C. Willet, M.D.

KEATS PUBLISHING
LOS ANGELES
NTC/Contemporary Publishing Group

The Homocysteine Revolution is intended solely for informational and educational purposes, and not as medical advice. Please consult a medical or health professional if you have questions about your health.

Library of Congress Cataloging-in-Publication Data

McCully, Kilmer S.
The homocysteine revolution : medicine for the new millennium / Kilmer S. McCully ; foreword by Andrew T. Weil.
p. cm.
Includes bibliographical references and index.
ISBN 0-87983-975-9
1. Arteriosclerosis—Etiology. 2. Homocysteine—Pathophysiology. 3. Vitamin B6—Physiological effect. 4. Folic acid—Physiological effect.
RC692.M33 1997
616.1'36071—dc21 96-29882
CIP

Published by Keats, a division of NTC/Contemporary Publishing Group, Inc. 4255 West Touhy Avenue, Lincolnwood, Illinois 60646-1975 U.S.A.

Printed and bound in the United States of America
International Standard Book Number: 0-87983-975-9
10 9 8 7 6 5 4 3 2 1

The Homocysteine REVOLUTION

To Annina

Contents

Foreword

Andrew T. Weil, M.D.

Medical detective stories are always fascinating, and Dr. Kilmer McCully has written a good one. Beginning with the chance observation that a young child with a rare inborn error of metabolism, dead of a stroke at age eight, had advanced arteriosclerosis, Dr. McCully describes his growing fascination with homocysteine as the causative agent. Until recently, homocysteine was an obscure amino acid, known only as a product of the normal breakdown of dietary protein. In this book, Dr. McCully reveals how he came to believe that it might be involved in the genesis of the disease that kills and disables more people prematurely than any other.

Arteriosclerosis is a hardening and stiffening of arteries throughout the body, especially those in the heart, neck, and legs. One component of it is atherosclerosis, the deposition of fat and cholesterol in arterial walls. The resulting "plaques" narrow arteries, become calcified, and provide sites for abnormal blood clots to form, often leading to medical catastrophes: heart attacks, strokes and amputated legs. Human beings are peculiarly susceptible to these degenerative processes in their arterial lifelines, and human beings in modern Western societies seem most at risk. My personal belief is that we are not destined to die of complications of arteriosclerosis in our forties, fifties and sixties. Such calamities are obviously a consequence of lifestyle in affluent nations and should be avoidable if we had better information about the factors involved in the underlying disease.

For several decades the medical establishment has focused on dietary fat and serum cholesterol as the key factors in atherosclerosis. A profusion of nonfat and low fat foods fills shelves of supermarkets, and the pharmaceutical industry has made a fortune selling cholesterol-lowering drugs. Nevertheless it appears that the origins of atherosclerosis and degenerative disease of the arteries are multifactorial, so that addressing serum cholesterol alone is not sufficient. Certainly there is no shortage of theories about other causative factors.

One theory holds that vitamin C deficiency is responsible, because that vitamin is needed for the making of healthy connective tissue, including that in the linings of arteries. According to the theory, plaque formation is actually the body's attempt to repair damaged areas of weakened artery walls. It would explain why humans and other primates are at risk for coronary heart disease, while most other animals are not; primates have lost the ability to synthesize vitamin C.

Another theory assigns a causative role to toxic emotions, especially anger and feelings of rage when frustrated. Recent research suggests that emotional factors may overshadow dietary ones in determining risk of heart attacks, but the cholesterol camp generally discounts this point of view.

Now there is the homocysteine theory. Elevated serum

homocysteine appears to be an independent risk factor for arterial disease. Questions remain about its importance relative to other factors, and good long-term studies need to be done to test the theory. The good news is that serum homocysteine, in most people, can be lowered with much less effort than serum cholesterol. A daily B-complex vitamin supplement, providing adequate amounts of folic acid and vitamins B6 and B12, will do the job. I do not think, however, that taking supplemental B-vitamins excuses us from attending to the other aspects of lifestyle that influence the risk of cardiovascular disease and premature death from heart attack.

In addition to explaining the genesis and nature of the homocysteine theory, Dr. McCully, one of its chief architects, also chronicles the remarkable resistance to the theory that he encountered until recently. His story offers a telling glimpse into the politics of medical research, and illuminates the tortuous way by which new ideas gain the attention of the medical establishment.

In this book Kilmer McCully also sketches new ramifications of the homocysteine theory, suggesting possible involvement of that amino acid in the causation of many other chronic diseases, including cancer. Again, I suspect that such diseases are multifactorial, with homocysteine possibly playing a role. Only research, including long-term studies of preventive strategies, will answer these questions.

The dietary and lifestyle recommendations that follow from the theory are sound. We should be eating more fresh fruits and vegetables, more whole grains, much less meat and other animal foods and much less processed food. Such changes will probably increase health and longevity for a number of reasons, including effects on the metabolism of homocysteine.

The Homocysteine Revolution contains a great deal of

information that will be new to most physicians and patients. This book will certainly stimulate discussion of a theory that is now gaining much greater attention from the world of medical science. It may even encourage medical investigators to initiate long term preventive studies for definitive proof of the homocysteine theory. Nevertheless it is not too early for all of us to apply the practical suggestions that Kilmer McCully makes to protect ourselves from arteriosclerosis and the other diseases of lifestyle that are so destructive to our society.

Tucson, Arizona
January 1997

Introduction

Walter C. Willet, M.D.

For nearly a century, diet has been considered an important cause of atherosclerosis and its consequence, heart attack. For most of this period, saturated fat and cholesterol have been held to be the responsible culprits, and their reduction has been the focus of dietary advice to the public. Kilmer McCully has indeed led a revolution because his work, and that of others inspired by his leads, has provided powerful evidence that widespread nutritional deficiencies are an important cause of heart disease in this country. Not surprisingly, this notion encountered great resistance, in part because nutritional dogma had maintained that deficiencies did not exist in the U.S.

Dr. McCully's initial observations began with an eight-year-old child with a rare genetic disorder who died of widespread and severe vascular disease similar to that of older adults. Through a series of astute observations, McCully pieced together biochemical and pathological documentation that high blood levels of homocysteine, a normal building block of protein, were responsible for the vascular disease. He then asked whether less extreme elevations in blood homocysteine levels such as those commonly found among apparently well individuals might, over several decades, increase risks of premature heart disease. An answer to this question required the expertise of epidemiologists, who study large populations for long periods of time. Only recently have such studies become available, and they have provided remarkably consistent confirmation of McCully's prediction that persons with higher blood levels of homocysteine have greater risks of heart disease. In contrast to the difficulty many individuals experience in reducing blood cholesterol levels, elevated homocysteine levels can usually be reduced with small amounts of folic acid and vitamins B-6 and B-12, either by improvements in diet or by taking an inexpensive multiple vitamin.

Dr. McCully carefully points out that many factors, including smoking, overweight and inactivity, also influence risk of coronary heart disease. Findings that homocysteine is among these factors do not negate the negative impact of saturated fat, although it is now apparent that replacing saturated fat with carbohydrate has at most a small benefit. Indeed, one of the important contributions of the homocysteine theory is that it has encouraged researchers to consider a wide range of dietary factors that could accelerate or delay the development of heart disease. Evidence has accrued that several of these, including some antioxidants, specific types of fatty acids and fiber, may also be important.

At what point does the homocysteine theory of heart disease developed by Dr. McCully become a fact rather than a theory? Although numerous lines of evidence strongly support the homocysteine theory, the most direct proof would be confirmation by one or more large trials in which individuals are randomized to a placebo or a combination of vitamins to lower homocysteine levels. Several such studies are now under way and may provide this level of proof. However, clear findings from such trials are not assured because they may not be of sufficient duration and also because beginning in 1998 our national food supply has been fortified with folic acid to reduce risk of birth defects.

For an individual, however, a prudent course is to act now and consume an adequate amount of folic acid and vitamins B-6 and B-12 on a daily basis. The sad fact is that Americans, on average, have been consuming only about half the current RDA for folic acid, mainly due to over-consumption of "empty calories" in the form of over-refined flour, animal fats and sugar, and insufficient intake of fruits and vegetables. Even with the recent fortification of flour, average intakes of folic acid will still be inadequate. Dr. McCully provides the outline for a diet that will not only help keep homocysteine levels low, but also is consistent with an overall healthy—and pleasurable—way of eating. For many of us, the optimal diet is difficult to maintain because of travel and eating away from home; thus a multiple vitamin, which is safe and inexpensive, provides a nutritional safety net.

Rarely do books combine an intriguing plot, in this case a fascinating scientific detective story, with information that can be of great personal value. Moreover, this is also the story of a personal struggle by a brilliant physician against a powerful and rigid scientific establishment. Although his career suffered setbacks, Dr. McCully continued to pursue his work on homocysteine, which is finally gaining its deserved appreciation. All this makes *The Homocysteine Revolution* a very special book.

combinations of vitamins to lower homocysteine levels. Several such studies are now under way and may provide the level of proof. However, clear findings from such trials are not assured because they may not be of sufficient duration and also because beginning in 1998 our national food supply has been fortified with folic acid to reduce rates of birth defects.

For an individual, however, a prudent course is to act now and consume an adequate quantity of folic acid and vitamins B6 and B12 on a daily basis. The sad fact is that Americans, on average, have been consuming only about half the current RDA for folic acid, mainly due to excessive consumption of "empty" calories in the form of overrefined flour, nutrient-poor fats and sugar and insufficient intake of fruits and vegetables. Even with the recent fortification of food, average intakes of folic acid will still be inadequate. Dr. McCully provides the outline for a diet that will not only help keep homocysteine levels low, but also is consistent with an overall healthy—and pleasurable—way of eating. For many of us, the optimal diet is difficult to maintain because of travel and eating away from home; thus a multiple vitamin, which is safe and inexpensive, provides a prudent [illegible].

Perhaps the best books combine an intriguing plot—in this case a fascinating scientific detective story—with information that could be of great personal value to every reader. This is also the story of a personal struggle by a brilliant physician against a powerful and dogmatic scientific establishment. Although his career suffered setbacks, Dr. McCully continued to pursue his work on homocysteine, which is finally gaining its deserved appreciation. All this makes *The Heart Revolution* a very special book.

Acknowledgments

I am indebted to the members of the Human Genetics Unit of the Massachusetts General Hospital, especially to John Littlefield, Vivian Shih and Harvey Levy, who introduced me to homocystinuria and excited my interest in the pathological findings in this newly discovered disease. I thank Giulio Cantoni and Harvey Mudd for introducing me to the arcana of methionine and homocysteine during my two years in their laboratory at the National Institutes of Health. Benjamin Castleman, Robert Scully, and James Caulfield are acknowledged for their support and for helping me to understand the pathology of arteriosclerosis. I gratefully acknowledge Louis Fieser, Paul Zamecnik, B.F. Skinner, Lewis Engel, James Bonner, and Konrad Bloch for encouraging my interest in medical research during my student years. During my fellowship years, Paul Zamecnik, Guido Pontecorvo, and James Watson skillfully guided me to a greater understanding and appreciation of molecular biology and microbial genetics. In developing my knowledge of the history of arteriosclerosis research, I was guided expertly by the unerring intellect and experience of Moses Suzman.

My interest in writing a book for the general reader was

first piqued during stimulating conversations with Stephen Raymond and Edward Gruberg, who wrote the first book on the homocysteine theory of arteriosclerosis. My scientific investigations were greatly aided by my collaborators, students, and technologists to whom I am grateful for their loyalty and dedication. In particular, Roberta Ricci, Pierre Clopath, Andrzej Olszewski, Marek Naruszewicz, and Michael Vezeridis were important contributors to the scientific studies. Finally, I am grateful to my friend and colleague, William Sunderman of the University of Connecticut, who helped me to chart a course through troubled waters.

The production and writing of this book were greatly facilitated by the expert editing by Phyllis Herman of Keats Publishing, Inc. and by Annette Francis of Bravo Books, Inc. For those details of obscure references and names I thank the resourceful Nicola Pallotti and Cheryl Banick of the Providence VA Medical Center library.

The Homocysteine REVOLUTION

CHAPTER 1

Medical Discovery

A Mysterious Case of Stroke in Childhood

In 1933, an eight-year-old boy was admitted to the Massachusetts General Hospital for the evaluation of four days of headache, drowsiness and vomiting. The boy was of Irish-American-ancestry and exhibited signs of retarded mental development. The lenses of both of the boy's eyes were dislocated, a congenital defect which interfered with his vision. One of the boy's brothers had a similar defect. Two weeks before admission to the hospital, the eight-year-old had been evaluated in the orthopedic clinic for a limp. The cause was found to be *coxa vara*, a congenital abnormality of the bone in the hip joint, which caused the leg to be shortened. After admission to the hospital, the boy's condition deteriorated severely. There were signs of a stroke, especially weakness and abnormal reflexes on the left side of the body. The blood pressure and temperature became elevated, but there were no signs of infection. Nothing could be done to prevent further deterioration of the boy's condition, and he died three days later.

After analyzing the boy's tissues, the pathologist established that the cause of death was arteriosclerosis of the carotid artery with cerebral infarct (hardening of the artery leading to the brain with death of brain tissue).

This obscure case, referred to as Case 19471, was published in the November 23 issue of the *New England Journal of Medicine* in 1933[1] and was subsequently forgotten for 32 years even though the findings were provocative. An apparently inherited abnormality of unknown cause was responsible for the death of an eight-year-old boy from a disease of aging, arteriosclerosis and stroke, usually found only in the elderly.

MEDICAL SLEUTH WORK

Thirty two years later, in 1965, a nine-year-old girl of Irish-American ancestry was evaluated at the pediatric clinic of the Massachusetts General Hospital because of slow mental development. The child's complexion was ruddy and flushed because of dilated blood vessels. The lenses of her eyes were dislocated, recalling several similar cases of a disease called homocystinuria, discovered just three years earlier in Belfast, Northern Ireland. These cases were identified by using new techniques to study the chemical composition of the urine of mentally retarded patients. In these cases, the urine was found to contain homocysteine, an amino acid derived from the normal breakdown of proteins in the body.

The young girl's mother told the pediatricians that an uncle had died suddenly of a similar disease in childhood over 30 years before and that the case was so unusual it was published in a medical journal. In searching the library, the pediatricians found the report describing Case

19471 in the November 23, 1933 issue of the *New England Journal of Medicine*.[1] This was the little girl's uncle.

The pediatricians took a sample of the young girl's urine to a laboratory for chemical analysis of amino acids, the basic building blocks of all the proteins of the body. By adding a few drops of the chemical sodium nitroprusside to detect homocysteine, the solution turned a deep magenta color. The test was positive for homocysteine.

By these laboratory tests the pediatricians verified that the nine-year-old girl with mental retardation had homocystinuria. They also concluded that her uncle, the eight-year-old boy who mysteriously died of a stroke in 1933, must also have had homocystinuria.

Cases of homocystinuria typically have mild mental retardation, tall stature, a ruddy complexion, light-colored hair and dislocation of the lenses of the eyes. The tall stature is caused by rapid growth in childhood, producing long legs, arms, fingers and toes. Many of the children with this disease die from blood clots developing in the brain, heart or kidneys, causing heart attack, stroke or kidney failure in childhood. The arteries in these cases are abnormal, with hardening and loss of elasticity of the artery walls.

"Chance Favors Only the Prepared Mind"—Louis Pasteur

In 1968 I had finally completed my many years of education, residency and fellowship in chemistry, medicine, biochemistry, molecular biology, genetics and pathology. After studying molecular genetics with the geneticist Guido Pontecorvo at Glasgow University in Scotland and with the discoverer of DNA structure, James Watson, at Harvard University, I completed my residency in pathology and was given an appointment and a research laboratory at Massachusetts General Hospital in Boston.

In order to study diseases of genetic origin, I decided to affiliate myself with the newly formed human genetics unit at the hospital. After several weeks of examining patients with genetic diseases, a case retrospectively diagnosed as homocystinuria was presented by the pediatricians. The fascinating story was told of the eight-year-old boy who had died of a stroke 35 years earlier. I decided to look at the pathology of the case because of the unusual feature of death in childhood from a disease previously attributed to aging. Was there a connection between abnormal homocysteine formation, blood clots and blood vessel disease in this boy?

By chance, I had a background of knowledge about homocysteine and other amino acids containing sulfur. Several years previously I had worked on amino acids and protein formation in the liver with Dr. Giulio Cantoni at the National Institutes of Health in Bethesda. In 1952 Cantoni had discovered adenosyl methionine, an important trace substance that is required for protein formation and other chemical reactions in the body. He found that this compound is formed from ATP, the source of chemical energy in the body, and methionine, with the help of enzymes in the liver. Methionine is an amino acid containing sulfur that is found in all proteins. Proteins are made up of 20 different amino acid building blocks. Methionine is chemically closely related to homocysteine. Adenosyl methionine, Cantoni's compound, transfers a carbon atom in the form of a methyl group to the sulfur atom of homocysteine to form methionine. This complicated process was later found to require the action of vitamins B12 and folic acid. During my two years in Cantoni's laboratory there were lengthy discussions about how adenosyl methionine and homocysteine function in the body.

Studying Homocystinuria

I had not even heard of homocystinuria that day in 1968 when the pediatricians presented the story of the eight-year-old boy to the human genetics group. The disease had been discovered only six years earlier by medical investigators in Belfast, Northern Ireland. Simultaneously cases of homocystinuria were discovered in Madison, Wisconsin and in Philadelphia by George Spaeth, an ophthalmologist who was a classmate of mine from Harvard Medical School. Spaeth had discovered homocysteine in the urine of one of his patients with congenital dislocation of the lenses. Still another physician, Dr. Harvey Mudd, had studied several more of these cases in Cantoni's laboratory at the National Institutes of Health. Mudd and his associates had shown that in homocystinuria the liver is unable to dispose of homocysteine normally because of a genetic error in the liver enzyme cystathionine synthase.

Spaeth and his associates had found that in some patients with homocystinuria the amount of homocysteine in the urine was dramatically decreased by moderately large doses of vitamin B6. The liver enzyme that Mudd had shown was abnormal in homocystinuria cases requires vitamin B6 for normal activity. This enzyme normally converts homocysteine to cystathionine, which is further processed in the liver to cysteine, another sulfur amino acid, and sulfate, for eventual excretion in the urine.

Because I knew something about homocysteine from

my experience in Cantoni's laboratory and because I wanted to use my new skills and knowledge as a pathologist, I decided to restudy the landmark case from 1933. After reading about it in the *New England Journal of Medicine,* I looked in the pathology department files for other data on the case. I found several original slides and a small lump of paraffin blocks containing tissues from the young boy. The blocks were melted together because they had been stored for many years in the hot attic of the old Allen Street building, long since demolished.

The paraffin blocks were remelted, separated and reprocessed by the pathology technicians to make a new set of glass slides for examination by microscopy. In viewing the slides, I confirmed what a pathologist had observed 35 years earlier. The walls of the carotid arteries leading to the brain were severely thickened and damaged by arteriosclerosis, a form of hardening of the arteries. Blood clots prevented blood from reaching the brain of the child, causing death of the right half of the brain.

This disastrous blood vessel disease had caused a stroke and killed the boy with what I now knew to be the newly discovered disease, homocystinuria. In addition to changes in the carotid arteries, I also found scattered, widespread changes in virtually all of the small arteries of the body. It was obvious to me that in some way the genetic error in this disease produced significant changes in all of the arteries. In addition, these changes looked to me, as a newly minted pathologist, very similar to the changes wrought by ordinary arteriosclerosis I had found in many of the elderly patients I saw during my residency.

There were many questions to be answered. How did I know that the hardening of the arteries was caused by the disease homocystinuria? Was there an effect on cholesterol and fat? Why was there no cholesterol deposited in the walls of the child's arteries? Was this disease of the blood vessels the same disease, arteriosclerosis, that is found in elderly people without homocystinuria? Did the genetic error in the liver enzyme of this child cause changes in other vital processes in the body? What had other medical scientists discovered about a connection between homocysteine and arteriosclerosis?

I learned that doctors in Belfast and in London had studied 10 cases of children affected by homocystinuria.[2] They found that many of these children had died from blood clots in the brain, heart and kidneys. They showed that hardening of the arteries resulting from fibrous plaques and loss of elasticity was of major importance in these cases and they considered that an indirect effect of abnormal methionine processing in the liver could have been the cause. Other doctors had found that the blood platelets, which contribute to blood clotting, are abnormally reactive in homocystinuria.

A group of doctors at Johns Hopkins Hospital in Baltimore also found that blood clots and thickening of the artery walls produced heart attacks and strokes in their patients with homocystinuria.[3] In describing the thickening of the artery walls, they also emphasized their severe loss of elasticity. Borrowing some of the slides from the cases from Belfast and from Johns Hopkins for comparison, I found that the changes in the arteries were identical to those in the 1933 case.

Neither group of doctors had used the term "arteriosclerosis" to describe the changes they found in the arteries of children with homocystinuria. Neither group related the changes in the arteries to the hardening of the arteries found in elderly people without homocystinuria. In fact, in the 1933 case, the pathologist had compared the changes in the arteries of the eight-year-old boy with the arteriosclerosis that he found in elderly patients without this inherited disease. By reading about these cases, it became obvious that children with homocystinuria have a severe disease of the arteries. It was not clear, however, how homocystinuria could produce changes in the arteries resembling arteriosclerosis without affecting cholesterol, lipoproteins or fats in the blood and in the artery walls.

MEDICAL DISCOVERY

Some time later, at a human genetics conference, a case of homocystinuria in a two-month-old baby boy was presented. The important difference from previous cases was that, in addition to homocysteine, this child was found to have another substance related to homocysteine, called cystathionine, in his urine. This finding indicated that the abnormality of the liver that was found in cases at the National Institutes of Health could not explain the liver abnormality in this baby.

By deciphering the baby's exact liver abnormality, the doctors discovered a new, previously unknown disease in which a different liver enzyme is abnormal.[4] This enzyme (methyltetrahydrofolate homocysteine methyl transferase) was unable to transform homocysteine into methionine using vitamin B12. A normal liver performs this conversion easily and rapidly. The new abnormality explained the presence of both homocystine and cystathionine in the baby's urine. In this boy the enzyme that is abnormal in other cases of homocystinuria was found to be normal, accounting for his liver's ability to produce cystathionine. Unfortunately, despite all of their efforts to treat the baby's disease with vitamin B12, vitamin B6, and another B vitamin, folic acid, he died within several days.

After hearing about the child, I immediately recalled the interesting case of homocystinuria documented in 1933, and decided to examine the autopsy protocol and tissue slides taken from the deceased baby. I predicted that the baby's blood vessels would show thickening of the artery walls caused by arteriosclerosis. If homocysteine, the amino acid itself, damages the arteries, the baby's arteries would manifest the same changes in the arteries as in the 1933 case. If the arteries were normal in the baby, then homocysteine must act indirectly to produce the arterial changes in patients with homocystinuria,[2] as doctors had theorized in 1965.

Rushing back to the pathology laboratory, I quickly located the report of the baby's autopsy. The protocol had been completed several weeks before, filed away and forgotten. I looked for the description of the arteries and was crestfallen to find that the report said nothing whatsoever about the arteries. To make matters worse, I knew that the resident who had completed the report was a very capable and conscientious doctor. However, some fat droplets were reported in the cells of the liver, and there were peculiar changes in the lining of the stomach. The resident's description of the biochemical abnormality in this new type of homocystinuria,[4] was detailed, accurate and well-written.

However, I was determined to find out what the baby's arteries looked like. Because of the severe liver disease and pneumonia in the lungs, the child had grown very little since birth and his organs were small. My fellow resident had carefully preserved all of the organs in a jar of formalin. I decided to restudy this case as carefully as I had studied the case from 1933. After the technicians had prepared a large collection of slides from the organs, I began to examine them carefully and systematically, making notes about the details of my findings.

Studying the arteries, I became very excited to discover that the changes of arteriosclerosis were there after all! Evidently my fellow resident had not examined the blood vessels carefully enough in preparing his autopsy report. He had not found severe damage to the arteries because he was not looking for these significant changes as I was.

I knew immediately that this discovery was extremely important and that I could investigate its significance because of my background of knowledge in biochemistry and molecular biology. I was so excited by this medical discovery that I had difficulty sleeping for almost two weeks. During that period, I woke up daily before sunrise thinking about what I had seen and how it related to my knowledge of homocysteine, arteriosclerosis and cholesterol. I had proven that in these rare genetic diseases, at least, the amino acid homocysteine caused damage and hardening of the arteries by a direct effect on the cells and tissues lining the arteries.

New Questions

If homocysteine causes damage to the arteries in children with rare inherited diseases, what does this discovery imply for the general population? In the 1950s and 1960s heart disease and stroke had reached epidemic proportions, becoming the number-one cause of death in America. Surely, the millions of people with heart disease could not all have rare inherited diseases that caused homocysteine to show up in the urine.

I wanted to find out how homocysteine is related to cholesterol and arteriosclerosis. The leading theory in

1968 was that a buildup of cholesterol in the "bad" form, low-density lipoprotein (LDL), somehow causes cholesterol to be deposited in the walls of the arteries. Both LDL and the "good" form of cholesterol, high-density lipoprotein (HDL), had been studied in the 1940s and 1950s at the University of California and at the National Institutes of Health in Bethesda. These studies had shown that a high level of LDL carried a high risk of developing heart disease. Similarly, a high level of HDL carried a degree of protection against developing heart disease. How does homocysteine fit into these theories?

Searching my memories from medical school, I recalled a lecture on the role of cholesterol in heart disease 13 years earlier, in 1955. At that time doctors at the Harvard School of Public Health had been studying cholesterol and experimental arteriosclerosis in monkeys. As I recalled, they had found that feeding the amino acid methionine to monkeys in a synthetic diet had caused the level of cholesterol in their blood to decline.[5] These investigators believed that this effect might have been beneficial in preventing cholesterol deposits from forming in the walls of the arteries. In contrast to this interpretation, I had found that a close chemical relative of methionine, homocysteine, was clearly causing damage to the arteries in children with homocystinuria.

A problem with the experiments with monkeys was that pure methionine was toxic when given in high doses. The animals lost weight, refused to eat normally and looked sickly. Because the animals could not eat their toxic diet, they could not eat the large amounts of cholesterol that were also included in it. When the monkeys' arteries were examined, no definite conclusion could be reached regarding whether methionine actually prevented or caused damage to the arteries. Because the doctors used a purified soy bean protein preparation, they believed that a deficiency of methionine could explain their results.

What was the effect of feeding homocysteine in its double form, homocystine, to experimental animals? Medical investigators at Duke University had done such a study in rats[6] several years earlier. They had found that, just as in the study in which methionine was fed to monkeys, homocystine in the diet caused the rats to lose weight and become sickly. Nothing was found in examining their tissues to suggest that homocystine damages the arteries in this type of experiment. The tissues looked like those of a starving animal except that deposits of iron were found in several organs. It was as if the added homocystine prevented the animals from eating altogether.

In discussing my findings and conclusions about homocysteine and arteriosclerosis with a biochemist colleague, we recalled a study of arteriosclerosis and vitamin B6 that had been published 20 years earlier.[7] Dr. James Rinehart and his associates at the University of California in San Francisco had published several papers showing that a partial deficiency of vitamin B6 in a synthetic diet fed to monkeys caused arteriosclerotic changes in the arteries if the experiment was carried out for a prolonged period, usually 6 to 18 months. Biochemists in Russia had discovered that the liver enzyme that converts homocysteine to cystathionine needs vitamin B6 for its action. Harvey Mudd had found that this enzyme is abnormal in children with homocystinuria. George Spaeth had found that some children with homocystinuria respond dramatically to moderately large doses of vitamin B6, preventing a buildup of homocysteine in their blood and urine. Could Rinehart's monkeys with vitamin B6 deficiency have had a buildup of homocysteine that damaged their arteries?

It was difficult to explain how homocysteine relates to

cholesterol in causing damage to arteries. In the first place, the children with different types of homocystinuria had normal blood cholesterol levels. Secondly, Rinehart's monkeys with vitamin B6 deficiency and arteriosclerosis had normal cholesterol levels. Finally, the investigators at Harvard School of Public Health had repeated Rinehart's experiments with vitamin B6 deficiency in monkeys and had found no evidence of cholesterol deposits in the arteries. They had prepared a diet that was so deficient in vitamin B6 that their monkeys lost weight, became anemic and died within several months before changes in the arteries could be detected.

At about this time, I was asked to describe the pathological findings in an interesting case at a clinical pathology conference. The discussion was held in the Ether Dome, where the use of ether had first been demonstrated publicly for surgical anesthesia. This was also the auditorium where 35 years earlier the case of the eight-year-old boy with arteriosclerosis (and later identified as homocystinuria) had been discussed. During the conference, a visiting cardiologist from South Africa, Dr. Moses Suzman, asked several interesting questions about my discussion of the pathological findings.

After the conference I met and chatted with Dr. Suzman, who was interested in my study of arteriosclerosis in children with homocystinuria. By this time, I was preparing my findings for publication in the *American Journal of Pathology*. Dr. Suzman told me that he knew James Rinehart when they were both research fellows at the Boston City Hospital. Rinehart had been trying to produce cirrhosis of the liver in monkeys by making them deficient in various vitamins. His experiments initially failed to produce cirrhosis, but he discovered that vitamin B6 deficiency caused arteriosclerosis if carried out for long enough periods of time. Dr. Suzman told me that in his practice in South Africa he routinely gave vitamin B6 and other vitamins to his cardiac patients because of Rinehart's discovery. Using this approach, Suzman's patients did extremely well, losing their symptoms of chest pain on exertion, increasing their exercise tolerance, improving their electrocardiograms and their diabetes and reducing their risk of heart attack.

Publication

In preparing my study for publication, I read several articles by doctors from Toronto who had been working with choline, trying to understand how this substance influences fat buildup in the liver. They had found that a deficiency of choline in the diet of rats caused arteriosclerotic changes in the rats' arteries and fat buildup in the liver.[8] Choline, a component of lecithin, was the same substance that had been studied in the 1930s, when it was learned that choline supplemented homocysteine in replacing methionine in growth experiments with animals. This finding of arteriosclerosis from choline deficiency raised the possibility that the arteriosclerotic changes were caused by a buildup of homocysteine in the rats' blood.

In the original publication of my medical discovery on homocysteine and arteriosclerosis, I concluded that homocysteine damages the arteries by a direct effect on the arterial cells and tissues of children with homocystinuria caused by two different genetic defects.[9] I went on to pose the question, "Is it possible, for example, that in patients with hereditary, dietary, environmental or other predisposition to arteriosclerosis—such as that observed in those who have diabetes, hypothyroidism, hypertension, radiation injury or who smoke cigarettes—damage to the arteries develops as the result of homocysteine build-up?" Finally I hypothesized that arteriosclerosis was caused by elevated blood homocysteine levels that were presumed to occur in vitamin B6-deficient monkeys and in choline-deficient rats.

It seemed obvious to me that this discovery was of tremendous potential importance in understanding the basic cause of arteriosclerosis in the general population. When I sent the manuscript for publication in 1969, it was accepted by the editor immediately without changes. I was astonished to receive hundreds of requests for reprints of this paper in succeeding weeks. Evidently, there were medical scientists all over the world who were interested in a new approach to understanding heart disease and arteriosclerosis.

Confirmation of the Discovery

Following the discovery of a significant new scientific or medical observation and interpretation, a period of questioning inevitably ensues. Other investigators who are knowledgeable in the field need time to read and understand the potential significance of the new observation. During the period of questioning, several basic issues are considered by other scientists. First and foremost, is the basic observation correct and valid? Second, is there independent evidence from a distinct but related set of observations that confirms the basic observation? Third, is the interpretation of the significance of the new observation reasonable and in accordance with other principles of medical science? Finally, do the basic observation and its interpretation suggest other independent means of proof and confirmation of the new discovery?

The essence of the new discovery in the case of homocysteine and vascular disease is the interpretation that, regardless of its cause, elevation of blood homocysteine causes arteriosclerosis by damaging the cells and tissues of the arteries. In the most frequently encountered form of homocystinuria, an abnormal liver enzyme (cystathionine synthase) causes elevation of blood homocysteine because the conversion of homocysteine to cystathionine (transsulfuration) is blocked. Damage to the arteries and arteriosclerotic changes in this disease were well described in the 1933 case[1] and in the cases from Belfast[2] and from Johns Hopkins.[3]

The form of homocystinuria caused by the abnormal liver enzyme (methyltetrahydrofolate homocysteine methyl transferase) that uses folic acid and vitamin B12 to convert homocysteine to methionine is much rarer. The first case in the world literature[4] of this form of homocystinuria (cobalamin C disease) was the key case that led to my discovery of the damaging effect of homocysteine on artery walls.[9] Because of its rarity, several years passed before the changes in the blood vessels in a second case were reported.[10] In this case, the changes in small blood vessels, especially arterioles, were found only in the brain. Nevertheless, this case was important because it confirmed my basic observation of arterial damage in the first reported case. Another five years passed before similar arterial damage was found in a third case (from Switzerland) of this rare form of homocystinuria.[11] These cases are important because they confirmed the basic observation that I had reported in 1969.

Another even more significant confirmation of my discovery of the relation between homocysteine and vascular disease was described in a third type of homocystinuria.[12] In this disease an abnormal liver enzyme (methylenetetrahydrofolate reductase) fails to convert folic acid to the form that is required for conversion of homocysteine to methionine by remethylation. In this case (from Chicago) damage to the arteries and arteriosclerosis were found to be virtually identical with that found in the other two types of homocystinuria. This independent confirmation of the connection between elevated blood homocysteine, vascular damage and arteriosclerosis in a third type of homocystinuria is particularly significant. This finding enabled one to conclude that in all of the three principle types of inherited homocystinuria, elevation of blood homocysteine causes arterial damage and arteriosclerosis regardless of the particular liver enzyme that is abnormal.

In the most frequent form of homocystinuria, cystathionine synthase deficiency, vitamin B6 is effective in correcting the abnormal metabolism of methionine and preventing elevation of blood homocysteine in about one-half of the cases. In the next most frequent form of homocystinuria, methylenetetrahydrofolate reductase deficiency, the B vitamin folic acid corrects the metabolic abnormality and prevents elevation of blood homocysteine in some cases. In the rarest form of homocystinuria, methyl transferase deficiency, vitamin B12 usually has little effect on the metabolic abnormality because of difficulties with absorption and function of vitamin B12 in the liver. In two of these three different types of an uncommon genetic disease, at least, therapy with specific vitamins offers some promise of preventing the arteriosclerosis associated with elevated blood homocysteine levels.

Questions and Initial Reaction

Is elevation of blood homocysteine significant to individuals with arteriosclerosis in the general population who do not have a form of homocystinuria? Is it possible that otherwise normal individuals may carry a silent genetic defect in the heterozygous form of a homocystinuria gene that may predispose them to elevation of blood homocysteine? Does the homocysteine approach imply that large segments of the population may have partial deficiencies of vitamins B6, B12 and folic acid? Is therapy with B vitamins a reasonable approach to prevention or treatment of arteriosclerosis in the general population? Can these provocative observations on the cause of arteriosclerosis in rare genetic diseases suggest ways to prove and to confirm the basic medical discovery by other independent means? What is the significance of homocysteine in regard to the cholesterol/lipid theory of causation of arteriosclerosis?

The initial reaction to my publication and lectures about the relation of homocysteine to arteriosclerosis took different forms according to the interest of the readers or audience. There was cautious acceptance of the idea that elevation of blood homocysteine was in some way the cause of vascular disease in the patients with homocystinuria. However, there was doubt that the vascular disease was indeed identical with arteriosclerosis as it is seen in the general population. In particular, the failure to find cholesterol crystals or lipid deposits in the arteries or elevation of blood cholesterol in children with homocystinuria made it especially troublesome for many to accept this discovery as relevant to arteriosclerosis as it is more commonly found. Finally, the suggestion that an amino acid, rather than cholesterol or fat, could be atherogenic, actually causing arteriosclerotic plaques, seemed difficult for many experts to accept.

Among those doctors and medical scientists who responded directly to publication of the discovery, several had specific knowledge about amino acid metabolism and vitamins B6, B12 or folic acid in disease processes. Several logical questions were asked about the effect of homocysteine on cells, tissues and metabolic processes in general. For example, there was an excellent question about whether the drug isoniazide could exacerbate vascular disease by causing elevation of blood homocysteine in patients who are given this drug for tuberculosis. Isoniazide is known to antagonize the action of vitamin B6, and some side effects of the drug are controlled by vitamin B6 supplements. Years later it was found that many drugs, including isoniazide, elevate blood homocysteine. In addition, the response of medical scientists with an interest in vascular disease and knowledge of amino acid metabolism indicated that they understood the potential benefit of this radically new approach to understanding the underlying cause of arteriosclerosis in the population.

From their questions and comments, it was apparent that doctors and medical scientists who adhered to the traditional cholesterol/fat concept of the cause of vascular disease were dubious about the significance of the new discovery. Since there was no indication of abnormality of cholesterol, lipids or fat metabolism in children with homocystinuria, how could this observation have implications for vascular disease in the general population? At this early stage, there was no public criticism of the new approach by adherents of the cholesterol/fat hypothesis. It seemed prudent for me to await developments in understanding of the connection between homocysteine and the cholesterol approach before discussing these questions in my publications. Besides, my knowledge of the biochemistry and pathophysiology of cholesterol, steroid hormones and fats would enable me to explore and understand the connection to homocysteine in the years to come.

A few medical authorities, both in the cholesterol field

and in the homocystinuria field, privately denounced the new homocysteine approach to understanding arteriosclerosis. They perceived that the fundamentally different nature of my new discovery threatened to undermine the conventional view of prevention and treatment of arteriosclerosis.

The vast majority of the medical community, however, totally ignored the new homocysteine theory, either because they had little knowledge of this complicated area of biochemistry and metabolism or because they believed there was too little evidence for the theory in previously published research. They believed that the homocysteine theory was of little general interest because it seemed to be applicable directly only to rare genetic diseases of little consequence to arteriosclerosis as it occurs in the general population.

IMPLICATIONS OF THE DISCOVERY

Why is the suggestion that elevated homocysteine levels cause arteriosclerosis a radical departure from the conventional concept of this disease? Does this new discovery force the medical community to rethink previously accepted theories about the underlying cause of arteriosclerosis? How does the homocysteine theory alter the strategy of public health experts for preventing arteriosclerosis? What are the implications for treatment of patients with heart attack, stroke, kidney failure or gangrene by the medical profession?

The primary implication is that arteriosclerosis is attributable to abnormal processing of protein in the body because of deficiencies of B vitamins in the diet. The homocysteine theory predicts that populations are at risk of the disease because the methionine of dietary protein is not prevented from forming excess homocysteine. This new theory predicts that a dietary imbalance between too much methionine from protein and a deficiency of vitamins B6, B12 and folic acid is the underlying cause of death and disability from vascular disease.

The homocysteine approach is radically different from the traditional view which relates arteriosclerosis to dietary consumption of excess fats and cholesterol. In the conventional view, the arteries are believed to be damaged by a buildup of cholesterol in the LDL component of plasma coupled with a related lowering of the HDL component. The view of the homocysteine theory is that arteries are damaged by the injurious effect of homocysteine on cells and tissues of arteries, setting in motion the many processes that lead to loss of elasticity, hardening and calcification, narrowing of the lumen and formation of blood clots within arteries. The homocysteine theory considers arteriosclerosis a disease of protein intoxication. The cholesterol/fat approach considers the disease to be caused by intoxication from fats.

If the underlying cause of arteriosclerosis were intoxication from eating too much fat and cholesterol, prevention might be easily achieved simply by decreasing consumption of the offending foods that are rich in these substances. However, if the underlying cause of this disease were intoxication by homocysteine formation from dietary protein because of deficiencies of B vitamins, prevention could only be achieved by consumption of foods that provide a limited quantity of methionine and an abundant supply of vitamin B6, B12 and folic acid. In summary then, the homocysteine theory considers arteriosclerosis a result of dietary imbalance from partial vitamin deficiencies whereas the cholesterol approach incriminates the toxicity of dietary fats.

In a disease as complex as arteriosclerosis, many factors besides diet are known to interact and contribute to its development and progression. Some of these factors are aging, the male gender, postmenopausal status in women, familial predisposition, smoking and other toxins, lack of exercise, high blood pressure and thyroid disease. While some correlations between these factors and LDL and HDL levels have been uncovered, there are many cases of severe or fatal arteriosclerosis in which plasma cholesterol, LDL and HDL are quite normal.[13]

Within the past decade medical investigators have begun to study blood homocysteine levels in populations and in selected groups of persons at high risk for arteriosclerosis. The exciting news is that an explosion of studies and an avalanche of new findings have begun to confirm the validity of the homocysteine theory. For the first time, it has become possible to conclude that all of the factors known to be of major importance in arteriosclerosis do in fact affect blood homocysteine levels in the ways predicted by the theory.

The further exciting news is that a young or middle-aged person who is interested in preventing vascular disease can use the homocysteine theory to reduce risk of arteriosclerosis in his or her later years. For the person with early or established vascular disease, the homocysteine approach offers a promising alternative to the traditional approach to medical therapy. Studies are currently under way in many medical centers and clinics to assess the potential benefits of the homocysteine approach to patients with vascular disease.

Finally, recent developments have suggested that damage to the arteries by homocysteine may depend upon the way in which homocysteine is carried by the LDL of plasma.[14] This new understanding has the potential for uniting the extensive field of knowledge about cholesterol and fats with the insights of the homocysteine theory of arteriosclerosis.

In future years the beneficial influence of the homocysteine approach on health and longevity promises to be tremendous. Already the continuing major declines in the risk of stroke and heart attack since the mid 1960s in America have been related to increased vitamin B6 in the food supply.[15] Recent studies have suggested that the addition of folic acid to the food supply could save a minimum of 50,000 American lives each year from heart disease alone.[16] A well-coordinated future effort to supply foods to the population with the proper balance between protein and vitamins B6, B12 and folic acid is anticipated to have a major impact on health and life expectancy. Finally, as explained in succeeding chapters, individuals can now acquire the knowledge necessary to prevent devastating damage to the arteries in later years.

REFERENCES

1. Case Records of the Massachusetts General Hospital, "Case 19471. Marked cerebral symptoms following a limp of three months' duration." *New England Journal of Medicine* 209: 1063-1066, 1933.
2. Nina A.J. Carson, C.E. Dent, C.M.B. Field and Gerald E. Gaull, "Homocystinuria. Clinical and pathological review of ten cases." *Journal of Pediatrics* 66:565-583, 1965.

3. R. Neil Schimke, Victor A. McKusick, Thomas Huang and Abou D. Pollack, "Homocystinuria. Studies of 20 families with 38 affected members." *Journal of the American Medical Association* 193:711-719, 1965.
4. S. Harvey Mudd, Harvey L. Levy and Robert H. Abeles, "A derangement in B12 metabolism leading to homocystinemia, cystathioninemia and methylmalonic aciduria." *Biochemical and Biophysical Research Communications* 35:121-126, 1969.
5. George V. Mann, Stephen B. Andrus, Ann McNally and Fredrick J. Stare, "Experimental atherosclerosis in Cebus monkeys." *Journal of Experimental Medicine* 98:195-218. 1953.
6. John V. Klavins, "Pathology of amino acid excess. Effects of administration of excessive amounts of sulphur containing amino acids: homocystine." *British Journal of Experimental Pathology* 44:507-515, 1963.
7. James F. Rinehart and Louis D. Greenberg, "Arteriosclerotic lesions in pyridoxine-deficient monkeys." *American Journal of Pathology* 25:481-491, 1949.
8. W. Stanley Hartroft, J.H. Ridout, E.A. Sellers and Charles H. Best, "Atheromatous changes in aorta, carotid, and coronary arteries of choline-deficient rats." *Proceedings of the Society for Experimental Biology and Medicine* 81:384-393, 1952.
9. Kilmer S. McCully, "Vascular pathology of homocysteinemia: Implications for the pathogenesis of arteriosclerosis." *American Journal of Pathology* 56:111-128, 1969.
10. A.D. Dyan and R.B. Ramsey, "An inborn error of vitamin B12 metabolism associated with a cellular deficiency of coenzyme forms of the vitamin." *Journal of the Neurological Sciences* 23:117-128, 1974.
11. E. Regula Baumgartner, H. Wick, R. Maurer, N. Egli and B. Steinmann, "Congenital defect in intracellular cobalamin metabolism resulting in homocystinuria and methylmalonic aciduria." *Helvetica Paediatrica Acta* 34:465-482, 1979.
12. Yashpal S. Kanwar, Jose R. Manaligod and Paul W.K. Wong, "Morphologic studies in a patient with homocystinuria due to 5,10-methylenetetrahydrofolate reductase deficiency." *Pediatric Research* 10:598-609, 1974.

13. Kilmer S. McCully, "Atherosclerosis, serum cholesterol and the homocysteine theory: a retrospective study of 194 consecutive autopsies." *American Journal of the Medical Sciences* 299:217-221, 1990.
14. Marek Naruszewicz, Ewa Mirkiewicz, Andrzej J. Olszewski and Kilmer S. McCully, "Thiolation of low-density lipoprotein by homocysteine thiolactone causes increased aggregation and altered interaction with cultured macrophages." *Nutrition, Metabolism and Cardiovascular Diseases* 4:70-77, 1994.
15. Kilmer S. McCully, "The homocysteine theory of arteriosclerosis: Development and current status." In: Antonio M. Gotto, Jr. and Rodolfo Paoletti, editors, *Atherosclerosis Reviews*, volume 11 (New York: Raven Press, 1983), pp. 157-246.
16. Carol J. Boushey, Shirley A.A. Beresford, Gilbert S. Omenn and Arno G. Motulsky, "A quantitative assessment of plasma homocysteine as a risk factor for vascular disease. Probable benefits of increasing folic acid intakes." *Journal of the American Medical Association* 274:1049-1057, 1995.

CHAPTER 2

Understanding the Causes of Arteriosclerosis

Arteriosclerosis and Its Origins

Some of the earliest knowledge about arteriosclerosis came from dissections of the human body that were carried out by the anatomists of Renaissance Italy. Leonardo da Vinci, the famous Italian artist, engineer and scientist, is generally credited with the first of these dissections in the 15th century. Some years later, Andreas Vesalius, a member of a prominent Belgian medical family and a founder of modern human anatomy, described abnormalities that he found in the aorta and artery branches during his dissections of deceased human subjects in Venice and Padua in the 16th century. Even in this early period, the abnormalities of the arteries, later called arteriosclerosis, were related to social standing. In dissections performed in 18th century Holland, those persons with the most severe abnormalities were found to be from the wealthy classes of Dutch merchants or professionals.

In the 19th century two of the founders of modern medicine, pathologists Karl Rokitansky and Rudolf Virchow, began the systematic study of changes in the tissues of deceased persons. In 1842 Rokitansky published his comprehensive and influential handbook of the changes that he had observed in the tissues of people who died of many different diseases. In a later edition of that handbook he suggested that the elements of the blood, including blood clots and blood serum, formed layers on the internal lining of the arteries.[1] With time, these layers incorporated blood elements into a tough, hardened, calcified artery wall that characterizes the striking changes of arteriosclerosis, according to Rokitansky.

In the mid- and late-19th century, Rudolf Virchow, the famous German pathologist who introduced microscopy of tissues to the study of pathology, offered his own version of the origin of arteriosclerosis.[2] He pointed out that in this disease the wall of the artery first undergoes a form of degeneration in which mucoid substances become deposited in the tissue. Then fatty substances from the blood enter the artery wall and become deposited, forming atheromas—raised swollen areas on the internal lining surface (intima) of arteries with arteriosclerosis. The inside of atheromas contains a porridge-like substance. The word *atheroma* is derived from the Greek words for porridge (*athere*) and swelling (*-oma*). The word atherosclerosis refers to the advanced form of the human disease characterized by multiple atheromas. Virchow also pointed out that arteriosclerosis, hardening of the artery wall, is caused by fibrous tissue and deposits of calcium salts. The word *arteriosclerosis* comes from the word *artery* and the Greek word for hardened (*sclere*).

In the 19th century the most common cause of death was infectious disease, especially pneumonia and tuberculosis. Virchow suspected that a type of infection or inflammation might contribute to arteriosclerosis. As evidence for this idea, he pointed out that cells associated with infections (leukocytes) are sometimes found in arteries with arteriosclerosis. He also likened the swellings of the artery wall, atheromas, to tumors of the blood vessels. He found that the cells of the arterial wall are stimulated in arteriosclerosis, thereby increasing in number and narrowing the channel within the artery.

DIET AND ARTERIOSCLEROSIS

In 1908, after learning the methods of tissue examination that were introduced by Rokitansky and Virchow, M.A. Ignatovsky, a young teacher in a military medical school in St. Petersburg, Russia, decided to apply these methods to investigating the cause of arteriosclerosis. Like the Dutch anatomists of the 18th century, he had observed that his patients with severe arteriosclerosis tended to be from the wealthy class, making their diet suspect. Doctors in England had also suspected the diet of the wealthy class, which contained a larger amount of meat, butter, eggs and milk than the diet of poorer classes. Ignatovsky decided to feed this type of high animal protein diet to rabbits to determine whether he could observe changes in the arteries similar to those of his patients with arteriosclerosis. The rabbit normally eats a diet without any animal protein, obtaining its protein entirely from grains and vegetables.

After feeding the animal protein diet to rabbits for several months, Ignatovsky found that the animals had developed hardening and plaques of the arteries and aorta. He demonstrated that these changes were very similar to the arterial plaques of patients with arteriosclerosis. Because of these findings, Ignatovsky suggested that a diet with abundant meat and dairy products could cause arteriosclerosis in his patients. In his publications he meticulously drew by hand beautiful illustrations showing the changes he had found in the rabbit arteries through direct examination and with his microscope. He published his findings in several prominent French, German and Russian medical journals.[3, 4] Infection could not explain the arterial changes, since no infectious agents were given to or found in his rabbits. Therefore, he suggested that it was the high protein diet that was responsible for the hardening of the rabbit arteries.

Several years later, at another medical school in St. Petersburg, two young doctors, Nikolai Anitschkov and S. Chalatov, became interested in Ignatovsky's findings. Previously, they had little success in producing arteriosclerosis in animals by injecting bacteria or by other methods. Although Ignatovsky had attributed his results to the protein in the meat and dairy products he fed the rabbits, the plaques in the rabbit arteries contained fats and cholesterol crystals. The German pathologist Ludwig Aschoff had also found cholesterol in human atheromas. The chemists of the late 19th century had isolated cholesterol in a pure form and determined its chemical structure. Anitsckow believed that the cholesterol in the meat and dairy products of the Ignatovsky diet could have produced the arteriosclerotic plaques in the rabbit arteries. Therefore, Anitschkov and Chalatov tried giving cholesterol to rabbits either mixed dry with rabbit chow or dissolved in vegetable oil.

After feeding rabbits this diet for several months, they found that the arteries of the animals developed the changes of arteriosclerosis similar to what Ignatovsky had observed. They found a great deal of fat and some cholesterol crystals in the artery walls. The liver and other organs also contained abundant fat and cholesterol, a condition known as cholesterolosis. They believed that Ignatovsky's results could have been produced by the cholesterol in the meat and eggs in his experimental diet and not by the animal protein. Their paper was published in a German medical journal in 1913.[5]

All of these studies, carried out in rival medical schools in pre-revolutionary St. Petersburg, clearly established that experimental arteriosclerosis could reliably be produced in animals by dietary manipulation. For the first time, the cause of arteriosclerosis could be related to a nutritional origin, replacing the somewhat vague concepts of causation by infection or inflammation that were inherited from the previous century. Of course, the results of the studies implied that arteriosclerosis in humans is also induced by nutritional modifications or abnormalities. It was not clear, however, from these early experiments, which factor or factors in the diet were responsible for the experimental disease in rabbits or for human arteriosclerosis and heart disease.

PROTEIN INTOXICATION AND ARTERIOSCLEROSIS

In 1922 Dr. Harry Newburgh, a full-time professor of clinical medicine and clinical research at the University of Michigan School of Medicine, began to devote a major portion of his efforts to his passion for clinical research on nutrition and the physiology of human disease.

Newburgh painstakingly reviewed the provocative results published by Ignatovsky, Chalatov and Anitschkov and other investigators of arteriosclerosis during the previous decade. He was intrigued that the disease arteriosclerosis could be induced in rabbits by manipulating their diet. He repeated the earlier Russian experiments and confirmed their results. He anticipated that a systematic investigation of the effect of meat protein would clarify the picture. He and his associates prepared lean beef muscle that was dried, powdered and extracted with solvents to remove all traces of fat and cholesterol. They fed increasing doses of the powdered meat protein to rabbits, along with white flour and bran. Newburgh found that the higher the protein content of the diet, the sooner and more severe were the arteriosclerotic changes in the rabbits' arteries.[6] Further experiments were needed to prove that some constituent of meat protein was producing these striking changes.

Newburgh reasoned that if meat protein in the diet produces arteriosclerosis in rabbits, he should be able to produce similar changes in the arteries by intravenously injecting one by one the individual amino acid components of protein into dogs or rabbits to discover which amino acid is the most damaging to the arteries. After these experiments were completed, he concluded that the arteries were not damaged by any single amino acid.

However, Newburgh discovered that cystine, the first amino acid to be identified in 1810 by William Wallaston, is toxic and very damaging to the kidneys when it is injected intravenously. (The name *cystine* is taken from the Greek word for bladder—*kystis*—because it was first isolated from human urinary bladder stones.) Cystine contains sulfur and is chemically related to homocystine, which does not occur in proteins. Several other amino acids in protein (lysine, histidine, tyrosine and tryptophan) also cause kidney damage when injected intravenously.[7]

Subsequent events explain why none of the amino acids of protein injected singly into animals was found to cause arteriosclerosis. The amino acid methionine, discovered in 1922 by Herman Mueller, and the amino acid homocysteine, discovered in 1932 by Vincent DuVigneaud, were not among the amino acids that Newburgh tested. At the time of his experiments, methionine was not known to be an essential component of proteins and homocysteine was completely unknown.

Newburgh's experiments were a "near miss" in medical science. If he had been able to give methionine or homocysteine by intravenous injection, the damaging effect of homocysteine on arteries would have been discovered in 1925! Nevertheless, Newburgh's discoveries were put to good use in treating patients with kidney failure and diabetes. The "Newburgh-Marsh low-protein diet" became the standard treatment for kidney failure until the introduction of artificial kidney dialysis and kidney transplantation over a generation later. Newburgh also introduced a low-carbohydrate, high-fat diet for treatment of severe diabetes in the era before the discovery of insulin.

VITAMINS AND ARTERIOSCLEROSIS

The first indication that a vitamin deficiency could be blamed for causing artcriosclerosis was the series of experiments with vitamin B6 deficiency in monkeys, as described in Chapter 1. In these experiments James Rinehart and his associates formulated a synthetic diet that contained no vitamin B6. After periods of vitamin B6 deficiency lasting 6 to 18 months, the monkeys' arteries were found to contain arteriosclerotic plaques characterized by loss of elasticity, hardening and narrowing of the lumen from fibrous tissue and deposits of mucoid substances containing tissue fluids.[8] Only with prolonged intermittent or partial deficiency of vitamin B6 were deposits of fats found in some of these plaques. When the synthetic diet contained added vitamin B6, no changes were observed in the arteries. Deficiencies of other vitamins did not cause arteriosclerotic plaques in monkeys.

Rinehart, like Virchow before him in the 19th century, suggested that mucoid degeneration is the earliest change in arteries with arteriosclerosis. He believed that fats from the blood plasma, including lipoproteins and cholesterol, could enter the artery wall and become deposited in association with the mucoid substance. In a meticulous study of the coronary arteries of persons who had died of arteriosclerosis and heart disease that was published in 1963, this sequence of events was generally confirmed in human subjects.[9]

Rinehart's results were independently reproduced and confirmed in dogs and monkeys at the Merck Institute.[10] Subsequent experiments in Japan also confirmed them, and the scientists there went on to show that the plaques induced by vitamin B6 deficiency regressed following intensive periods of vitamin B6 treatment.[11] The experiments with animals suggested that a widespread deficiency of vitamin B6 in the human population could be a factor in causing arteriosclerosis. Rinehart's early results suggested that the amount of vitamin B6 in human blood samples was suboptimal. Furthermore, the amount of vitamin B6 that was necessary to prevent weight loss in vitamin B6-deficient monkeys (50 mcg per kilogram of body weight) was considerably greater than that consumed by humans (20 mcg per kilogram of body weight) according to nutritional surveys.

Why was this significant discovery of the relation between vitamin B6 and arteriosclerosis neglected in the 1950s and 1960s? Although Rinehart related his findings to the importance of vitamin B6 in the breakdown of proteins, there was no theory which could explain why a vitamin deficiency produces changes in artery walls. Furthermore, vitamin–B6 deficient monkeys and dogs had normal blood cholesterol levels and only a small amount of fat and cholesterol was found in a few of the plaques of the arteries. When James Rinehart died in 1955, no investigator was able to continue his pioneering work.

When scientists at the Harvard School of Public Health took up the question of vitamin B6 and arteriosclerosis,[12] they made their animals so deficient in vitamin B6 that the animals lost weight, became severely anemic and died within 4 to 9 months. Rinehart had subjected his monkeys to intermittent periods of complete vitamin B6 deficiency or prolonged periods of partial vitamin B6 deficiency, allowing the animals to survive for periods as long as 23 months. Arteriosclerotic plaques require prolonged periods of intermittent or partial vitamin B6 deficiency of 6 to 12 months to allow the change in arterial cells and arterial elasticity and hardening to develop. Finally, vitamin B6-deficient animals develop plaques that are easily seen only by microscopy. The Harvard scientists used a method of staining with fat-soluble dyes to search for fatty plaques in the lining. Rinehart had found no fatty plaques there and neither did the Harvard scientists.

The seemingly minor differences between Rinehart's experiments and the Harvard experiments, however, led to a drastically different interpretation of their significance. The Harvard scientists concluded that vitamin B6 deficiency produces no arteriosclerosis in monkeys, even though their animals died of deficiency before the changes could have developed and the method they used to study the arteries would not have detected the significant changes Rinehart had found. Furthermore, the Harvard scientists could not accept the finding that arteriosclerotic plaques were developing in the monkeys without the apparent involvement of cholesterol and fats. The result of this contradictory interpretation of Rinehart's discovery was that other scientists lost interest and felt that this area of investigation was not promising.

Cholesterol, Fat and Arteriosclerosis

Since the early years of the 20th century, the prevailing theory about arteriosclerosis has been that cholesterol and fats in the diet are responsible for the buildup of cholesterol in the plasma and for the deposition of cholesterol in arteriosclerotic plaques.

Prompted by the demonstration of cholesterol crystals and fatty deposits in arteriosclerotic plaques by Ludwig Aschoff and by the finding of similar plaques in rabbits that were fed cholesterol by Nikolai Anitschkov, many medical scientists incriminated dietary cholesterol and fats in the causation of arteriosclerosis. Nutritional surveys of susceptible populations showed a general correlation between the fat content of the diet and the incidence of arteriosclerosis.[13] However, other surveys showed that consumption of dietary sugar, white flour and protein from foods of animal origin also correlated with the incidence of arteriosclerosis. Finally, a more detailed examination of dietary composition revealed a correlation between consumption of unsaturated oils of plant foods or fish with protection against arteriosclerosis.

The populations of Asian countries are less susceptible to arteriosclerosis than populations of western countries, suggesting that racial factors may be of importance in causing the disease. Early studies, however, showed that Asian populations consuming a Western diet, such as Americans of Japanese ancestry in Hawaii and California, developed increased cholesterol in the blood and increased risk of arteriosclerosis, compared with their relatives living in Asia. Indonesian stewards aboard Dutch ships were found to develop increased blood cholesterol and increased risk of arteriosclerosis after eating the Dutch diet.[13] These studies suggest that dietary factors are more important than racial factors in the cause of arteriosclerosis.

Another line of evidence supporting the correlation between elevated blood cholesterol and susceptibility to arteriosclerosis is derived from the study of genetic diseases affecting blood lipoproteins. The clearest example of such a disease is familial hypercholesterolemia, a rare condition occurring in one person per million. In this disease all cells of the body are unable to process and internalize LDL normally. As a result, the level of LDL and cholesterol in the blood becomes extremely elevated, leading to rapidly progressive and sometimes fatal arteriosclerosis.

Another example of a genetic disease affecting blood lipoproteins is dense LDL hypertriglyceridemia, in which small dense aggregated LDL particles are correlated with a high risk of arteriosclerosis. In yet another example, the condition affecting a group of individuals with familial dyslipidemic hypertension is believed to be of genetic origin. These individuals have small dense LDL particles, hypertension, diabetes mellitus and reduced HDL levels, greatly increasing their risk of arteriosclerosis.

In addition to familial diseases of cholesterol and lipoprotein processing and diets containing abundant fats, sugars and animal protein, other major factors contributing to human arteriosclerosis have been identified. These factors include advanced age, male gender, postmenopausal status, smoking and other toxins, hypertension, diabetes, hypothyroidism and lack of exercise. The influence of these major risk factors for arteriosclerosis on levels of blood cholesterol, LDL and HDL has been intensively studied for many years. The general results of these studies have shown that there is a correlation between these major risk factors and the elevation of LDL and total cholesterol and the decrease of HDL in the blood.

A problem with the risk factor approach is that a majority of individuals with arteriosclerosis have no abnormality of total blood cholesterol or lipoprotein fractions. Practicing physicians know that many of their patients with severe or fatal arteriosclerosis, including myocardial infarction, kidney failure or gangrene of the toes, have normal cholesterol and lipoprotein levels. Furthermore, no comprehensive theory has been developed which satisfactorily explains how arteriosclerosis risk factors affect cholesterol levels or how elevated LDL and decreased HDL levels initiate formation of arteriosclerotic plaques.

The development of a reliable and versatile clinical blood test for measurement of cholesterol in plasma (the Lieberman-Burchard test) greatly aided the study and understanding of the importance of cholesterol in human arteriosclerosis. The development of ultracentrifugation, electrophoresis and chromatography to determine blood lipoprotein fractions enabled medical scientists to explore and evaluate the importance of LDL, HDL and other lipoprotein fractions in the cause of arteriosclerosis.

In studying the formation of cholesterol in the body, scientists discovered that most of the cholesterol in the blood is formed by biochemical processes in the liver. Cholesterol is an important major constituent of the membranes of all cells of the body. Furthermore, cholesterol is needed for the production of the sex hormones estrogen and androgen in the ovary and testis. Cholesterol is also needed for production of stress and mineral hormones of the adrenal gland. Finally, cholesterol is excreted in the bile in the form of bile salts that are made from cholic acid, the degradation product of cholesterol, and two amino acid derivatives, glycine and taurine. The amount of cholesterol that is formed in the liver is carefully controlled and adjusted according to the needs of the different organs of the body. If the amount of cholesterol is increased in the diet, a healthy, well-functioning liver makes less cholesterol for the needs of the body. If the amount of cholesterol in the diet is decreased, the liver makes more cholesterol. In this way the body regulates very precisely how much cholesterol is produced for its needs.

OXIDATION, CHOLESTEROL AND ARTERIOSCLEROSIS

If cholesterol is produced within the body to make cell membranes, steroid hormones and bile salts, how could an excess of dietary cholesterol induce arteriosclerosis? In the 1950s the tantalizing clues that were uncovered by Ignatovsky, Newburgh and Rinehart to incriminate dietary protein receded into the background of medical thinking and were largely ignored because no theory could explain how protein intoxication or vitamin deficiency could produce arteriosclerosis. On the other hand, the cholesterol/fat approach became the favorite of the medical/pharmaceutical establishment because of the gradual development of knowledge in this field. Yet the cholesterol/fat hypothesis also needed a comprehensive theory to explain how cholesterol, a normal chemical constituent of the body, could, when overeaten in the diet, induce a generalized disease of the arteries by causing an increased level of LDL and a decreased level of HDL in the plasma. Two related questions are (1) how does a diet high in saturated animal fats promote arteriosclerosis and (2) how does a diet high in unsaturated plant or fish oils protect against the disease?

In trying to understand how cholesterol and lipoproteins of plasma could cause arteriosclerotic plaques, medical scientists considered the nature of these plaques as they occur in human disease and in experimental animals. In the early stages of human arteriosclerosis, a mucoid change occurs in the artery wall, and soon thereafter fatty substances from the plasma enter the artery wall, forming "lipid streaks." These early changes are seen as flat areas on the lining of arteries containing fats as demonstrated by fat-soluble stains. Wandering cells of the blood called monocytes enter the lining of the artery and take up lipoproteins, transforming them into "foam cells" that contain abundant fat droplets. As the disease progresses, however, changes in the artery wall occur to produce loss of elasticity and hardening caused by fibrous tissue and deposits of calcium salts. In later stages of human arteriosclerosis the calcified plaques of fibrous tissue give the walls of most affected arteries a tough, brittle, hardened consistency that is very difficult to cut either with scissors or with a scalpel blade. Only in the aorta and some large arteries do the excessive deposits of fats and proteins cause soft atheromas to become prominent. The idea that arteries in human arteriosclerosis are narrowed only by greasy fatty deposits is simply not true for most arteries. The main changes, as pointed out by Rokitansky, Virchow and other scientists in the 19th century, involve increased fibrous tissue and calcium deposits, making the artery wall hardened, brittle and tough, hence the name arteriosclerosis.

One of the problems with the cholesterol-feeding experiments of Anitschkov and similar experiments by other scientists is that the arterial plaques in the animals contained too much fat and cholesterol in comparison with the plaques found in the human disease. Another problem with the cholesterol/fat experiments is that the LDL fraction of lipoprotein is largely innocuous when injected directly into arteries or other tissues, failing to damage artery walls. Moreover, added LDL is not readily taken up by cell cultures of macrophages to form the foam cells that are known to be key players in the formation of arteriosclerotic plaques. Some further change seems to occur that makes the LDL of individuals with arteriosclerosis injurious to the lining surface of arteries. This change in LDL leads to the formation of foam cells, fatty streaks and subsequent transformation of these early abnormalities into advanced plaques that are brittle, tough and hardened by fibrous tissues and calcium deposits.

Early attempts to identify which component of LDL is injurious to artery walls led to the testing of many chemical relatives of cholesterol. A group of cholesterol compounds that contain extra oxygen atoms was found to be highly toxic when tested in cell cultures and in fragments of aorta maintained in culture.[14] Moreover, several of these oxidized cholesterol compounds, called oxycholesterols, produced injury to artery walls, deposition of fat and arteriosclerotic plaques when fed to rabbits. One of the most toxic and injurious of these oxycholesterols is cholestane triol, which contains three added oxygen atoms per cholesterol. Oxycholesterol was also found greatly to reduce cholesterol formation by cultured cells because of its toxic effects on the enzymes of these cells.

In a series of studies of oxycholesterols, medical scientists at Albany Medical College showed that highly purified cholesterol, chemically freed of all traces of oxycholesterols and protected from the oxygen of air, does not produce arteriosclerosis when administered to rabbits or monkeys.[15] The method that these scientists used to purify cholesterol was developed in the 1950s by Professor Louis Fieser, a prominent chemist at Harvard when I was a student in his organic chemistry course. He selected several of his students (including me) to help him develop this method. We added bromine to cholesterol to produce dibromocholesterol, which was highly purified by repeated crystallization. When the bromine was removed by acid, extremely pure cholesterol was then protected from the oxygen of air by storage under nitrogen gas in the deep freezer.

These experiments with oxycholesterols showed not only that these chemical derivatives are highly effective in producing arteriosclerosis in animals, but they also showed that highly purified cholesterol, freed of all traces of oxycholesterols and protected from the oxygen of air, does *not* injure the arteries of animals. This important discovery means that the experiments of Anitschkov and other scientists who had fed cholesterol to animals have to be reinterpreted. Unless these scientists took precautions to prevent the exposure of the cholesterol that they used in their experiments to the oxygen of air, their experiments could be interpreted as showing that oxysterol contaminants (other than cholesterol itself) were producing arteriosclerosis in their experimental animals. In addition, these oxycholesterols have been discovered in foods in association with fats of animal origin, particularly those foods which have been heated in the presence of air. Finally, these oxycholesterols have been discovered in the LDL fraction of human blood plasma and in the arteriosclerotic plaques of human arteries.

Modification of LDL by Arterial Cells

Following the discovery of the toxic effects of oxycholesterols, scientists studied the process by which LDL reacts with oxygen in the body. Experiments with cells cultured from arteries (endothelial cells, smooth muscle cells) and from blood (macrophages/monocytes) showed that these cells are able to add oxygen to LDL particles.[16] These living cells use oxygen in a way that causes LDL to become dense and to contain oxycholesterols, oxidized fats and oxidized proteins. In experiments using solutions without exposure to living cells, this modified LDL is formed by free radical oxygen damage in LDL samples that are incubated with copper or iron salts. Several compounds containing sulfur, including homocysteine, have been found to hasten this modification of LDL when solutions are exposed to the oxygen of air.

The experiments in which LDL is exposed to living cells in culture or exposed to metal salts in solution show that oxygen causes LDL to change into a form that is readily taken up by macrophanges to form foam cells in cultures. There is doubt, however, that this process occurs in this way in individuals with arteriosclerosis. Modified LDL does not occur in plasma, and antioxidant substances in plasma prevent formation of modified LDL. It is much more likely that LDL is taken up by arterial cells and that oxygen is added to LDL within these cells during the early stages of formation of arteriosclerotic plaques. Other experiments with animals have shown that there is a generalized disturbance in the way that all tissues of the body handle oxygen in arteriosclerosis.

The studies of Drs. Michael Brown and Joseph Goldstein in the 1970s showed that cells cultured from individuals with familial hypercholesterolemia lack a cell membrane receptor that is responsible for internalization and processing of LDL.[17] As the result of this failure to process LDL normally, extremely high levels of cholesterol and LDL build up in the blood of these individuals. The victims of this disease frequently develop heart disease and arteriosclerosis in their teens and 20s. These studies show that the receptor for LDL on cell membranes is an important factor in controlling how cells process and utilize the cholesterol and other consitituents of LDL.

The process by which cells take up LDL has been studied intensively by medical scientists because of the importance of foam cells in arteriosclerotic plaques. Wandering cells of the blood (monocytes) ordinarily take up very little LDL, as shown by experiments with cultures of these cells. When the LDL is first modified by artificial chemical reactions (such as acetylation or carbamylation), however, the cells eagerly take up modified LDL by means of a membrane protein called a “scavenger receptor.” As the result of this process, the cells take up abundant modified LDL and store cholesterol within their cytoplasm to form “foam cells.” In the progression of arteriosclerotic plaques, foam cells release cholesterol and fats into early plaques.

In advanced plaques, cholesterol crystals and fatty deposits are formed by the continued release of cholesterol and fats from foam cells. The artificial chemical modification of LDL is very unlikely to be of importance in human arteriosclerosis, however, since this chemical process does not occur in living cells and tissues.

While these studies of the interaction of LDL with cells and its modification by reaction with oxygen have illuminated important aspects of the formation of arteriosclerotic plaques, there remain many unanswered questions about the relation of these processes to the underlying causes of arteriosclerosis in the general population. What chemical modification of LDL occurs in human arteriosclerosis that leads to its internalization and formation of foam cells in early plaques? How do dietary fats and cholesterol affect the process of modification of LDL by the cells of developing arteriosclerotic plaques? Is there any relation between changes in LDL processing or LDL modification and the effects of protein intoxication on artery walls as studied by Ignatovsky, Newburgh and Rinehart? How can the process of LDL internalization and modification by reaction with oxygen within arterial cells be altered by dietary changes, drug therapy or other measures for the prevention or treatment of arteriosclerosis? Current scientific investigation of the cholesterol/fat hypothesis is focused on answering these questions.

BLOOD CLOTTING AND ARTERIOSCLEROSIS

An increased tendency to form blood clots within arteries, a process called thrombosis, is characteristic of human arteriosclerosis. During the progression of plaques, the blood clots that form in areas of damage to the arterial lining contribute to the narrowing of the artery lumen. Small blood clots that adhere to the surface of plaques gradually become incorporated into the plaque, increasing the thickness of the plaque over a period of weeks and months. In advanced arteriosclerosis, therefore, incorporated areas of blood clots, deposits of cholesterol and fats, fibrosis and deposits of calcium salts form complicated arteriosclerotic plaques. If this process is gradual and progressive, the function of vital organs is affected over a period of months or years. For example, when the arteries to the legs are gradually and progressively narrowed by these advanced complicated plaques, the amount of blood flow in the toes becomes progressively compromised and greatly diminished. The result of this process is that the tissues of the toes and feet gradually die, a condition known as gangrene. This painful condition is commonly treated by surgical grafting of artificial arteries in order to restore blood flow to the toes and feet. If grafting is unsuccessful, or if the arteriosclerosis is too far advanced for surgical therapy, amputation of the toes, foot or leg may become necessary because of pain and life-threatening gangrene. A similar progression of advanced arteriosclerotic plaques commonly affects the arteries leading to the brain, heart and kidneys, causing gradual loss of function of these vital organs.

A more dramatic and sudden effect of arteriosclerosis occurs when a large blood clot forms in an artery that is already severely narrowed by plaques. In the coronary artery a thrombosis of this type deprives a portion of heart muscle of blood flow, causing death of part of the heart. This condition results in acute heart attack, a complication known as acute myocardial infarction. Careful studies have shown, however, that complete coronary occlusion by thrombosis is the end result of a complex series of changes in the wall of the artery including degeneration of plaque contents, rupture of arterial wall tissue and bleeding into the affected plaque.[9] When the carotid artery to the brain is affected by sudden and complete occlusion by thrombosis at the site of advanced arteriosclerotic plaques, a stroke is caused by death of brain tissue.

The propensity for individuals with arteriosclerosis to develop blood clots which gradually or suddenly reduce blood flow in vital arteries has led to the use of anticoagulant drugs to control this complication. Aspirin is a drug that decreases the reactivity of blood platelets, the cell-like components of blood that are required for blood clotting. Population studies have suggested that small daily doses of aspirin may prevent the occurrence of thrombosis in individuals susceptible to coronary heart disease or stroke. Another approach is to use drugs, such as tissue plasminogen activator [TPA] or streptokinase, that activate plasminogen, a normal blood enzyme that helps to dissolve blood clots. These drugs help to limit damage to the heart or brain when given promptly after formation of an occlusive thrombus in a coronary or carotid artery. By helping to dissolve the blood clot that is occluding the artery, the blood flow is reestablished, reducing the size of the damaged area in the heart or brain.

The injury to arterial cells and tissues in the early stages of arteriosclerosis triggers complex cellular and molecular interactions, known as the response-to-injury hypothesis.[18] The injury of the lining cells of arteries triggers a reaction by blood-clotting factors and platelets that leads to the formation of fibrin, the principal component of blood clots. This reaction causes the platelets and arterial cells to release protein growth factors that stimulate growth of the muscle cells of artery walls. This injury also causes white blood cells to adhere to the site of injury, forming more foam cells and releasing more growth factors and other cell-signalling molecules called cytokines. The result of these complex interactions is increased growth of the muscle cells of the artery wall, production of fibrous tissue and ground substance by these cells and the deposition of fatty substances, including cholesterol, from LDL within the site of arterial injury.

Lipoprotein(a) is a genetically determined component of lipoprotein that has been found to be correlated with susceptibility to arteriosclerosis in several studies.[19] Because of its close chemical relation to the enzyme plasminogen, which normally controls blood clotting, lipoprotein(a) is widely assumed to be a factor in promoting blood clotting. Thus, because of its chemical composition and structure, this substance is likely to be involved both in the deposition of fats in arteriosclerotic plaques and in limiting the ability of the body to dissolve blood clots. The therapeutic action of streptokinase or tissue plasminogen activator in heart attack or stroke depends on activation of the plasminogen of blood plasma to dissolve blood clots. However, some doubt has been cast upon the importance of lipoprotein(a) in arteriosclerosis by failure to find an association between elevated lipoprotein(a) and risk of myocardial infarction.[20]

Shortcomings of the Cholesterol/Fat Approach

During its 80-year reign, the cholesterol/fat explanation of the cause of arteriosclerosis became, despite its many shortcomings, the favorite of the medical-pharmaceutical establishment. A reason for its wide acceptance is that it offers a general explanation for the correlation between elevated levels of LDL and decreased HDL and susceptibility to arteriosclerosis. The approach also offers a general explanation of the correlation between composition of the fatty constituents of the diet and susceptibility to the disease. It does not, however, address adequately the other correlations between susceptibility to arteriosclerosis and the consumption of animal protein and highly processed foodstuffs, including sugars and white flour. The approach also explains the experimental induction of elevated LDL levels and deposition of fat in arteriosclerotic plaques in experimental animals. Insufficient attention, however, has been paid to the key role of oxycholesterols in the experimental disease.

Some of the shortcomings of the cholesterol/fat approach are of major significance. Perhaps its most important failure is the lack of explanation for the rapid escalation of incidence of arteriosclerosis, heart disease and stroke during the mid-20th century in America and its subsequent dramatic decline beginning in the mid-1960s. Detailed studies of the composition of the American diet failed to reveal a correlation between cholesterol and fat content and the major changes produced by arteriosclerosis. In general, the fat and cholesterol content of the American diet has changed very little during recent decades which saw a two- to three-fold decline in the incidence of heart disease, stroke and other manifestations of arteriosclerosis. Moreover, there were no significant changes in blood levels of LDL and cholesterol during this period. Other factors, including changes in medical therapy and lifestyle factors such as smoking and exercise, cannot explain why the incidence of arteriosclerotic disease has declined.

Another related shortcoming of the cholesterol/fat approach is its failure to demonstrate a correlation between the cholesterol and fat composition of the diet and the level of LDL in susceptible populations as exemplified by the 50-year-old Framingham Heart Study. Experiments with animals also fail to demonstrate a correlation between dietary cholesterol and the level of cholesterol in the LDL of plasma. The feeding experiments in which cholesterol was added to the diet of animals were compromised by failure to consider the potent effects of the oxycholesterol contaminants of the added cholesterol.

In accordance with its position as the leading cause of mortality in America, arteriosclerotic heart disease and stroke have been the subject of intensive clinical investigation over the past four decades. Starting with the Heart-Diet Pilot and the Coronary Drug Project in the 1960s and 1970s, continuing with the Multiple Risk Factor Intervention Trial, the Coronary Primary Prevention Trial, and other studies of the 1980s, a tremendously expensive and detailed effort was made to evaluate the efficacy of cholesterol-lowering drugs, hormones, vitamins and diets in the prevention of coronary heart disease. During this long period of clinical trials, low-cholesterol/fat diets; a series of drugs such as cholestyramine, clofibrate, gemfibrizol, colestipol and lovastatin; hormones such as estrogens and dextrothyroxine; and the vitamin niacin have been evaluated for their ability to lower serum cholesterol and LDL levels and to raise the HDL level. While modest reductions in cholesterol or LDL were observed in some studies, the overall reductions in coronary heart disease and mortality have been slight or negligible in most studies. More recently, aggressive anti-cholesterol and anti-LDL therapy has been claimed to provide some evidence of modest regression of plaques, as shown by angiographic X-ray studies of coronary arteries.[21] Despite the decades-long effort by thousands of medical investigators, however, coronary heart disease stubbornly remains the leading cause of death in America, and aggressive diet and drug therapy have shown only marginal to modest efficacy in combating the disease.

At a practical level, physicians know that the majority of their patients with coronary heart disease, stroke and other forms of arteriosclerotic disease have no evidence of elevated cholesterol or LDL levels. In a study of 194 consecutive autopsy studies of mostly male veterans, for example, I found that only 8 percent of cases with severe arteriosclerosis had total cholesterol levels greater than 250 mg/dL, and the mean blood cholesterol level in the group with the severest disease was 186.7 mg/dL.[22] This study did confirm that cholesterol levels are positively correlated with severity of arteriosclerosis in patients with minimal, moderate or severe disease. In this study two-thirds of the patients with severe arteriosclerosis had no evidence of elevated blood cholesterol, diabetes or hypertension.

It is significant that the 80-year history of the cholesterol/fat approach has yet to provide a coherent and comprehensive scientific theory which explains in detail how cholesterol, a normal constituent of the body, or excess dietary fat in the diet of susceptible populations produces arteriosclerotic plaques. The current explanations of the modification of LDL[16] and the response-to-injury hypothesis[18] do not offer a comprehensive theory that links these pathogenic processes to known causative factors in the disease.

Recent epidemiological surveys have suggested that diets or supplements containing abundant vitamin E are of benefit in reducing the risk of coronary heart disease in both women and men.[23] Vitamin E is a potent fat-soluble antioxidant vitamin that may act by modifying the reaction of LDL with oxygen. Recent studies, however, have shown that another antioxidant vitamin precursor, beta-carotene, lacks a preventive effect on coronary heart disease, as predicted by the LDL modification hypothesis. Similarly, the findings that premenopausal women and postmenopausal women taking estrogens are protected against arteriosclerotic heart disease are not readily explained by the modified LDL hypothesis. No adequate epidemiological test of the response-to-injury hypothesis has yet been devised, so this explanation of the genesis of arteriosclerosis remains primarily a detailed description of cellular and molecular events in the progression of arteriosclerotic plaques.

Nutritional Deficiency and Arteriosclerosis

The entire history of the cholesterol/fat hypothesis explaining the cause of arteriosclerosis is based on the unproven assumption that the disease is produced by overconsumption of the normal dietary constituents cholesterol and fat. Only in the case of the oxycholesterols is there compelling evidence to suggest that a trace or contaminant constituent associated with fat and cholesterol in the diet is actually injurious and capable of initiating arteriosclerotic plaques. Overconsumption of cholesterol and fats in the diet, however, may be linked to concomitant underconsumption of nutritional constituents, in particular, the nonfat, water-soluble and indigestible fiber components of the diet.

The idea that vitamin deficiencies (vitamins B6, B12 and folic acid) could be responsible for or participate in the cause of the most common disease in America has not until recently been taken seriously by the medical community. Yet the overconsumption of fats, sugars and highly processed foods that are depleted of these vitamins is just the circumstance which could lead to widespread nutritional deficiencies of the water-soluble vitamins that are easily destroyed or depleted by food processing. In this way the concept of underconsumption of vital nutrients that are lost or destroyed in food processing, preservation or preparation is diametrically opposed to the assumption that overconsumption of a major dietary constituent could be the underlying cause of arteriosclerosis.

The cholesterol/fat approach has become so widely embraced for so long by the nutritional and food industry establishments that a different concept of the cause of arteriosclerosis has been difficult for many to accept. Because of the ingrained nature of conventional thinking, any approach based on other considerations, discoveries and theories that differ from conventional wisdom has been considered unthinkable and unacceptable.

The National Cholesterol Education Program of 1987 was founded by a consensus development conference on cholesterol and heart disease sponsored by the National Heart, Lung and Blood Institute of the National Institutes of Health in Bethesda in 1984. The focus of the recommendations of the "consensus conference" was to recognize that blood cholesterol, when elevated, increases the risk of arteriosclerotic heart disease. The National Cholesterol Education Program further went on to declare that dietary or drug therapy which succeeds in lowering blood cholesterol will reduce the burden of arteriosclerosis and heart disease in America. Nowhere in the proceedings of the "consensus conference" or in the National Cholesterol Education Program was there any consideration of the possibility that the underlying cause of the disease could be related to nutritional deficiencies. The idea that the food industry might cause the nation's number-one killer disease by creating a food supply that is seriously deficient in B vitamins has been considered preposterous by many.

The vitamin deficiency approach to the prevention of arteriosclerosis has until recently been regarded by the medical community as old-fashioned, ineffective, outmoded and without sufficient foundation in scientific evidence. The idea that expensive drugs or drastic diets to control elevated blood cholesterol could be ineffective in preventing vascular disease is generally considered unthinkable by the pharmaceutical-medical complex. The proposed comprehensive program of drug therapy to prevent elevated blood cholesterol levels in as many as 50 million individuals is potentially enormously profitable to the pharmaceutical industry. Moreover, recent efforts have been directed to another enormously profitable measure, using aggressive drug and dietary therapy in children in an effort to combat elevated blood cholesterol levels in childhood. The unproven assumption is that this strategy could prevent arteriosclerotic disease, especially coronary heart disease, in adulthood. In contrast, the vitamin deficiency concept of the cause of arteriosclerosis promises to be extremely effective without yielding excessive profits to the pharmaceutical companies that manufacture unpatentable, unprofitable and inexpensive vitamin additives to the food supply. This strategy will not allow the pharmaceutical industry to reap the bonanza of profits entailed in the anticholesterol drug market.

The risk factor approach has made important advances in understanding the relative importance of diet, family history, gender, smoking, lack of exercise, aging, obesity, diabetes, hypertension, elevated blood cholesterol and LDL and kidney failure in the causation of arteriosclerosis. However, this approach has not yet produced a coherent scientific theory that explains how these factors lead to and cause the arteriosclerotic plaques and blood-clotting abnormalities that produce the human disease. New thinking and new strategies, provided by the discovery of the connection between homocysteine and vascular disease as described in the chapter which follows, are needed to develop a scientifically coherent and persuasive theory of the underlying cause of arteriosclerosis in susceptible populations.[24]

REFERENCES

1. Karl Rokitansky, *Lehrbuch der Pathologische Anatomie*, Zweiter Band, Specielle Pathologische Anatomie (Wein: Wilhelm Braumuller, 1856), pp. 305-315.
2. Rudolf Virchow, *Die Cellularpathologie*, Dreite Ed (Berlin: August Hirschwald, 1862), pp. 351-360.
3. M.A. Ignatovsky, "Influence de la Nourriture Animale sur L'Organisme des Lapins," [*Archives of Experimental Medicine and Pathological Anatomy*] 20: 1-20, 1908.
4. M.A. Ignatovsky, "Uber die Wirkung des Tierischen Eiweisses auf die Aorta und die parenchymatosen Organe der Kaninschen," [*Virchow's Archive for Pathological Anatomy, Physiology and Clinical Medicine*] 198:248-270, 1909.
5. N. Anitschkov and S. Chalatov, "Uber experimentelle Cholesterinsteatose und ihre Bedeutung fur die Entstehung einiger pathologische Prozesse." *Centralblatt fur Allgemeine Pathologie und Pathologische Anatomie* 24:1-9, 1913.
6. L. Harry Newburgh and Sarah Clarkson, "The production of atherosclerosis in rabbits by feeding diets rich in meat." *Archives of Internal Medicine* 31:653-676, 1923.
7. L. Harry Newburgh and P.L. Marsh, "Renal injuries by

amino acids." *Archives of Internal Medicine* 36:682-711, 1925.

8. James F. Rinehart and Louis D. Greenberg, "Vitamin B6 deficiency in the Rhesus monkey with particular reference to the occurrence of atherosclerosis, dental caries and hepatic cirrhosis." *American Journal of Clinical Nutrition* 4:318-325, 1956.
9. G.R. Osborn, *The Incubation Period of Coronary Thrombosis* (London: Butterworths, 1963), pp. 1-143.
10. Charles W. Mushett and Gladys Emerson, "Arteriosclerosis in pyridoxine-deficient monkeys and dogs." *Federation Proceedings* 15:526, 1956.
11. Fumio Kuzuya, "Reversibility of atherosclerosis in pyridoxine-deficient monkeys." Proceedings of the 4th International Conference of Atherosclerosis (Berlin: Springer Verlag, 1977), pp. 275-277.
12. George V. Mann, "Blood changes in experimental primates fed purified diets: pyridoxine and riboflavin deficiency." *Vitamins and Hormones* 26:465-485, 1968.
13. Ancel Keys, "Coronary heart disease—the global picture." *Atherosclerosis* 22:149-192, 1975.
14. John D.B. MacDougall, S. Biswas and Robert P. Cook, "The effects of certain C27 steroids on organ cultures of rabbit aorta." *British Journal of Experimental Pathology* 46:549-553, 1965.
15. Hideshige Imai, Nicholas T. Werthessen, C. Bruce Taylor and K.T. Lee, "Angiotoxicity and arteriosclerosis due to contaminants of USP-grade cholesterol." *Archives of Pathology and Laboratory Medicine* 100:565-572, 1976.
16. Daniel Steinberg, Sampath Parthasarathy, Thomas E. Carew, John C. Khoo and Joseph L. Witztum, "Beyond cholesterol: Modifications of low-density lipoprotein that increase its atherogenicity." *New England Journal of Medicine* 320:915-924, 1989.
17. Michael S. Brown and Joseph L. Goldstein, "Expression of the familial hypercholesterolemia gene in heterozygotes: Mechanism for a dominant disorder in man." *Science* 185:61-63, 1974.

18. Russell Ross, "The pathogenesis of atherosclerosis: A perspective for the 1990s." *Nature* 362:801-809, 1993.
19. Angelo M. Scanu and Gunther M. Fless, "Lipoprotein(a). Heterogeneity and biological relevance." *Journal of Clinical Investigation* 85:1709-1715, 1990.
20. Paul M. Ridker, Charles H. Hennekens and Meir J. Stampfer, "A prospective study of lipoprotein(a) and the risk of myocardial infarction." *Journal of the American Medical Association* 270:2195-2199, 1993.
21. H. Robert Superko and Ronald M. Krauss, "Coronary artery disease regression. Convincing evidence for the benefit of aggressive lipoprotein management." *Circulation* 90:1056-1069, 1994.
22. Kilmer S. McCully, "Atherosclerosis, serum cholesterol and the homocysteine theory: A study of 194 consecutive autopsies." *American Journal of the Medical Sciences* 299:217-221, 1990.
23. Meir J. Stampfer, Charles H. Hennekens, JoAnn E. Manson, Graham A. Colditz, Bernard Rosner and Walter C. Willett, "Vitamin E consumption and the risk of coronary disease in women." *New England Journal of Medicine* 328:1444-1449; 1450-1456, 1993.
24. Kilmer S. McCully, "Homocysteine and vascular disease." *Nature Medicine* 2:386-389, 1996.

CHAPTER 3

Beyond Cholesterol: The Homocysteine Theory of Arteriosclerosis

Beyond Cholesterol

The failure of proponents of the cholesterol/fat approach to formulate a comprehensive coherent theory of the origin of arteriosclerosis is the principal reason that new discoveries and new thinking are desperately needed to understand the causes of the leading killer and disease in America. In addition, the most glaring inadequacies of the cholesterol/fat approach, failure to correlate disease with cholesterol or lipoprotein abnormalities in the majority of cases; failure to predict or explain dramatic increases and decreases in the incidence of arteriosclerosis; failure to relate dietary cholesterol to cholesterol levels in blood; failure to lower risk substantially by lowering cholesterol levels through diet, drugs and lifestyle changes all indicate an urgent need for a new, comprehensive and effective approach for prevention and treatment of arteriosclerosis.

The very beneficial reduction in the incidence of myocardial infarction since the 1960s in America has contributed to modest gains in life expectancy. Yet despite these favorable trends, arteriosclerosis remains the leading cause of death by coronary heart disease, stroke and kidney failure. Several years ago, a conference at the National Institutes of Health was unable to explain the decline in morbidity from coronary heart disease by changes in dietary fat and cholesterol, changes in blood cholesterol levels, changes in medical therapy or changes in smoking, exercise or other aspects of lifestyle.[1]

The favorable trend in the incidence of arteriosclerotic heart disease in the U.S. is not observed in all countries. In the countries of Eastern Europe in the post-communist era, there have been alarming increases in incidence of coronary heart disease. In Russia the life expectancy has fallen considerably, and coronary heart disease incidence has increased. There are similar alarming trends among the Japanese, who are experiencing increases in coronary heart disease, and among primitive peoples from various parts of the world. Asian populations, such as the Japanese, Chinese and Indonesians, and primitive peoples, such as the Eskimos and Bantus, have in the past been protected against arteriosclerosis because of their dietary traditions. Increases in heart disease among these formerly protected populations in recent years is very likely to have been caused by the introduction of the dietary practices of industrialized, developed countries. Increased consumption of meat, eggs and dairy products, together with increased reliance on highly processed and packaged foods, are widely believed to be at least partially responsible for this trend.

The traditional cholesterol/fat approach to the prevention and treatment of arteriosclerosis is based on the assumption that cholesterol and fats are toxic, producing damage via lipoproteins to artery walls. The prescription for preventing heart disease, according to this approach, is twofold. First, reduce dietary fat and cholesterol, and second, lower the blood levels of cholesterol and LDL. Advocates of this approach have suggested limiting total dietary fats to 30 percent of calories and consuming fewer than 300 mg per day of cholesterol.[2] If reduction of fat is beneficial, according to this approach, then even more drastic diets containing severely restricted fat and cholesterol should be even better. Such drastic diets have been shown to benefit persons with coronary heart disease and arteriosclerosis, causing apparent relief of symptoms[3] and modest evidence of reversal or regression of arteriosclerotic plaques.[4]

I suggest that a completely new approach to understanding the cause of arteriosclerosis is inherent in the medical discovery of the damaging effect of homocysteine on arterial walls and the production of arteriosclerosis in children with homocystinuria, as described in Chapter 1.

In the homocysteine approach, the underlying cause of the disease is interpreted as an imbalance between the methionine of dietary protein and the dietary intake of vitamins B6, B12 and folic acid that are necessary to prevent homocysteine accumulation in the cells and tissues of the body. The particular challenge in developing a new theory of arteriosclerosis, based on the medical discovery of the connection between homocysteine and arteriosclerosis, is to integrate the new findings with the vast body of knowledge about fats and cholesterol acquired in the past 80 years. The challenge is not to discard the cholesterol/fat approach, but to integrate past knowledge with new interpretations.

THE HOMOCYSTEINE THEORY OF ARTERIOSCLEROSIS

The development of the homocysteine theory of arteriosclerosis is based on the results of animal experimentation, the study of homocysteine in cells and tissues, and evidence from the study of human subjects and populations at risk of arteriosclerosis.[5] In essence the homocysteine theory relates the underlying cause of arteriosclerosis to a buildup of homocysteine in the blood caused by dietary, genetic, toxic, hormonal and aging factors in susceptible populations.

The importance of the homocysteine theory is that it explains many observations of the disease that cannot be explained by the cholesterol/fat hypothesis. Furthermore, the theory explains why the diet of developed, industrialized countries accelerates the age of onset and the pace of progression of the disease. Obviously, factors other than diet will vary among populations, but these factors cannot explain dramatic increases or decreases of disease incidence occurring within a single population. For example, genetic, hormonal and aging factors are relatively constant in populations that may experience two- or threefold changes in the incidence of the disease. These dramatic changes are attributable principally to changes in dietary factors.

The dietary factors that determine whether blood homocysteine levels are elevated are the total methionine content of dietary protein and the content of vitamins B6, B12 and folic acid in the diet. In the diagram of Figure 1, the conversion of homocysteine to methionine is controlled by vitamins B12 and folic acid, which remethylate homocysteine to methionine. This process is reversible, converting homocysteine back to methionine. The only source of homocysteine in the body is from the methio-

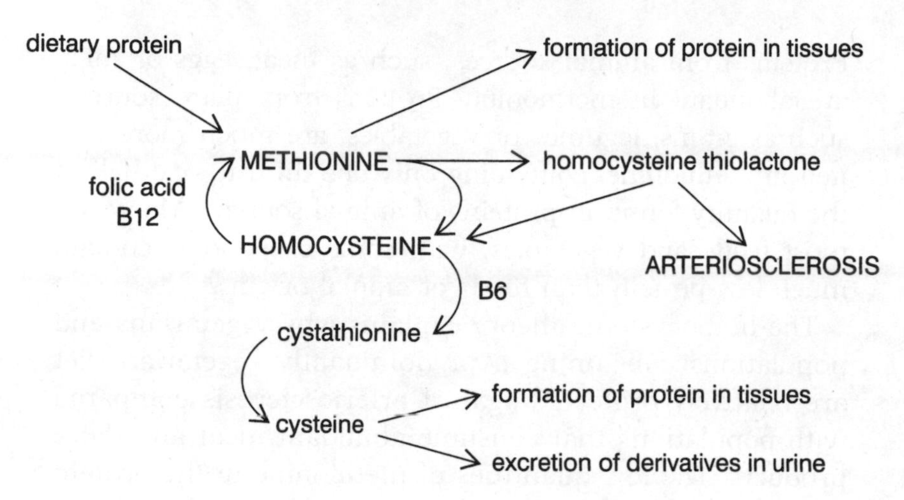

Figure 1. **Homocysteine in Cells and Tissues**

nine of dietary proteins. The conversion of homocysteine to cystathionine is controlled by vitamin B6. This process is irreversible, and the only way to dispose of excess homocysteine is by converting cystathionine to cysteine for excretion in the urine in the form of sulfate and other compounds containing sulfur.

Folic acid and vitamin B12 protect arteries against the damaging effect of homocysteine by conversion to methionine, which does not cause damage unless it is reconverted back to homocysteine. Vitamin B6 protects arteries by converting homocysteine to cysteine and other compounds that are excreted in the urine.

The amino acid methionine is present in all proteins. Methionine is known as an essential amino acid because all animals, including man, require a supply of methionine from dietary protein for proper growth and maintenance of all cells and tissues of the body. The only source of homocysteine is from the methionine of dietary proteins. Dietary proteins vary in the amount of methionine that they supply.

Proteins from animal sources, such as meat, eggs or milk, are abundant in methionine. Proteins from plant sources, such as grains, legumes or vegetables, are much more limited in methionine, containing only one third to one half of the quantity found in proteins of animal sources. Moreover, most fruits and vegetables, with some exceptions, contain much less protein than foods of animal origin.

The homocysteine theory explains why vegetarians and populations consuming a predominantly vegetarian diet are relatively protected against arteriosclerosis compared with populations that consume abundant meat and dairy products. The low quantities of methionine in the protein of plant-based foods put less strain on the body's resources for conversion of homocysteine to methionine or for excretion of homocysteine derivatives in the urine. In contrast, the high quantity of methionine in the protein of animal-based foods requires increased amounts of vitamins B6, B12 and folic acid to keep blood levels of homocysteine down to a safe range.

The homocysteine theory explains why the diets of industrialized, developed countries are so likely to hasten the onset and progression of arteriosclerosis. Vitamins B6, B12 and folic acid are each exquisitely sensitive to destruction by the harsh physical or chemical treatments involved in food processing, refining and preservation. In milling wheat into white flour, for example, 50 to 90 percent of vitamin B6 is destroyed.[6] Losses of vitamin B6 amount to 40 to 50 percent in canning meats and fish and 60 to 75 percent in canning vegetables. Losses of vitamin B6 from the freezing of vegetables average 15 percent. Losses of folic acid from cereals, dairy products, meats and vegetables range from 25 to 75 percent when fresh raw foods are compared with refined, processed and preserved foods. Vitamin B12 is obtained only from foods of animal origin, and the small amount of the vitamin required per day (3 micrograms) is easily supplied in most diets. Thus, strict vegetarian diets can on rare occasions lead to serious vitamin B12 deficiency. More commonly, elderly people or those with inflammation of the stomach fail to absorb sufficient vitamin B12 to prevent a borderline deficiency.

Losses of vitamin B6 and folic acid during the refining, processing and preservation of foods are likely to cause widespread marginal or frankly deficient dietary intakes in populations consuming a high proportion of calories from these foods. The homocysteine theory of arteriosclerosis attributes the origin of the disease to the inadequate dietary intake of vitamin B6 and folic acid and the consequent failure to prevent the damage to arteries caused by elevated blood levels of homocysteine. In primitive peoples or in other populations, such as in some Mediterranean countries where diets are rich in fresh or minimally processed foods, the likelihood of vitamin B6 and folic acid deficiency is negligible, the consumption of foods with abundant methionine is low, and the susceptibility to arteriosclerosis is also low.

Figure 2 illustrates the processes by which homocysteine causes arteriosclerosis. In the liver, methionine, obtained from the breakdown of proteins, is continually converted to homocysteine and back to methionine. This conversion process (remethylation) is dependent upon vitamins B12 and folic acid, and deficiencies of these vitamins lead to a buildup of homocysteine. A second process (transsulfuration), which converts homocysteine to cystathionine, cysteine and other compounds for excretion in the urine requires vitamin B6. Deficiency of vitamin B6 leads to a buildup of homocysteine because the body has no other way to eliminate excess homocysteine by excre-

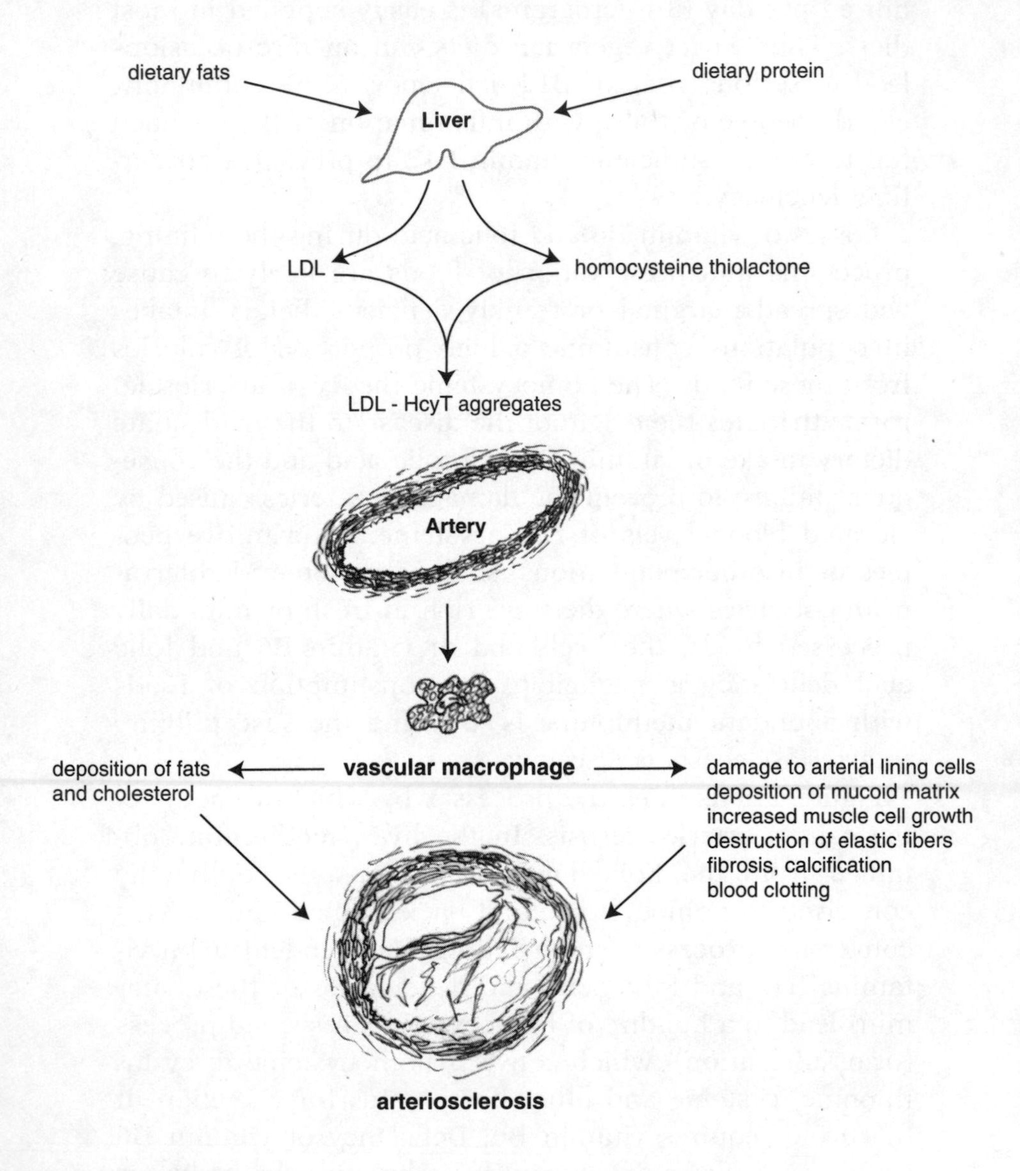

Figure 2. **Homocysteine Theory of Arteriosclerosis**

tion in the urine. Vitamins B6, B12 and folic acid must be obtained from food because, like other vitamins, the body cannot make these essential substances from other nutrients.

Current thinking about how homocysteine causes plaques in the arteries theorizes that a buildup of homocysteine in the body leads to overproduction of a highly reactive form of homocysteine that causes LDL to become aggregated.[7] This reactive form, homocysteine thiolactone, is made from methionine in the liver by an enzyme that participates in protein formation and by other less well-understood processes. The LDL-homocysteine thiolactone aggregates are released into the blood from the liver. Then these aggregates are taken up by macrophages of the artery wall, many of which are derived from wandering monocytes of blood, to form foam cells of early arteriosclerotic plaques. These foam cells degrade the LDL-homocysteine thiolactone aggregates and release fat and cholesterol into developing plaques. The foam cells also release homocysteine thiolactone into surrounding cells of the artery wall, affecting the way cells handle oxygen. As a result, highly reactive oxygen radicals accumulate within cells, damaging the lining cells of arteries, promoting blood clot formation and stimulating growth of arterial muscle cells which form fibrous tissue, mucoid matrix and degenerative elastic tissue.[8]

The homocysteine theory explains why populations that consume foods of animal origin with abundant methionine and foods that are highly processed, refined and preserved with depletion of B vitamins are susceptible to arteriosclerosis. Other factors, known as risk factors, are of major importance in influencing the onset and progression of the disease. As previously noted, these major risk factors include family history, advanced age, male gender, postmenopausal status, cigarette smoke and other toxins, certain drugs and hormones, diabetes and kidney failure, thyroid deficiency, hypertension, lack of exercise and elevated blood cholesterol. How do these factors control homocysteine and its damaging effect on arteries? Is there evidence that these major risk factors influence the way homocysteine is processed in the body?

Homocysteine and Genetic Risk Factors

A family history of early-onset heart disease is related to predisposition to the disease because of genetic inheritance from mother and/or father. As explained in Chapter 2, familial diseases of cholesterol and lipoproteins predispose to arteriosclerosis by causing extreme elevations of blood cholesterol or production of small, dense LDL particles in plasma. In recent years familial factors affecting homocysteine have been discovered among individuals with early-onset heart disease, stroke or peripheral vascular disease. In general, these familial or genetic factors cause greater susceptibility by increasing the quantities of dietary folic acid, vitamin B6 or B12 needed to prevent a buildup of homocysteine in the blood.

As explained in Chapter 1, deficiencies of three different enzymes are known to cause homocystinuria, elevation of blood homocysteine and generalized arteriosclerosis. When defective genetic copies of the DNA codes for one of these three enzymes are inherited from both parents, the pure form of the disease, known as the homozygous state, is produced in the affected child. When only a single defective genetic copy of the DNA which codes for one of these enzymes is inherited from one parent (a condition known as the heterozygous state), a mild or hidden form of the disease is produced in the affected child. While the full-blown disease, homocystinuria, is rare in the homozygous form (about 1 in 50,000 to 1 in 150,000), the mild or hidden form in the heterozygous state is much more common, about 1 or 2 per 100.

In the most common form of homocystinuria caused by homozygous deficiency of cystathionine synthase, about one-half of the children respond to moderately high doses of vitamin B6 by eliminating homocystine through the urine and by the reduction of blood homocysteine to normal levels. In the heterozygous or hidden state of the disease, blood levels of homocysteine may be normal. However, after receiving an oral dose of methionine, the precursor of homocysteine, the blood levels of homocysteine become more elevated after two to six hours than what is observed in normal individuals without this hidden genetic defect.

The heterozygous state for cystathionine synthase deficiency can also be detected by direct analysis of the abnormal enzyme function in cultured cells or in liver biopsy tissue. One early study failed to detect increased risk of heart disease in heterozygotes for cystathionine synthase deficiency. Recent studies have also failed to detect the heterozygous state of this defective enzyme in a small sample of familial, early-onset cases of arteriosclerosis, using molecular genetic analysis.[9] Studies are currently under way to detect the true incidence of defective genes for cystathionine synthase in the population, using direct analysis of the gene on chromosome 21 by methods of molecular biology.

The next most common cause of homocystinuria, as Chapter 1 explains, is the defective enzyme methylenetetrahydrofolate reductase. In the homozygous state, in which defective copies of this gene are inherited from both parents, the affected child has homocystinuria that responds to increased doses of folic acid. In addition, this genetic defect produces an unstable form of the enzyme that loses its normal activity when heated in a test tube experiment. In the heterozygous state, in which a single copy of the defective gene is inherited from one parent, a subtle hidden change causes a slight elevation of blood homocysteine and increased risk of coronary heart disease. Recent studies, using techniques of molecular biology, have estimated that the frequency of this heterozygous condition is as high as 38 percent among French Canadians.[10] The importance of these findings is that a significant proportion of the population requires an increased amount of dietary folic acid to prevent mild elevation of blood homocysteine.

The third type of genetic defect in homocystinuria, deficiency of methyl transferase, is quite rare, and there are no current estimates of the frequency of this defective gene in populations. Taken together, the hidden genetic factors, heterozygous cystathionine synthase deficiency and heterozygous methylenetetrahydrofolate reductase deficiency, have been estimated to be factors in one-third or more of cases of early-onset arteriosclerosis in which no abnormality of cholesterol or lipoproteins is found.[11, 12]

Homocysteine and Aging

One of the strongest risk factors for development of arteriosclerotic heart disease, stroke and peripheral vascular disease is aging. The overall risk and incidence of arteriosclerosis closely parallel the aging process, leading to the dictum, "you are as old as your arteries." The incidence and risk of all forms of arteriosclerotic disease are highly correlated with age. It is in the seventh, eighth and ninth decades of life that arteriosclerotic disease affects large segments of susceptible populations, strongly affecting life expectancy. Accordingly, declines in the rate of coronary heart disease and stroke since the 1960s in America have been correlated with modest increases in life expectancy.

The aging process affects the ability of the body to dispose of excess homocysteine. A number of studies have shown a gradual increase in blood homocysteine levels, starting in the seventh decade and increasing in the eighth and ninth decades, closely paralleling the aging process. Typically, the levels of blood cholesterol also rise gradually throughout adult life, reaching a peak in the seventh and eighth decades and levelling off or declining thereafter.

The factors that control blood homocysteine levels in aging are only partially understood. It is clear that food consumption declines with aging, and the dietary intake of vitamins B6, B12 and folic acid parallels this decline. As one ages, the ability to consume food and burn calories gradually declines. The decline in blood levels of vitamin B6 with aging is quite striking, leading to levels only one-fourth to one-third the levels found in babies and young children.[13] This major decline in vitamin B6 is only partially counteracted by vitamin B6 supplementation, suggesting that absorption and retention of the vitamin within the body are affected by the aging process. Folic acid and vitamin B12 levels also decline somewhat with aging, and dietary intake, absorption and retention of these vitamins are also affected by the aging process.

A recent survey of elderly subjects enrolled in the Framingham Heart Study showed that consumption and blood levels of vitamins B6, B12 and folic acid determine the elevation of blood homocysteine in an aging population.[14] The effect was particularly striking in the case of folic acid, where both low plasma levels and low intake of the vitamin were correlated with significant elevation of the level of blood homocysteine. The level of blood homocysteine was significantly correlated with age in the 67- to 96-year-old age groups.

Homocysteine and Elevated Blood Cholesterol

For many years elevation of blood cholesterol has been known as a major risk factor for arteriosclerosis. As explained in Chapter 2, the underlying causes for elevation of blood cholesterol in arteriosclerosis are insufficiently understood. Epidemiological and nutritional surveys have shown that dietary fat and cholesterol are related to blood cholesterol in a general way. Many other factors influence blood cholesterol, however, and these factors are also only partially understood. Dietary cholesterol causes the liver and other tissues to decrease their synthesis of blood cholesterol. When dietary cholesterol is decreased, the liver begins to make more cholesterol to keep the blood cholesterol at levels sufficient for the body's needs.

Drastic diets limiting fat content to less than 10 percent of calories and cholesterol to less than 200 milligrams per day have only partial success in lowering blood cholesterol and preventing or reversing arteriosclerotic heart disease, as explained in Chapter 2. Careful examination of these diets reveals a major reliance on foods of vegetable and fruit origin with emphasis on fresh, raw or minimally processed foods, and the quantities of dietary fats and sugars are strictly limited. These diets contain greater quantities of vitamins B6, B12 and folic acid than diets that rely on foods of animal origin, fats and sugars. Moreover, the switch from protein of animal origin to protein from plant sources limits the quantity of methionine that must be prevented from forming homocysteine by these three vitamins, as illustrated in Figure 1. Thus diets with drastically reduced calories from fats are those predicted to be beneficial by the homocysteine theory of arteriosclerosis.

How does limiting the dietary intake of the methionine found in animal protein and increasing dietary sources of vitamins B6 and folic acid help to prevent elevation of blood cholesterol? Experiments with animals have shown that homocysteine, in its reactive thiolactone form, is capable of increasing the formation of fats in the form of triglycerides and cholesterol in the form of low-density lipoprotein in the liver. Thus diets that emphasize less intake of methionine by consuming proteins of primarily plant origin and greater intake of vitamins B6 and folic acid from minimally processed or raw foods will decrease formation of homocysteine and its secondary effect on triglyceride and lipoprotein formation in the liver.

Dietary fats and dietary sugars of all kinds are examples of calorically rich, highly processed foodstuffs that contain no vitamins, minerals or proteins. For this reason fats and sugars are sometimes referred to as "empty calories." The greater the consumption of dietary fats and sugars, therefore, the greater is the reliance on the remainder of the diet to supply sources of vitamins B6 and folic acid. A diet that contains 40 percent of calories from sugars and 40 percent of calories from fats leads to a nutritional imbalance in which chronic deficiency of folic acid and vitamin B6 fails to prevent overproduction of homocysteine from the methionine of proteins. Such a diet also may contain excessive amounts of animal protein, leading to further buildup of homocysteine because of limited body stores of the essential B vitamins.

The homocysteine theory of arteriosclerosis explains why populations that consume a high proportion of dietary calories as fats, sugars and other highly processed, refined and preserved foods have increased risk of the disease. These diets also exacerbate the tendency of blood cholesterol and lipoprotein levels to increase with age. In contrast, the diets of primitive peoples living their indigenous lifestyle contain few processed, refined or preserved foods with excessive calories from fats and sugars. The natural intake of vitamin B6 and folic acid from native diets is high, protecting the arteries from the damaging effect of excessive homocysteine and preventing excessive rise in blood levels of cholesterol and lipoproteins.

As primitive peoples begin to eat more processed foods, they begin to experience increased cholesterol and lipoprotein levels, increased homocysteine levels and increased risk of heart disease,[15] though recent studies have suggested that genetic factors may protect South African blacks from elevation of blood homocysteine compared with whites consuming the same diet.[16]

The Male Gender, Postmenopausal Women and Hormones

In susceptible populations men have a much higher risk of coronary heart disease than women of the same age. The onset of the disease in men typically occurs in the fifth or sixth decade of life, whereas in women the onset of coronary heart disease is typically delayed until the sixth decade, after menopause. The disease rapidly increases in postmenopausal women until, in the seventh and later decades, the severity and incidence become similar to that of men. The protection against arteriosclerotic heart disease in women is related to estrogen production by the ovaries. The gradual loss of estrogen secretion by the ovaries after menopause or the sudden loss of estrogen secretion following surgical removal of the ovaries causes the arteriosclerotic process to increase rapidly in women of susceptible populations. Recent studies have suggested a protective effect of estrogen against coronary heart disease in postmenopausal women taking hormone replacement therapy.

Studies over the years have consistently shown that women have slightly lower levels of homocysteine in the blood (about 6 to 10 micromoles per liter) than men (about 8 to 12 micromoles per liter). After menopause, however, the blood levels of homocysteine increase in women to values similar to those found in men of the same age. Blood homocysteine levels continue to rise gradually with age, reaching higher values of 10 to 14 micromoles per liter in both women and men in the eighth and ninth decades of life.

It is clear that the blood levels of homocysteine in women and men correlate with relative susceptibility to arteriosclerotic heart disease. Thus in women before menopause the protection against arteriosclerosis is explained by the effect of estrogens and other ovarian hormones on blood levels of homocysteine. The precise reasons for this effect are incompletely understood at a biochemical level, but differences in enzyme activities in the liver and the lower mass of muscle in women compared with men have been suggested to be factors. After menopause or surgical removal of the ovaries, decreased secretion of estrogens and other ovarian hormones contributes to increased blood levels of homocysteine and increased susceptibility to coronary heart disease.

In contrast to the protective effect of natural ovarian hormones on susceptibility to arteriosclerosis, the administration of synthetic estrogens and progesterones in contraceptive hormones has been found to increase the risk of developing blood clots and arteriosclerotic plaques in young women. The use of low-dose contraceptive hormones has reduced the risk of these complications in recent years. These synthetic contraceptive hormones have been found to cause mild episodic increases in blood homocysteine levels, explaining the slightly increased risk of blood clots and arteriosclerotic plaques in the women who take them. Young women who smoke cigarettes and take contraceptive hormones are at greater risk of arteriosclerosis than nonsmoking women who take these hormones.

The reason synthetic contraceptive hormones lead to increased levels of blood homocysteine is that they antagonize the functions of vitamin B6 in the body. This effect is shown by the greater quantities of dietary or supplemental vitamin B6 needed to restore chemical imbalances in the processing of several amino acids in the liver. In experiments with human volunteers and with animals, diets that are deficient in vitamin B6 have been found to cause elevation of blood levels of homocysteine and excretion of trace amounts of homocystine and small quantities of cystathionine in the urine. Women who smoke while taking contraceptive hormones are at greater risk of blood clots and arteriosclerosis because cigarette smoke also antagonizes vitamin B6 in its vital functions in the body, increasing further the quantity of dietary or supplemental vitamin B6 needed to prevent elevation of blood homocysteine levels.

Recently the antiestrogenic, chemotherapeutic drug tamoxifen has been found to decrease the risk of fatal heart attacks by 50 percent in women under treatment for breast cancer. Tamoxifen causes a moderate reduction in blood levels of cholesterol and lipoproteins, and studies of blood homocysteine levels show a decrease of 30 percent in women under treatment for 9 to 18 months.[17] Tamoxifen may act in the body by affecting estrogen function, by increasing the effectiveness of folic acid or by facilitating the processing of oxygen by an antioxidant effect within arterial wall cells, causing a reduction in blood homocysteine and its damaging effect on arteries. Although tamoxifen may benefit the arteries of women under treatment for cancer, the drug is not advised for women without cancer because of its sometimes toxic side effects.

Homocysteine, Drugs and Toxins

In the 1950s and 1960s a study of English workers in the rayon manufacturing industry showed that among production workers exposed to the industrial solvent carbon disulfide the risk of developing coronary heart disease doubled compared with workers and employees not exposed to the solvent. Carbon disulfide is known to antagonize vitamin B6 by chemically combining with an active form of the vitamin in the liver.[18] This effect explains why carbon disulfide increases the risk of coronary heart disease since it leads to increases in blood homocysteine levels by decreasing its conversion to cystathionine.

Cigarette smoke contains small quantities of carbon disulfide among the 600 or more toxic chemicals it contains. Cigarette smoke also contains large quantities of carbon monoxide. Cigarette smoke, like carbon disulfide, antagonizes vitamin B6, probably because of the reaction of carbon monoxide with a form of the vitamin in the liver, causing inactivation. The result of the toxic actions of both carbon disulfide and cigarette smoke is that deficiency of active forms of vitamin B6 decreases the ability of the liver to dispose of homocysteine by conversion to cystathionine, leading to elevated blood homocysteine levels and damage to artery wall cells.

In the 1970s dermatologists began using the chemotherapeutic drug azaribine to treat cases of psoriasis that were resistant to treatment by other methods, especially coal tar and ultraviolet light. A number of patients receiving azaribine developed blood clots in peripheral arteries, heart attacks and strokes soon after starting the drug. When the blood homocysteine was analyzed, the levels were found to have been considerably increased by the drug. Azaribine was found to antagonize vitamin B6, causing excretion of homocysteine and other amino acids in the urine and producing elevation of blood homocysteine. Because of these findings the Food and Drug Administration withdrew its approval of the use of azaribine in the treatment of psoriasis in 1976, the first such recall in history.[19]

Methotrexate, a chemotherapeutic drug widely used for the treatment of leukemia and cancer, has also been found to increase the blood levels of homocysteine. Methotrexate exerts its pharmacological action in the body by antagonizing folic acid, resulting in a buildup of homocysteine because of decreased conversion to methionine.

The widely used anesthetic gas nitrous oxide ("laughing gas") also causes elevation of blood homocysteine levels. Nitrous oxide acts in the body by antagonizing vitamin B12, preventing the conversion of homocysteine to methionine. Other important drugs, including anticonvulsants and diuretics, have been found to increase the blood levels of homocysteine, but the effect of this elevation on risk of blood clots and vascular disease has not been determined.[20] Some anticonvulsants like phenytoin act by antagonizing folic acid, reducing the conversion of homocysteine to methionine. The reasons for the action of other drugs on the elevation of blood homocysteine and the relative risk of arteriosclerosis remain to be determined in many cases.

Diabetes and Kidney Failure

Diabetes mellitus (sugar in the urine) is a very common disease that strongly predisposes affected persons to rapidly advancing arteriosclerosis. Sufferers from diabetes frequently are affected by heart attack, stroke, kidney failure, blindness and gangrene of the toes and feet, all caused by severe arteriosclerosis. In fact, arteriosclerosis is the leading cause of death among diabetics.

Diabetes is a complex disease related to insufficient production of insulin by the pancreatic islets or the inability of insulin to transport blood sugar (glucose) into cells for production of energy. As a result, all cells of the body become starved for sugar and switch into a starvation mode of cellular activity. The excess blood sugar in diabetes reacts chemically with the hemoglobin of red blood cells and with the membranes around small blood vessels and capillaries, narrowing the lumen and interfering with the passage of red blood cells. In the kidney, the clogging of small arteries gradually leads to failure of kidney function, a frequent complication of diabetes.

A very striking effect of kidney failure, whether from diabetes or from other causes, is a remarkable buildup of homocysteine in the blood.[21] The levels of homocysteine may become extremely high, reaching two to three times the normal value, and the degree of elevation parallels the severity of kidney failure. These high levels of blood homocysteine subject all arteries of the body to damage and rapidly progressive arteriosclerosis. In the case of kidney failure from diabetes, the remarkable buildup of homocysteine leads to the vascular complications that result in disability and death from the disease. Recent studies of persons with early diabetes without kidney failure have not revealed an abnormality of homocysteine blood levels.

The effect of various treatments on blood levels of homocysteine has been studied in persons with kidney failure. Dialysis with an artificial kidney machine causes a temporary fall in the blood homocysteine level, but after one to two days, the blood homocysteine returns to its previously elevated level. Using vitamin therapy, the most effective treatment is with large doses (5 milligrams per day) of folic acid, which partially decreases the homocysteine level. Supplementation with vitamin B12 or vitamin B6 does not decrease the homocysteine level further. The exact cause of elevation of blood homocysteine in kidney failure, whether from diabetes or from another disease, is insufficiently understood.

Homocysteine and Thyroid Hormone

For many years deficiency of thyroid hormone secretion has been known to predispose to arteriosclerotic heart disease. In persons with a serious deficiency of thyroid hormone, the ability of the cells of the body to use oxygen is impaired. The basal metabolic rate is slowed in hypothyroidism, and the liver begins to make increased quantities of cholesterol and triglycerides. As a result the cholesterol and lipoprotein levels become elevated, and the risk of coronary heart disease increases. Administration of potent thyroid hormone preparations such as thyroxine to persons with severe hypothyroidism and elevated blood cholesterol increases the risk of heart attack. Subtle or marginal deficiencies of thyroid hormone, detected by measuring basal metabolic rate, are found to be widespread in populations with a high risk of arteriosclerotic heart disease.

In West African studies of thyroid deficiency and goiter resulting from insufficient dietary iodine, analysis of the amino acids of plasma revealed elevation of blood homocysteine levels.[22] These findings have been confirmed by several subsequent studies of patients with thyroid abnormalities. The patients at increased risk for arteriosclerotic heart disease with hypothyroidism have elevated blood homocysteine levels, and patients with overactive thyroid glands and hyperthyroidism have decreased levels of plasma homocysteine compared with normal values. In experiments with rats, following surgical removal of the pituitary gland, the growth response of the animals to homocysteic acid, the fully oxidized form of homocysteine, was found to require thyroid hormone.[23]

The Scientific Evidence for the Homocysteine Theory

Animal Studies

Chapter 1 explained that feeding homocystine or its precursor methionine to monkeys or rats causes weight loss and lower levels of blood cholesterol because of the toxicity of these amino acids. Before designing my first research project, I considered these questions: How could the elevation of blood levels of homocysteine be produced in animals? Would the elevation of blood homocysteine cause arteriosclerosis and blood clots in animals as it did in children with homocystinuria? How could homocysteine be given to animals that could not eat a toxic diet? Which chemical form of homocysteine should be given to animals to reproduce or mimic the disease homocystinuria in children?

Since no medical investigator had looked for arteriosclerosis after homocysteine was given to animals, I decided in 1969 that the first experiment should be done by direct injection into rabbits. Although the method was somewhat artificial, homocysteine was injected subcutaneously in a dilute solution of glucose and water. In this way, a known amount of homocysteine would be absorbed gradually over a period of hours, simulating the situation in children with homocystinuria. The thiolactone form of homocysteine was injected because it is stable in solution and readily converted to homocysteine by normal enzymes of plasma and tissues. An experiment with radioactively labelled homocysteine thiolactone showed that the amino acid is rapidly converted into a series of labelled compounds in the serum.

Our first results showed that, just as was expected, early arteriosclerotic plaques were found in the coronary arteries of yearling rabbits after only three weeks of twice-daily injections of homocysteine thiolactone![24] When young weanling rabbits were injected once daily for five weeks, early arteriosclerotic plaques were found in the coronary arteries, aorta and arteries of the other organs. If the animals were fed cholesterol and also injected with homocysteine, the arteriosclerotic plaques were found to contain fat deposits. If the animals were given a diet that was deficient in vitamin B6 and also injected with homocysteine, the plaques became more prominent and more widespread. We had for the first time produced arteriosclerosis by injection of an amino acid, reproducing many of the features of arteriosclerotic plaques found in children with homocystinuria, both in rabbits fed cholesterol and in rabbits given a vitamin B6-deficient diet. When these results were presented at a national meeting, nobody made a comment; the audience maintained a "stony silence," in the words of Dr. Moses Suzman, following one of his lectures on homocysteine and arteriosclerosis.

This response to what I thought was an extraordinary experiment confirming my conclusions about the arteriosclerotic effect of an amino acid was very disappointing. Investigators interested in the traditional approach of feeding cholesterol and fat to animals totally ignored our results and went back to studying cholesterol and lipoproteins some more. One group of investigators in the homocystinuria field offered to collaborate by repeating my experiments in their laboratory, sending me the slides from the arteries of their rabbits to examine independently. In my opinion, their results also showed early arteriosclerotic plaques in young rabbits, just as we had found two years earlier. However, these investigators published a contradiction of our earlier findings in their paper in 1974, claiming that the plaques were "spontaneous and of no significance." They illustrated their report not with the slides they had sent me, but with a photograph of a normal artery![25]

I felt totally betrayed by this episode. If only I had photographed their slides before returning them, I could have published an illustrated rebuttal. Subsequently, the investigators refused further collaboration and returned to their studies of sulfur amino acids in children with homocystinuria and in newborn children. The only way I could counteract the effect of this contradictory report was to repeat my experiments with rabbits, giving larger doses of homocysteine for longer periods of time.

The original experiments with rabbits[24] were designed to study the effect of moderate doses of homocysteine thiolactone, comparable with the dose that a human adult might receive when eating a diet consisting predominantly of animal protein. Our results had shown early arteriosclerotic plaques, as I had predicted. If the dose of homocysteine thiolactone was increased fivefold to overload the capacity of the rabbits' tissues to eliminate the amino acid, would more dramatic effects be observed? I remember very well receiving an emergency call to see several rabbits that had died after one month of injections with high doses of homocysteine thiolactone. When the animals were examined, I found that blood clots had formed in the veins of the legs and abdomen and travelled to the lungs, causing bleeding and dead areas of the lungs. In animals that were given injections of vitamin B6 as well as homocysteine, no blood clots formed and the animals survived until the experiment was finished after two months.[26]

These results were tremendously exciting because high doses of homocysteine thiolactone had produced in animals the dramatic complication of blood clots in the lungs that had killed some of the children with homocystinuria. However, the experiment was quite artificial because the amino acid had been injected rather than fed in the diet. I needed to design an experiment that would force the rabbits to eat large quantities of homocystine or methionine which had been found to be toxic when fed in an experimental diet by other investigators.

In order to make the experiments resemble the human situation more closely, a synthetic diet was made with agar containing special chemical forms of these amino acids and fed to rabbits. Different groups of rabbits received homocysteine thiolactone in the perchlorate form, methionine converted to methyl homocysteine thiolactone by acid and homocystine treated with hydrogen peroxide. To our great surprise, these forms of homocysteine and methionine stimulated the growth of the rabbits, producing giant rabbits! My associates in the pathology department made several visits to the animal farm to observe them.

At the conclusion of the experiment, when the arteries

of the rabbits were examined, arteriosclerotic plaques were found that closely resembled the arteriosclerosis found in children with homocystinuria. We had not only reproduced the vascular disease associated with the genetic disease homocystinuria, we had also produced the complication of blood clot formation and embolism to the lungs. Finally, we had also suppressed the formation of blood clots by vitamin B6, although the vitamin did not prevent the formation of arteriosclerosis that was produced by injecting the very large doses of homocysteine thiolactone or methionine.[26]

After publication of our findings, scientists in Japan repeated our experiments and made very similar observations on the formation of blood clots and arteriosclerosis, completely confirming our findings.[27] These scientists also repeated the experiments of Rinehart with vitamin B6 deficiency in monkeys, observing arteriosclerosis after prolonged periods of partial deficiency of the vitamin. They went on to show that vitamin B6 therapy caused reversal and regression of the arteriosclerosis that had been induced by vitamin B6 deficiency. Because their report was published in Japanese in a Japanese journal, however, I was not aware of their important confirmation of our results until I received a review in English from the author some years later.

Another important experiment was conducted with baboons that were given homocysteine thiolactone by continuous intravenous injection.[28] In this expensive experiment the arteries were found to have been damaged by homocysteine, producing arteriosclerotic changes that were very similar to what we had found in the rabbits that were given subcutaneous injections of homocysteine. The blood platelets were found to have formed very early blood clots at the sites of injury in the arteries, and larger blood clots and arteriosclerotic plaques were found within only two weeks in the arteries of some baboons that were given high doses of homocysteine thiolactone. Scientists in Prague were able to produce similar damage to arteries by force-feeding methionine or homocysteine to rats by stomach tube.[29]

Although a few scientists failed to observe arteriosclerotic plaques in animals that were given homocysteine, probably because of different methods of analyzing the tissues, many subsequent studies have confirmed that homocysteine produces arteriosclerosis and blood clots in a variety of experimental animals. For example, recent experiments in France in which large doses of casein (the calcium form of milk protein) were fed to minipigs, showed early changes in the aorta caused by the destruction of elastic tissue activated by the enzyme elastase, a result of the elevation of blood homocysteine.[30] In an earlier experiment with vitamin B6-deficient pigs, arterial damage and arteriosclerosis were also related to elevation of blood homocysteine levels.[31]

These experiments with a variety of experimental animal species provide abundant evidence that induction of elevated blood levels of homocysteine by direct injection, dietary feeding or by chronic partial vitamin B6 deficiency reproduces the essential features of arteriosclerosis that are observed in children with hereditary homocystinuria. The inadequate, flawed or misinterpreted experiments of a few investigators who failed to observe these effects in animals delayed acceptance of the homocysteine theory. The positive results of the many scientists who had had success in this field support the validity of the theory.

Studies of Cells and Tissues

Why should elevated blood levels of homocysteine cause damage and arteriosclerotic changes in the arteries? How does an amino acid normally produced in the body affect artery cells and tissues, narrowing and obstructing the normal flow of blood through the lumen of the artery? How does homocysteine affect the biochemical functioning and growth of cells and tissues? How does excess homocysteine lead to the formation of blood clots within arteries and veins? These are some of the questions that have been addressed by medical scientists during the quarter-century that has elapsed since discovery of the homocysteine theory of arteriosclerosis.

One of the earliest attempts to answer these questions involved growing cells in culture from the skin of children with homocystinuria. Since the enzyme deficiency of cystathionine synthase in homocystinuria involves a genetic defect in all cells of the body, the cultured cells were found also to be deficient in this enzyme. In observing the growth of these cultured cells, the matrix substance produced by the abnormal cells was found to be clumped and aggregated, compared with the finely fibrillar matrix substance produced by normal cells.[32] This effect recalled the observation that the aorta of children with homocystinuria contains a matrix substance of reduced solubility.[33] When homocysteine thiolactone was added to normal cell cultures, some of the fibrillar matrix became clumped, showing that homocysteine changed the aggregation of ground substance to reduce its solubility. As explained in Chapter 2, one of the earliest changes in arteriosclerotic plaques is an accumulation of mucoid matrix substance of decreased solubility in areas of damage to arterial tissues.

When homocysteine thiolactone is added to cell cultures

from children with homocystinuria, the cells show extreme toxicity, detaching from the culture dish and losing viability. If vitamin B6 is also added to the cell cultures from children who respond to vitamin B6 therapy, the toxic effect of homocysteine is overcome, allowing the cells to multiply rapidly. By using homocysteine thiolactone labelled with radioactive sulfur, a new pathway was discovered by which the sulfur is converted to sulfate without forming cystathionine since the enzyme for this conversion is absent from these cell cultures.[34] Proof of this new pathway was demonstrated by a study of how homocysteine is processed by the livers of guinea pigs deprived of vitamin C. In this study, the reaction of oxygen with the sulfur atom of homocysteine was shown to require vitamin C in order to form PAPS (phosphoadenosine phosphosulfate), the coenzyme that attaches sulfate groups to the mucoid matrix of cells.[35]

Another very interesting feature observed in cell cultures from children with homocystinuria is the distinctive pattern of growth, which resembles the pattern of growth of cancer cells in culture. Furthermore, the muscle cells of arteries grow in a similar pattern in early arteriosclerotic plaques. As explained in Chapter 2, the 19th-century German pathologist Rudolf Virchow likened the increased numbers of muscle cells in atheromas to tumors of the blood vessels. In some way, abnormal homocysteine production induces cells to lose control of growth processes, causing growth of muscle cells in arteriosclerotic plaques. Recent experiments have shown that homocysteine damages cultured endothelial cells and increases the growth of smooth muscle cells.[36] These effects on the cells of artery walls explain in a general way the early phases of production of arteriosclerotic plaques.[5]

The observations of growth stimulation in normal guinea pigs and rabbits[26] and the abnormal growth pattern of cultured cells from children with homocystinuria[34] suggest that homocysteine is involved in stimulating the growth of normal cells and tissues. Many of the children with homocystinuria grow rapidly in childhood, achieving taller stature than their unaffected relatives. As previously noted, these children also have long arms, legs, fingers and toes as a result of the accelerated growth. Experiments with rats from which the pituitary gland is removed surgically show that a homocysteine compound containing extra oxygen (homocysteic acid) stimulates growth. This growth response simulates the response to growth hormone and is correlated with release of an insulin-like growth factor into the plasma, provided that thyroid hormone is also given.[23] Insulin-like growth factor is known to promote the growth of cartilage and bone in growing animals by increasing the sulfate content of matrix substances. This process is under the control of growth hormone and is mediated by the formation of PAPS from homocysteine.[35]

The fundamental nature of the participation of homocysteine in normal growth suggests a relationship to the disturbances of growth in cancer cells. Experiments with radioactively labelled homocysteine thiolactone revealed a complete inability of malignant cells to add oxygen to homocysteine and to form sulfate.[37] Normal cells and cells from children with homocystinuria perform this conversion easily, rapidly and completely. As a result of this specific abnormality, cancer cells accumulate excess homocysteine thiolactone which reacts with and alters the structure and function of proteins, mucoid substances and chromatin, the nuclear material containing DNA. This study suggested a new interpretation of the origin of cancer cells and led to the discovery of the new anticancer compounds, thioretinaco and thioretinamide, which are described in Chapter 6.

Because of the relation of homocysteine to the growth

process in normal and malignant cells, a study was performed in young and adult rats and guinea pigs, comparing the effectiveness of the liver in processing homocysteine. The results show that the livers of older animals accumulate homocysteine thiolactone and the livers of younger animals prevent oxygen from converting homocysteine to the dimer form, homocystine.[38] These findings show that homocysteine is processed differently in aged animals, explaining the gradual rise of blood homocysteine levels with age[14] and the decreased ability of tissues to form adenosyl methionine from methionine and ATP. The implications of these findings for the aging process are described in Chapter 6.

The liver cells of children with homocystinuria caused by each of the three enzyme deficiencies known to produce abnormal homocysteine processing are found to accumulate droplets of fat within the cytoplasm. A very striking abnormality of the cytoplasmic organelles (mitochondria) is also found in homocystinuria. The mitochondria are the structures within the cell cytoplasm for utilization of oxygen in the burning of food for production of chemical energy in the form of ATP. In homocystinuria the mitochondria become enlarged, assume bizarre shapes, and become aggregated one with another. A similar effect has been produced in the mitochondria of both normal and hypertensive rats by administering either methionine or the oxycholesterol, cholestane triol.[39] This fundamental abnormality of energy production by the mitochondria is a key process by which the cells become damaged and increase the formation of fats and cholesterol in arteriosclerosis.[8]

Because of the prominence of blood clots in children with homocystinuria and in animals given homocysteine, medical scientists have studied the effects of homocysteine on blood clotting in the body. Early studies showed that blood platelets, the circulating cell fragments in the blood that orchestrate the clotting process, are overreactive, showing increased adherence to glass beads in test tube experiments. Later experiments showed that freshly synthesized homocysteine thiolactone in the uncharged, salt-free form is extremely active in causing aggregation of blood platelets.[40] In addition, homocysteine has been found to activate multiple blood-clotting proteins and to increase formation of thromboxane, the hormone-like fatty acid derivative (prostaglandin A), causing an increased tendency to form blood clots. Finally, homocysteine increases the binding of lipoprotein(a), a lipoprotein fraction related to the clotting process, to fibrin, the protein component of blood clots.[41] These studies show that homocysteine hastens blood clotting by affecting platelets, protein-clotting factors, lipoproteins and prostaglandins that cooperate in the complex activation process within blood vessel walls and circulating blood components.

These diverse experiments with cells and tissues support the homocysteine theory of arteriosclerosis by describing the pathogenic processes by which a buildup of homocysteine in plasma, cells and tissues leads to arterial damage and arteriosclerotic plaques. In Figure 2 (page 64), components of lipoprotein-homocysteine thiolactone aggregates are taken up by cells of the artery wall, forming foam cells. These cells degrade and store fats and cholesterol from the LDL component, releasing them gradually to form the cholesterol crystals and fatty deposits of advanced arteriosclerotic plaques. The homocysteine thiolactone component is released from foam cells and affects the oxygen utilization process of adjacent arterial cells, causing increased formation of damaging free radical substances. In turn the disturbance of oxygen processing causes increased growth of muscle cells, formation of mucoid matrix from the sulfur atom of homocysteine, destruction of elastin fibers by activation of elastase, production of fibrous collagen fibers, calcium deposits and activation of blood clotting.[8] These diverse studies of the effects of homocysteine on cells and tissues explain the principal processes by which a buildup of homocysteine causes formation of arteriosclerotic plaques.

Human Studies

One day in 1973 Dr. Bridget Wilcken, a pediatrician from England, visited my laboratory in Boston. She had read several of my articles describing my findings on homocysteine and arteriosclerosis. She was travelling to Australia to join her husband, internist Dr. David Wilcken, who was interested in the possibility of investigating homocysteine in patients with coronary heart disease. During her visit, we discussed ways in which evidence for the homocysteine theory could be established by studying human subjects. Subsequently, in 1976, the Wilckens published a study that showed that, in a group of 25 patients with coronary heart disease, the blood homocysteine became highly elevated in seven patients following an oral dose of methionine, compared with high elevation of blood homocysteine in only one of 22 normal subjects.[42] This significant human study was the first of many subsequent studies of homocysteine and arteriosclerosis to be published by the Drs. Wilcken and their colleagues during the past 20 years, and it was the first study of its kind in the medical literature.

Beginning in the mid-1980s epidemiological studies of human populations were begun for the purpose of comparing the blood levels of homocysteine in patients with coronary heart disease, stroke, peripheral vascular disease and kidney failure with the blood homocysteine levels of normal subjects. The result of these studies is a consensus among medical investigators that elevation of blood homocysteine level is a strong independent risk factor for the development of arteriosclerotic disease.[43] Levels of blood homocysteine greater than 14 micromoles per liter are associated with increased risk of arteriosclerosis, and the higher the homocysteine level, the higher the risk. The consequences of this risk are demonstrated by the finding of a three-fold increase in risk of heart attack in a five-year prospective study of 14,000 U.S. physicians.[44]

Elevated blood homocysteine is estimated to account for at least 10 percent of the risk of coronary heart disease in the U.S. population. Accordingly, reduction of blood homocysteine levels by the addition of folic acid to the food supply is estimated to prevent as many as 50,000 deaths from coronary heart disease annually.[43] In 1996 the U.S. Food and Drug Administration adopted new guidelines requiring the addition of folic acid to enriched foods such as flour, pasta and other grain-based foods. This action promises to help counteract elevated homocysteine levels and the consequent risk of vascular disease, continuing the decline in mortality from heart disease and stroke that was attributed to the addition of synthetic vitamin B6 to the food supply beginning in 1961.[5]

An early study of patients with cerebrovascular disease and stroke demonstrated increased levels of blood homocysteine before and after an oral dose of methionine compared with normal subjects.[45] A recent study of over 1,000 subjects from the Framingham Heart Study showed that the higher the level of blood homocysteine, the greater the degree of narrowing of carotid arteries to the brain.[46] A subsequent study found that increased risk of early-onset (before age 55) heart disease, cerebrovascular disease and peripheral vascular disease correlates with blood homocysteine levels greater than 14 micromoles per liter.[47] In comparison with traditional risk factors, elevation of blood homocysteine was found to be a greater risk factor (22-40-fold) than elevated blood cholesterol (1.2-3.1-fold), high blood pressure (8-18-fold) or cigarette smoking (3.5-fold) in the selected group of patients with early-onset arteriosclerosis.

A large cross-sectional study of vascular disease risk in over 16,000 subjects estimated the relation between blood homocysteine level and other established risk factors.[48] The homocysteine level correlated with male gender, age, cigarette smoking, lack of exercise, blood pressure, heart rate, blood cholesterol and triglyceride levels. For example, the homocysteine level in male smokers, aged 65 to 67, is almost 5 micromoles per liter greater than in nonsmoking women, aged 40 to 42. In another study of 199 male coronary heart disease patients, elevated blood homocysteine, high blood pressure, decreased HDL, increased LDL, fibrinogen (blood clotting protein), plasminogen (clot dissolving enzyme) and viscosity of plasma were all found to correlate with coronary heart disease risk.[49] A study of 304 patients with coronary heart disease revealed that risk of disease correlated with homocysteine levels, diabetes, smoking, male gender, age and low levels of vitamin B6.[50]

A total of 209 published studies of the epidemiological relation between homocysteine and arteriosclerosis were reviewed recently.[43] The consensus of these studies is that elevated blood homocysteine is a strong independent risk factor for arteriosclerosis. A detailed study of coronary arteries by X-ray angiography in 163 males with angina pectoris concluded that the degree of narrowing of the coronary artery by arteriosclerotic plaques correlates better with blood levels of homocysteine than with blood levels of cholesterol.[15] A study of a susceptible population estimated a 40 percent increase in risk of arteriosclerotic heart disease for each increase of 4 micromoles per liter of blood homocysteine.[51]

The risk of blood clots in the leg veins for pulmonary embolism (blood clots in the lungs) has also been correlated with blood homocysteine levels. Recent studies have shown that 10-20 percent of patients with recurrent blood clots in leg veins have elevated levels of blood homocysteine.[52, 53] The risk of blood clots in young individuals with elevated blood homocysteine was shown to be inherited as a genetic predisposing factor in 26 of 30 families studied.[52] Familial predisposition to elevated blood homocysteine levels in arteriosclerosis has also been documented in numerous other published studies.[11,12,47,54]

The reason that the U.S. Food and Drug Administration decided to require the addition of folic acid to foods is that mothers consuming 400 mcg per day of folic acid, either in the diet or from vitamin supplements, have a greatly reduced risk of giving birth to babies with neural tube defects of the brain and spine such as anencephaly or spina bifida. Recent studies have shown that these same women have a high level of blood homocysteine, predisposing their babies to birth defects.[55] The effect of folic acid in preventing these birth defects, therefore, may be related to the lowering of blood homocysteine levels in early pregnancy.[9,55]

PREVENTION OF ARTERIOSCLEROTIC HEART DISEASE AND THE HOMOCYSTEINE THEORY

Considering the overwhelming evidence that elevated blood levels of homocysteine are associated with increased risk of arteriosclerosis, what is the evidence that lowering homocysteine levels decreases the risk of vascular disease? Is there proof that therapy with vitamins B6, B12 and folic acid reduces the risk of vascular disease by reducing homocysteine levels? Despite repeated suggestions over a quarter-century based on the homocysteine theory of arteriosclerosis that large-scale trials should be initiated to answer this question, no definitive information is yet available in the published medical literature. Only with the relatively recent results of human epidemiological studies in the 1990s has there begun to be interest by governmental agencies in funding trials of this type.

The first suggestion that control of blood homocysteine levels might reduce risk of arteriosclerosis came from studies of children with homocystinuria. A study of homocystinuria caused by cystathionine synthase deficiency revealed that about one-half of 629 patients responded to large doses (500-1000 mg per day) of vitamin B6.[56] The risk of blood-clot formation was significantly decreased by vitamin B6 in the responding patients, compared with the patients who showed no response to vitamin B6.

In 1962 Dr. John Ellis of Texas discovered that many victims of carpal tunnel syndrome, a painful disorder of the wrist and hand, respond symptomatically to moderately large doses of vitamin B6 (100-200 mg per day) after two to three months. Many patients with carpal tunnel syndrome, particularly if it involves both hands, have deficient blood levels of vitamin B6 and they respond favorably to vitamin B6 therapy. Dr. Ellis observed that few of his patients receiving vitamin B6 developed angina or heart attack. In a retrospective study of his patients over a five-year period, the risk of chest pain or heart attack was found to have decreased by 75 percent, compared with patients of other physicians in the county who received no vitamin B6.[57] Furthermore, there was an apparent increase in longevity of 7 to 17 years in patients who had taken vitamin B6, compared with patients who had not taken the vitamin.

Although no prevention trials based on the homocysteine theory of arteriosclerosis have been published in the medical literature, there is increasing interest by investigators worldwide in designing and completing a definitive prospective study of this type. The necessary elements for the success of such a trial were discussed by medical scientists working in the homocysteine field at the First International Conference on Homocysteine Metabolism in Ireland in 1995. At least three proposals have been submitted to the National Institutes of Health for consideration for funding within the past two years. Governmental funding agencies over the past quarter-century have repeatedly ignored proposals for a large-scale trial of the homocysteine theory because of resistance by adherents of the cholesterol/fat approach. As a result, funding has concentrated on control of multiple risk factors and a variety of potentially toxic drugs that have yielded inconclusive or disappointing results.

The recent flood of findings on homocysteine and arteriosclerosis in human populations will trigger a series of prospective trials of the homocysteine theory, probably within the next decade. A complicating factor is the addition of vitamin B6 and folic acid to foods, breakfast cereals and other widely distributed sources, potentially accelerating the well-established decline in vascular disease since the 1960s.

ARTERIOSCLEROSIS AND THE HOMOCYSTEINE THEORY

The development of the homocysteine theory has enabled medical scientists to appreciate the significance of the seminal discoveries of the early pioneers in arteriosclerosis research, M.A. Ignatovsky, Harry Newburgh and James Rinehart. The origin of arteriosclerosis is now understood to be a toxic effect of a by-product of protein breakdown, the amino acid homocysteine. The importance of fats and sugars in the genesis of the disease is now understood to be related to loss of vitamins B6 and folic acid through processing, refining and preservation of foods, creating an imbalance between the abundant methionine of foods of animal origin and the amount of these essential vitamins necessary to prevent a buildup of homocysteine in the body.

The role of antioxidants in arteriosclerosis is related to the effects on oxidative modification of LDL, the carrier of homocysteine by LDL-homocysteine aggregates. The uptake of these aggregates by the cells of the artery wall causes deposition of fats and cholesterol and results in damage to artery wall cells by interfering with normal oxygen processing and allowing accumulation of damaging free radical substances.[8] The unsaturated oils of fish do in fact decrease blood homocysteine levels in men with elevated blood fat levels.[58] In a study of men with elevated cholesterol levels, the administration of vitamins B6, B12, folic acid, riboflavin, choline and troxerutin, an antioxidant of plant origin, decreased both blood homocysteine and LDL levels.[59] Choline is a constituent of lecithin that helps to convert homocysteine to methionine in the body.

The homocysteine theory offers an explanation for observations on human arteriosclerosis that are difficult to explain by the cholesterol/fat approach. The dramatically declining incidence of heart attack and stroke in America, despite relatively constant dietary fat and cholesterol intake and constant blood levels of cholesterol, is explained by the effect of synthetic vitamin B6 in preventing the disease.[5] The low incidence of arteriosclerosis in Eskimos, despite high dietary fat and cholesterol, is explained by the effect of unsaturated fish oils and the abundant vitamin B6 of fish in suppressing blood homocysteine levels. The decreased incidence of heart attack in Europe during World Wars I and II is explained by the scarcity of animal foods, such as meat and eggs, and the reliance of the population on vegetables, decreasing the amount of methionine in the diet and increasing natural sources of vitamin B6 and folic acid.

The effects of drugs, toxins and hormonal status in risk of arteriosclerosis are explained by their effects on blood levels of homocysteine, since effects on LDL and blood cholesterol levels may not be consistently observed. The important effect of kidney failure on risk of arteriosclerosis is explained by large increases in blood homocysteine levels, since cholesterol and LDL levels may be unaffected in many cases. The high risk of arteriosclerosis of the coronary arteries after heart transplantation is explained by the prominent increase in blood homocysteine levels.[60,61]

As explained more fully in Chapter 6, the greater risk of arteriosclerosis with advancing age is attributed to the loss of a key player in the processing of homocysteine and methionine by all cells of the body, thioretinaco ozonide. The loss of this substance from the membranes of all cells is responsible for the gradual increase in blood levels of homocysteine with age, increasing the risk of arteriosclerosis. The decline in the processing of foods in the liver and other organs by reaction with oxygen leads to the accumulation of damaging oxygen radicals in all aging tissues.[62]

While the homocysteine theory of arteriosclerosis needs

further development in some respects, the basic elements of the theory that have already been discovered explain the principal processes underlying the genesis of the disease. These principles have already been applied to prevent arteriosclerosis in susceptible individuals and populations. In Chapter 5 the therapeutic measures currently available to individuals at risk for arteriosclerosis are explained in light of the existing knowledge of its cause, the altered processing of homocysteine.

REFERENCES

1. Proceedings of the Conference on the Decline in Coronary Heart Disease Mortality, Richard J. Havlik and Manning Feinleib, Editors. (Bethesda: NIH Publication No. 79-1610, 1979), pp. 1-399.
2. Peter O. Kwiterovich, *The Johns Hopkins Complete Guide for Preventing and Reversing Heart Disease* (Rocklin, Calif.: Prima Publishing, 1993), pp. 163-176.
3. Nathan Pritikin and Patrick M. McGrady, Jr., *The Pritikin Program for Diet and Exercise* (New York: Grosset & Dunlap, 1979), pp. 79-105.
4. Dean Ornish, S.E. Brown, L.W. Scherwitz, J.H. Billings, W.T. Armstrong, T.A. Ports, S.M. McLanahan, R.L. Kirkeide, R.J. Brand and K.L. Gould, "Can lifestyle changes reverse coronary heart disease?" *Lancet* 336:129-133, 1990.
5. Kilmer S. McCully, "Homocysteine theory of arteriosclerosis: Development and current status." In: Antonio M. Gotto, Jr. and Rodolfo Paoletti, editors, *Atherosclerosis Reviews*, Volume 11 (New York: Raven Press, 1983), pp. 157-246.
6. Henry A. Schroeder, "Losses of vitamins and trace minerals

resulting from processing and preservation of foods." *American Journal of Clinical Nutrition* 24:562-573, 1971.

7. Marek Naruszewicz, Ewa Mirkiewicz, Andrzej J. Olszewski and Kilmer S. McCully, "Thiolation of low-density lipoprotein by homocysteine thiolactone causes increased aggregation and altered interaction with cultured macrophages." *Nutrition, Metabolism and Cardiovascular Diseases* 4:70-77, 1994.
8. Kilmer S. McCully, "Homocysteine and vascular disease." *Nature Medicine* 2:386-389, 1996.
9. Arno G. Motulsky, "Nutritional ecogenetics: Homocysteine-related arteriosclerotic vascular disease, neural tube defects and folic acid." *American Journal of Human Genetics* 58:17-20, 1996.
10. Phyllis Frosst, Henk J. Blom, R. Milos, Philippe Goyette, C.A. Shephard, Rowena G. Matthews, Godfried J.H. Boers, Martin den Heijer, Leo A.J. Kluijtmans, Lambert P.W.J. vanden Heuvel and Rima Rozen, "A candidate risk factor for vascular disease: A common mutation in methylenetetrahydrofolate reductase." *Nature Genetics* 10:111-113, 1995.
11. Paul N. Hopkins, Lily L. Wu, Steven C. Hunt, Brent C. Jones, G. Michael Vincent and Roger R. Williams, "Higher plasma homocysteine and increased susceptibility to adverse effects of low folate in early familial coronary heart disease." *Arteriosclerosis, Thrombosis and Vascular Biology* 15:1314-1320, 1995.
12. Jacques J. Genest, Jr., Judith R. McNamara, Barbara Upson, Deeb N. Salem, Jose M. Ordovas, Ernst J. Schaefer and M. Rene Malinow, "Prevalence of familial hyperhomocysteinemia in men with premature coronary artery disease." *Arteriosclerosis and Thrombosis* 11:1129-1136, 1991.
13. A. Hamfelt, "Age variation of vitamin B6 metabolism in man." *Clinica Chimica Acta* 10:48-54, 1964.
14. Jacob Selhub, Paul F. Jacques, Peter W.F. Wilson, David Rush and Irwin H. Rosenberg, "Vitamin status and intake as primary determinants of homocysteinemia in an elderly population." *Journal of the American Medical Association* 270:2693-2698, 1993.

15. Johan B. Ubbink, W.J. Hayward Vermaak, J.M. Bennett, Piet J. Becker, D.A. van Staden and S. Bissbort, "The prevalence of homocysteinemia and hypercholesterolemia in angiographically defined coronary heart disease." *Klinische Wochenschrift* 69:527-534, 1991.
16. Johan B. Ubbink, J. Hayward Vermaak, Rhena Delport, Annatjie vander Merwe, Piet J. Becker and Hendrik Potgeiter, "Effective homocysteine metabolism may protect South African blacks against coronary heart disease." *American Journal of Clinical Nutrition* 62:802-808, 1995.
17. G. Anker, P.E. Lonning, Per Magne Ueland, Helga Refsum and E.A. Lien, "Plasma levels of the atherogenic amino acid homocysteine in postmenopausal women with breast cancer treated with tamoxifen." *International Journal of Cancer* 60:365-368, 1995.
18. Edward J. Calabrese, "Environmental validation of the homocysteine theory of arteriosclerosis." *Medical Hypotheses* 15:361-367, 1984.
19. William Drell and Arnold D. Welch, "Azaribine—homocystinemia—thrombosis in historical perspective." *Pharmacy and Therapeutics* 41:195-206, 1989.
20. Per Magne Ueland and Helga Refsum, "Plasma homocysteine, a risk factor for vascular disease: Plasma levels in health, disease and drug therapy." *Journal of Laboratory and Clinical Medicine* 114:473-501, 1989.
21. Joy A. Friedman and Johanna T. Dwyer, "Hyperhomocysteinemia as a risk factor for cardiovascular disease in patients undergoing hemodialysis." *Nutrition Reviews* 53:197-201, 1995.
22. Yves Ingenbleek, Denis Barclay and Henri Dirren, "Nutritional significance in serum amino acid patterns in goitrous patients." *American Journal of Clinical Nutrition* 43:310-319, 1986.
23. Pierre Clopath, Virginia C. Smith and Kilmer S. McCully, "Growth promotion by homocysteic acid." *Science* 192:372-274, 1976.
24. Kilmer S. McCully and Bruce D. Ragsdale, "Production of

arteriosclerosis by homocysteinemia." *American Journal of Pathology* 61:1-11, 1970.

25. Shiela Donahue, John A. Sturman and Gerald Gaull, "Arteriosclerosis due to homocysteinemia. Failure to reproduce the model in weanling rabbits." *American Journal of Pathology* 77:167-174, 1974.
26. Kilmer S. McCully and Robert B. Wilson, "Homocysteine theory of arteriosclerosis." *Atherosclerosis* 22:215-227, 1975.
27. Fumio Kuzuya and N. Yoshimine, "Homocysteine theory of arteriosclerosis." *Domyakukoka* (*Journal of Japan Atherosclerosis Society*) 6:135-139, 1978.
28. Laurence A. Harker, Russell Ross, Sherrill J. Slichter and C. Ronald Scott, "Homocystine-induced arteriosclerosis. The role of endothelial cell injury and platelet response to its genesis." *Journal of Clinical Investigation* 58:731-741, 1976.
29. Josef Hladovec, "Experimental homocystinemia, endothelial lesions and thrombosis." *Blood Vessels* 16:202-205, 1979.
30. Pierre Rolland, Alain Friggi, Andre Barlatier, Philippe Piquet, Valerie Latrille, Marie M. Faye, Joel Guillon, Philippe Charpiot, Heidi Bodard, Odette Ghirnighelli, Raymond Calaf, Roger Luccioni and Danielle Garcon, "Hyperhomocysteinemia-induced vascular damage in the minipig." *Circulation* 91: 1161-1174, 1995.
31. Lori A. Smolin, T.D. Crenshaw, D. Kurtycz and N.J. Benevenga, "Homocysteine accumulation in pigs fed diets deficient in vitamin B6: Relationship to atherosclerosis." *Journal of Nutrition* 113:2122-2133, 1983.
32. Kilmer S. McCully, "Importance of homocysteine-induced abnormalities of proteoglycan structure in arteriosclerosis." *American Journal of Pathology* 59:181-193, 1970.
33. Nina A.J. Carson, C.E. Dent, C.M.B. Field and Gerald E. Gaull, "Homocystinuria. Clinical and pathological review of ten cases." *Journal of Pediatrics* 66:565-583, 1965.
34. Kilmer S. McCully, "Macromolecular basis for homocysteine-induced changes in proteoglycan structure in growth and

arteriosclerosis." *American Journal of Pathology* 66:83-95, 1972.
35. Kilmer S. McCully, "Homocysteine metabolism in scurvy, growth and arteriosclerosis." *Nature* 231:391-392, 1971.
36. Jer-Chia Tsai, Mark A. Perrella, Masao Yoshizumi, Chung-Ming Hsieh, Edgar Haber, Robert Schlegel and Mu-En Lee, "Promotion of vascular smooth-muscle growth by homocysteine: A link to atherogenesis." *Proceedings of the National Academy of Sciences USA* 91:6369-6373, 1994.
37. Kilmer S. McCully, "Homocysteine thiolactone metabolism in malignant cells." *Cancer Research* 36:3198-3202, 1976.
38. Kilmer S. McCully, "Growth disorders and homocysteine metabolism." *Annals of Clinical and Laboratory Science* 5:147-152, 1975.
39. Dietrich Matthias, Curt H. Becker, R. Riezler and Paul H. Kindling, "Homocysteine induced arteriosclerosis-like alterations of the aorta in normotensive and hypertensive rats following application of high doses of methionine." *Atherosclerosis* 122:201-216, 1996.
40. Kilmer S. McCully and Angelina C.A. Carvalho, "Homocysteine thiolactone, N-homocysteine thiolactonyl retinamide and platelet aggregation." *Research Communications in Chemical Pathology and Pharmacology* 56:349-360, 1987.
41. Peter C. Harpel, Victor T. Chang and Wolfgang Borth, "Homocysteine and other sulfhydryl compounds enhance the binding of lipoprotein(a) to fibrin: A potential link between thrombosis, atherogenesis and sulfhydryl compound metabolism." *Proceedings of the National Academy of Sciences USA* 89:10193-10197, 1992.
42. David E. Wilcken and Bridget Wilcken, "The pathogenesis of coronary artery disease. A possible role for methionine metabolism." *Journal of Clinical Investigation* 57:1079-1082, 1976.
43. Carol J. Boushey, Shirley A.A. Beresford, Gilbert S. Omenn and Arno G. Motulsky, "A quantitative assessment of plasma homocysteine as a risk factor for vascular disease." *Journal of the American Medical Association* 274:1049-1057, 1995.
44. Meir J. Stampfer, M. Rene Malinow, Walter C. Willett,

Laura M. Newcomer, Barbara Upson, Daniel Ullmann, Peter V. Tishler and Charles H. Hennekins, "A prospective study of plasma homocyst(e)ine and risk of myocardial infarction in U.S. physicians." *Journal of the American Medical Association* 268:877-881, 1992.

45. Lars E. Brattstrom, Jan Erik Hardebo and Bjorn L. Hultberg, "Moderate homocysteinemia—a possible risk factor for arteriosclerotic cerebrovascular disease." *Stroke* 15:1012-1016, 1984.
46. Jacob Selhub, Paul F. Jacques, Andrew G. Bostom, Ralph B. D'Agostino, Peter W.F. Wilson, Albert J. Belanger, Daniel H. O'Leary, Philip A. Wolf, Ernst J. Schaefer, and Irwin H. Rosenberg, "Association between plasma homocysteine concentrations and extracranial carotid artery stenosis." *New England Journal of Medicine* 332:286-291, 1995.
47. Robert Clarke, Leslie Daly, Killian Robinson, Eileen Naughton, Seamus Cahalane, Brian Fowler and Ian Graham, "Hyperhomocysteinemia as an independent risk factor for vascular disease." *New England Journal of Medicine* 324:1149-1155, 1991.
48. Ottar Nygard, Stein Emil Vollset, Helga Refsum, Inger Stensvold, Aage Tverdal, Jan Erik Nordrehaug, Per Magne Ueland and Gunnar Kvale, "Total plasma homocysteine and cardiovascular risk profile. The Hordaland homocysteine study." *Journal of the American Medical Association* 274:1526-1533, 1995.
49. Arnold von Eckardstein, M. Rene Malinow, Barbara Upson, Jurgen Heinrich, Helmut Schulte, Rainer Schonfeld, Ekkehart Kohler and Gerd Assmann, "Effects of age, lipoproteins and hemostatic parameters on the role of homocyst(e)-inemia as a cardiovascular risk factor in men." *Arteriosclerosis and Thrombosis* 14:460-464, 1994.
50. Killian Robinson, Ellen L. Mayer, Dave P. Miller, Ralph Green, Frederick van Lente, Anjan Gupta, Kandice Kottke-Marchant, Susan R. Savon, Jacob Selhub, Steve E. Nissen, Michael Kutner, Eric J. Topol and Donald W. Jacobsen, "Hyperhomocysteinemia and low pyridoxal phosphate, com-

mon and independent reversible risk factors for coronary artery disease." *Circulation* 92:2825-2830, 1995.

51. E. Arnesen, Helga Refsum, K.H. Bonas, Per Magne Ueland, O.H. Forde and J.E. Nordrehaug, "Serum total homocysteine and coronary heart disease." *International Journal of Epidemiology* 24:704-709, 1995.
52. Isabella Fermo, Silvana Vigano'D'Angelo, Rita Paroni, Guiseppina Mazzola, Giliola Colori and Armando D'Angelo, "Prevalence of moderate hyperhomocysteinemia in patients with early-onset venous and arterial occlusive disease." *Annals of Internal Medicine* 123:747-753, 1995.
53. Martin den Heijer, Ted Koster, Henk J. Blom, Gerard M.J. Bos, Ernst Briet, Pieter H. Reitsma, Jan P. VandenBroncke and Frits R. Rosendaal, "Hyperhomocysteinemia as a risk factor for deep vein thrombosis." *New England Journal of Medicine* 334:759-762, 1996.
54. Godfried H.J. Boers, Antony G.H. Smals, Frans J.M. Trijbels, Brian Fowler, Jan A.J.M. Bakkeren, Henny C. Schoonderwaldt, Wim J. Kleijer and Peter W.C. Kloppenborg, "Heterozygosity for homocystinuria in premature peripheral and cerebral occlusive arterial disease." *New England Journal of Medicine* 313:709-715, 1985.
55. Johan B. Ubbink, "Is an elevated circulating maternal homocysteine concentration a risk factor for neural tube defects?" *Nutrition Reviews* 53:173-175, 1995.
56. S. Harvey Mudd, Fleming Skovby, Harvey L. Levy, Karen D. Pettigrew, Bridget Wilcken, Reed E. Pyeritz, G. Andria, Godfried H.J. Boers, Irvin L. Bromberg, Roberto Cerone, Brian Fowler, Hans Grobe, Hildgund Schmidt and Leslie Schweitzer, "The natural history of homocystinuria due to cystathionine beta synthase deficiency." *American Journal of Human Genetics* 37:1-31, 1985.
57. John M. Ellis and Kilmer S. McCully, "Prevention of myocardial infarction by vitamin B6." *Research Communications in Molecular Pathology and Pharmacology* 89:208-220, 1995.
58. Andrzej J. Olszewski and Kilmer S. McCully, "Fish oil decreases serum homocysteine in hyperlipemic men." *Coronary Artery Disease* 4:53-60, 1993.

59. Andrzej J. Olszewski, Wictor B. Szostak, Magda Bialkowska, Stefan Rudnicki and Kilmer S. McCully, "Reduction of plasma lipid and homocysteine levels by pyridoxine, folate, cobalamin, choline, riboflavin and troxerutin in atherosclerosis." *Atherosclerosis* 75:1-9, 1989.
60. P. Ambrosi, A. Barlater, G. Habib, Danielle Garcon, B. Kreitman, Pierre H. Roland, S. Saingra, D. Metras and Roger Luccioni, "Hyperhomocysteinemia in heart transplant recipients." *European Heart Journal* 15:1191-1195, 1994.
61. Peter B. Berger, James D. Jones, Lyle J. Olson, Brooks S. Edwards, Roger P. Frantz, Richard Rodeheffer, Bruce A. Kottke, Richard C. Daly and Christopher G.A. McGregor, "Increase in total plasma homocysteine concentration after cardiac transplantation." *Mayo Clinic Proceedings* 70:125-131, 1995.
62. Andrzej J. Olszewski and Kilmer S. McCully, "Homocysteine metabolism and the oxidative modification of proteins and lipids." *Free Radical Biology and Medicine* 14:683-693, 1993.

CHAPTER 4

Reaction, Resistance and Acceptance of the Homocysteine Theory

THE NATURE OF SCIENTIFIC DISCOVERY

The curious history of reaction and resistance to the homocysteine theory of arteriosclerosis demands explanation. Why should a quarter-century of medical science elapse and a whole new generation of scientists mature before the significance of an important new theory of disease is recognized? Is there some flaw or internal inconsistency in the homocysteine theory that has prevented its timely acceptance and implementation? No disease has been investigated more thoroughly and painstakingly in the 20th century than arteriosclerosis. Although research on cancer has attracted the attention of generations of medical scientists, the sheer volume of effort devoted to understand arteriosclerosis exceeds even that devoted to understanding cancer. In view of tremendous interest by medical scientists, why has a significant new theory of the underlying cause of arteriosclerosis been widely ignored and criticized by others for so long?

An outstanding scientist who attempted to answer questions about the nature of scientific discovery in another context was James Bryant Conant, chemist, educator, scientific administrator, public servant and president of Harvard University from 1933 until 1953. In his capacity as chemist and historian of science, Conant investigated and wrote an influential analysis of the reaction of early 19th-century chemists to the discovery of oxygen, the nature of combustion and the overthrow of the phlogiston theory of combustion. Phlogiston was a supposed property of matter that was consumed during combustion. Conant showed that adherents of the phlogiston theory ridiculed the discovery of oxygen and its combination with combustible materials to produce heat and fire. He analyzed their thinking, human nature and motives in an effort to understand their resistance to the new theory.

One of Conant's protegés, Thomas Kuhn, became interested in the nature of scientific discovery and the reaction of the scientific community to the development of a significant new scientific theory. Kuhn began his investigation of this topic as a junior fellow at Harvard. The result was his influential book *The Structure of Scientific Revolutions,* published as a monograph in 1962.[1] Although I did not know Kuhn when I was a student at Harvard College in the early 1950s, I was familiar with Conant's case studies of the history of science. In fact, one of the reasons I attended Harvard was the preeminence of Conant in chemistry, education and scientific leadership. I met Conant briefly several times as a student at Harvard and decided to concentrate in chemistry and biochemistry as an undergraduate.

The main concept Kuhn developed in his monograph is the insight that science often progresses by episodic revolutions in thinking rather than by incremental analysis of scientific problems. Kuhn pointed out that the history and development of science are intertwined with the personalities, motivations, human nature and thinking habits of practicing scientists. The ascendance of a particular scientific theory depends upon how well it explains a recognized set of observations and facts established by scientists over a period of years. When a new discovery is considered incompatible with current scientific theory, a crisis occurs in the field of investigation because of the anomalous new discovery. Adherents of the established scientific theory marshal the facts at their command and energetically gather new information that may support the existing theory. Only when sufficient data and facts are gathered by proponents of the new theory to demonstrate the incompatibility of the prevailing theory does the crisis in scientific understanding lead to the new theory's acceptance and the previous theory's overthrow. Kuhn termed this resolution of conflict between incompatible theories a "paradigm shift." In the resolution period following a paradigm shift, Kuhn found that scientists gather further information to support the new theory and reexamine and reinterpret the previous body of knowledge as to its compatibility with the new theory.

Albert Szent-Gyorgi, the brilliant 20th-century biochemist, described scientific discovery as a process that begins with analyzing the same facts other scientists examine but concludes with a new concept based on fresh observation. In this process, the discoverer realizes that the significant new observation will force reexamination and reinterpretation of an existing body of information about a scientific challenge. The more significant the challenge and the more extensive the backlog of previous knowledge in the field, the more significant is the new discovery and the more likely it is that the new theoretical interpretation will precipitate a "paradigm shift" in the sense described by Kuhn.

It is rare in the history of science that a previously widely held theory is totally rejected and discarded by proponents of a significant new scientific theory. An example of this rare occurrence in chemistry is the overthrow of the phlogiston theory of combustion, which was totally forgotten in the wake of Lavoisier's discovery of the reaction of oxygen with combustible materials. Another example, in biology and medicine, is the theory of spontaneous generation, which was overthrown by Pasteur's famous demonstrations and arguments concerning microorganisms before the French Academy of Science. Closely allied with the overthrow of the theory of spontaneous generation was the introduction of the germ theory of disease by Pasteur, leading to the science of microbiology, the early efforts to control contagious diseases in the 19th century and the discovery of antimicrobial therapy of infectious disease in the 20th century.

More commonly, new scientific theories that are based on new discoveries force scientists to reinterpret a large body of existing information according to the principles of the new theory. An example from physics is Albert Einstein's theory of relativity, prompted by the discovery of X-rays, radioactive decay and the constancy of the speed of light. One consequence was the overthrow of the concept of transmission of light by a hypothetical, but unproven, substance called the "ether of space." Another consequence was that the known dual nature of matter, with both wave-like and particle-like properties, was reinterpreted and reincorporated by Einstein into the theories of relativity, quantum mechanics and structure of matter that underlie the development of modern physics.

In the case of the homocysteine theory of arteriosclerosis, the discovery of the atherogenic effect of homocysteine resulting from the study of children with homocystinuria and the reproduction and demonstration of vascular disease in hyperhomocysteinemic animals did not immediately precipitate a scientific crisis in thinking about arteriosclerosis. There was at first insufficient knowledge about how homocysteine damages arteries, insufficient knowledge about homocysteine levels in subjects with arteriosclerosis in its different manifestations and insufficient knowledge about how homocysteine relates to fats, cholesterol and lipoproteins in their effects on vascular disease. Only when the accumulation of knowledge about homocysteine reached a critical level was it possible to explain and reinterpret the long history of research on arteriosclerosis. Only within the past few years, in the 1990s, has it become possible to consider that the homocysteine theory may constitute a "paradigm shift" in understanding about the cause of arteriosclerosis in susceptible populations in the sense described by Kuhn.

CONTROVERSY OVER THE HOMOCYSTEINE THEORY

Why was the homocysteine theory of arteriosclerosis controversial and widely ignored when it was first developed? Why was the introduction of a new concept of arteriosclerosis based on a medical discovery about the damaging effect of homocysteine on arteries a threat to the conventional wisdom about the disease? Why was this new concept of arteriosclerosis as a disease of protein intoxication from dietary imbalance involving vitamins so difficult for medical scientists in the cholesterol, fat and lipoprotein fields to accept? Why was a new approach that had the potential to explain many otherwise imponderable observations about arteriosclerosis so widely ignored?

As explained in Chapter 1, the initial reaction to the medical discovery about homocysteine and vascular disease was one of interest and fascination on the part of medical scientists who were looking for a new approach to otherwise inexplicable observations about arteriosclerosis. Within the next five years, however, influential scientists in the homocystinuria field and in the cholesterol-lipoprotein field began to question the significance of the new approach. Some scientists perceived that it threatened to revise thinking radically about the underlying cause of the most pervasive degenerative disease in developed countries.

Perhaps the most controversial aspect of the new homocysteine theory, when it was first developed, was that cholesterol, fats and lipoproteins were relegated to a secondary role in understanding the underlying cause of arteriosclerosis. The discovery of the atherogenic effect of homocysteine in children with different forms of homocystinuria was considered an anomaly since arteriosclerosis was then observed to be caused without the evident participation of cholesterol, fats, or lipoproteins.

In the mid-20th century, elements of a crisis gradually developed in the conventional cholesterol/fat concept of the underlying cause of arteriosclerosis. A number of significant observations were found to be incompatible with the traditional approach, including the failure to relate blood cholesterol to dietary cholesterol and fat, the occurrence of arteriosclerosis in many individuals without abnormalities of blood cholesterol and lipoproteins, the failure to correlate major declines in risk of heart disease and stroke with changes in blood cholesterol or dietary cholesterol and the failure of several major trials of cholesterol lowering by diet or drug therapy to show decreased disease or increased longevity. The recent modest success of statin drug therapy in lowering blood cholesterol and reducing disease risk is compromised by the evidence of liver and muscle toxicity and carcinogenicity of these drugs in animals[2] and by the evidence that these drugs inhibit formation of ubiquinol, a key component of energy production in heart and other cells.[3] The success of vitamin E in prevention of arteriosclerosis, originally proposed by the Shute Clinic in Canada in the early 1950s, is contrasted with the recent failure to show a protective effect of beta-carotene in disease prevention.

As pointed out by Kuhn, a crisis in scientific theory, such as the accumulation of the significant anomalies in the cholesterol/fat approach, never leads to rejection of the previous theory unless a plausible alternative theory is available to take its place. The cholesterol/fat approach persisted as the leading theory to explain the underlying cause of arteriosclerosis for many years because no other theory was available to explain the vast accumulation of observations and facts concerning the disease. The homocysteine theory of arteriosclerosis, when first introduced in 1975[4] and when first developed comprehensively in 1983,[5] did not attempt to explain the many anomalous observations in the cholesterol/fat field. This is because there was no comprehensive biochemical theory that related the observations on homocysteine and vascular disease to observations in the cholesterol/fat field. As Chapter 6 explains, such a comprehensive theory was not introduced until 1993.[6]

Another reason the homocysteine theory of arteriosclerosis was not accepted is that the anomalous observation of vascular disease in children with homocystinuria was based on genetic diseases which are rare in the general population. If these diseases affected only 1 child in 100,000, how could the observation be applied to the population as a whole? Furthermore, the heterozygous state of homocystinuria caused by cystathionine beta synthase deficiency occurs at most in 1 to 2 percent of the population, and early studies failed to show increased risk of arteriosclerosis in these heterozygotes. Only with the recent observation of the high incidence—38 percent—of the heterozygous state of the enzyme methylenetetrahydrofolate reductase in a susceptible population[7] does it become plausible that the homocysteine theory applies to a population at risk. This mutation could affect a major segment of the population by increasing the quantity of dietary folic acid that is necessary to prevent buildup of blood homocysteine.

Chapter 2 noted that scientists at the Harvard School of Public Health failed to confirm Rinehart's discovery of arteriosclerosis in monkeys with chronic vitamin B6 deficiency because of the experiment's flawed design and interpretation. Although other groups of investigators also observed arteriosclerosis in vitamin B6-deficient monkeys and pigs, the influence of the Harvard experiments brought into question the whole theory of vitamin deficiency as a cause of arteriosclerosis in the general population. Similarly, when medical scientists reported that they could not confirm our finding of early arteriosclerotic plaques in rabbits injected with homocysteine, the effect of their report was to question the entire validity of the homocysteine theory. Only with subsequent experimentation in animals over the next decade did it become apparent that elevated blood homocysteine is associated with arteriosclerosis in animals in the overwhelming majority of studies.

The original experiments of Rinehart and Greenberg in

vitamin B6-deficient monkeys suggested that the blood levels of B6 in the human population were in the deficient range that caused arteriosclerosis in monkeys. Despite published reports in the earlier literature that suggested that a widespread deficiency of vitamin B6 in the population could account for arteriosclerosis,[8] this finding was generally dismissed by nutritionists as lacking adequate foundation. Only with recent studies showing widespread deficiencies of vitamin B6, folic acid and vitamin B12 in the elderly[9] and in cardiac patients[10] is there increasing acceptance of Rinehart's finding that vitamin deficiency may be the underlying cause of the disease. Since fat and cholesterol were found only in small quantities in the arteriosclerotic plaques of a few of Rinehart's monkeys and the predominant plaques were fibrous and fibrocalcific, most scientists who adhered to the cholesterol/fat theory regarded the experimental results as atypical of the human disease. The logical conclusion of this line of thinking was that since the experimental plaques contained little fat and cholesterol, vitamin B6 deficiency was not relevant to arteriosclerosis.

Many medical scientists who investigate patients with arteriosclerosis are only generally familiar with the detailed pathological findings in arteriosclerosis. Except for scientists with experience in human pathology, many investigators have an incomplete concept of the cellular and tissue components of arteriosclerotic plaques. Many pathologists and medical scientists who investigate the cellular and tissue aspects of the disease, on the other hand, may have an incomplete understanding of the biochemical and physiological details of how cholesterol and lipoproteins are formed in the body. The controversy over acceptance of the homocysteine theory of arteriosclerosis is partly related to misinterpretation of the significance of fat and cholesterol deposits in plaques and their role in the development of plaques. The idea that plaques are filled with or obstructed only by greasy fat deposits is incorrect for the vast majority of plaques. As discussed in Chapter 2, many arteriosclerotic plaques, even in advanced disease, are of the fibrous and fibrocalcific type that are found in subjects with homocystinuria and in monkeys with vitamin B6 deficiency. Typically arteriosclerotic plaques are tough, inelastic, thickened and heavily encrusted with calcium deposits, making them difficult to dissect with scalpel or scissors. In advanced plaques, their complex structure also includes cholesterol crystals, fatty deposits, areas of degeneration or death of tissue, blood clots, protein deposits, the growth of small blood vessels into the artery wall and areas of bleeding that predispose to complete blockage by formation of blood clots.

If a medical investigator is convinced that cholesterol and fats are the underlying cause of arteriosclerotic plaques, then any observations or experimental results in which cholesterol and fatty deposits are inconspicuous are dismissed as irrelevant. On the other hand, experts in the development of plaques agree that lipoproteins do participate in the early stages of plaque formation by forming foam cells. If the exact nature of the interaction between tissue changes in the arteries produced by homocysteine and the deposits of cholesterol and lipoproteins is incompletely understood, the participation of homocysteine in the process is perceived as questionable, leading to controversy about the significance of homocysteine in the development of plaques.

Adherents of the cholesterol/fat hypothesis correctly point out that elevated cholesterol levels are associated with increased risk of arteriosclerosis, particularly at levels greater than 240 milligrams per deciliter. Practicing physicians know, however, that the majority of their patients with arteriosclerosis have normal or desirable cholesterol levels in the 180–220 range. In my autopsy study of almost 200 veterans, the group with the most severe disease had a mean cholesterol of 186, and two-thirds had no evidence of diabetes, high blood pressure or elevated cholesterol levels.[11] The response to these facts by cholesterol and fat experts is that even though blood cholesterol level is low in some cases, cholesterol must cause the disease because of the correlation of risk with elevated levels. One of the attractive features of the homocysteine theory is that a dietary, genetic, toxic or age-related factor (homocysteine) is able to explain many of the cases of severe arteriosclerosis in patients with lifelong normal or desirable cholesterol levels. The failure to acknowledge this disparity between the cholesterol and homocysteine approaches leads to another source of controversy about the underlying cause of the disease.

Another reason for controversy over the homocysteine theory is the inherent complexity and inscrutable nature of the degenerative diseases of aging. Although cholesterol levels increase after puberty and in the adult years, the reasons for this increase are only partially understood. Furthermore, in the elderly population there is little correlation between cholesterol levels and risk of arteriosclerosis, as shown by the Framingham Heart Study. As explained more fully in Chapter 6, the gradual rise in homocysteine levels with aging is the result of a gradual shift in the way the body processes homocysteine. This shift to higher levels with aging suggests a new explanation of the biochemical basis of the aging process. The detailed processing of methionine and homocysteine in aging is at the heart of how aging cells and tissues are impaired in their ability to use food and oxygen for the production of chemical energy in the body.

Resistance to the Homocysteine Theory

In the 28 years since its first discovery, the principles of the homocysteine theory have been explained repeatedly and have been supported by scientific studies in different disciplines from laboratories all over the world.[4,5,6] Although medical experts have had extensive opportunity to read about and understand these principles, the medical community in America has been unwilling, until the past half-decade, to consider the theory seriously. One reason, as explained in the previous section, is that the homocysteine theory relegates cholesterol and fats to a secondary role in causation and incriminates deficiencies of vitamins B6, folic acid and B12 and an imbalance between dietary protein and these vitamins as the underlying cause of arteriosclerosis.

Other reasons for the reluctance to accept the homocysteine theory are (1) incomplete understanding by some investigators of the pathological changes and pathogenesis of the disease, (2) the inherent complexity of degenerative diseases associated with aging, (3) inability or unwillingness to acknowledge that a completely different complex area of biochemistry other than cholesterol and fats is involved in the cause of the disease, (4) misinterpretation of aspects of experimental arteriosclerosis induced by cholesterol in animals, (5) failure to appreciate the significance of cholesterol oxides in plaque formation, (6) the observed correlation between damage to arteries and deposition of cholesterol and fats in developing plaques, (7) the inherent difficulty in attributing disease in populations to specific nutritional factors and (8) the failure of previous science to advance a theory explaining the significance of the protein intoxication approach to understanding the origin of arteriosclerosis.

When treating manifestations of arteriosclerosis, heart attack, stroke, kidney failure or gangrene of feet and legs, the medical profession frequently encounters the disease in its late stages. Usually decades of gradual narrowing of coronary, carotid, renal or iliac arteries by arteriosclerosis have occurred silently before symptoms occur. In attempting to treat a serious disease late in its course, difficult problems are encountered by physicians and surgeons. Drug therapy may be ineffective in reversing decades of damage and gradual narrowing of the arteries. Surgical therapy by angioplasty or by bypass grafts may be temporarily effective in relieving symptoms in the late stages of the disease, but the process may recur and cause narrowing of the treated arteries or the grafted segments. Treatment of associated prediposing conditions such as diabetes or high blood pressure may help to delay the onset of further complications of arteriosclerosis, but therapy for these conditions is frequently only partially successful.

Efforts by medical practitioners or nutritional experts to arrest the progress of arteriosclerosis by controlling blood cholesterol and lipoproteins through dietary modification and drug therapy are fraught with difficulty. Changing lifelong habits of poor diet and nutritional abuse are frequently ineffective in elderly patients. Drug therapy to lower blood cholesterol is complicated by toxic side effects in some cases and by failure of the cholesterol and lipoprotein levels to respond satisfactorily in other cases. Because medical practitioners encounter the disease after major complications have already occurred and because the disease is so far advanced, efforts at prevention of further progression, therefore, are frequently ineffective.

Because of their training and orientation, some medical and surgical practitioners in the arteriosclerosis field have traditionally neglected nutritional and preventive measures when treating patients with advanced disease. Because of the difficulties in treating advanced disease, the use of proper nutrition is limited. Because of some unsubstantiated claims by nutritionists and because of reluctance to accept the causative role of nutritional imbalance between proteins and vitamins, many medical practitioners have been reluctant to accept a new approach. Furthermore, nutritional scientists concentrated for many years on treating those diseases caused by extreme and serious deficiencies of vitamins; for example, they used niacin therapy for pellagra, vitamin C therapy for scurvy and vitamin B12 therapy for pernicious anemia. Only in recent years have they begun to concentrate on the role of partial vitamin deficiencies and subtle nutritional imbalances in degenerative diseases.

Because the cholesterol approach to the treatment and prevention of arteriosclerosis has prevailed for 80 years, the pharmaceutical industry has concentrated on developing better drugs to lower blood cholesterol levels. The current generation of the "statin" drugs used for this purpose impairs the function of the liver and other organs in the formation of cholesterol in the body. These drugs have had modest success in preventing the complications of arteriosclerosis in recent trials, but the price in terms of safety is potential toxicity to the liver, muscles and optic lenses and the threat of cancer, indicated by their carcinogenic effects in animals.[2,3] Another price is the high cost of those drugs which are now recommended for a large segment of the population, including children who may be at risk for developing elevated cholesterol levels as adults. The pharmaceutical industry has concentrated on developing these lucrative drugs because the prevention of arteriosclerosis by improving diet or adding vitamin supplements to enriched foods offers little economic incentive. The pharmaceutical industry is reluctant to support the homocysteine theory because little profit can be made from marketing vitamins and because the theory obviates the need for expensive cholesterol-lowering drugs.

Furthermore, the nutritional community and the food industry have been resistant to the homocysteine theory for several reasons. First, the theory implicates the modern food supply in the cause of arteriosclerosis because highly processed foods are deficient in vitamins and nutritionally imbalanced. The marketing of these foods, deficient in B vitamins, is profitable because of their long shelf life and ease of distribution. Second, the homocysteine theory obviates the need for marketing low-cholesterol foods, polyunsaturated oils and "light" foods which are popular and profitable. To reduce the toxic buildup of homocysteine, the food industry would instead need to concentrate on marketing and distributing fresh, minimally processed foods which are more perishable and fragile than packaged, boxed, frozen, canned or highly preserved foods. A future threat to the food supply is the proposal to market irradiated foods which are seriously deficient in vitamins B6, folic acid and vitamin B12 because of the exquisite sensitivity of these vitamins to damage by the oxidizing effects of radiation. On the other hand, there has been a major improvement in the marketing and transporting of fresh vegetables and fruits in the past 30 years, possibly contributing to the decline in heart attacks and strokes because of the increased availability of these foods all year long.

The traditional approach to addressing the nutritional cause of arteriosclerosis has been to incriminate dietary cholesterol and fats. This approach is based on the facts that feeding cholesterol to animals induces arteriosclerosis and elevated blood lipoprotein levels and diets high in the fats and cholesterol of animal origin are correlated with susceptibility to the disease. This ingrained pattern of thinking about the cause of arteriosclerosis, sometimes termed the "cholesterol myth," has a certain direct appeal because of its apparent cause-and-effect relationship. Unfortunately, nutrition and its relation to induction of disease are highly complex and difficult to interpret.

The homocysteine theory of arteriosclerosis has less direct appeal because the production of the disease is related to a subtle imbalance of dietary proteins and vitamins, relegating the increase of lipoprotein and cholesterol levels in some cases to secondary effects. In addition, the simple concept that foods with high sugar or high fat content are highly processed with little vitamin content has been difficult for adherents of the cholesterol/fat approach to accept.

My Personal Story

New scientific theories are related to the social, cultural and personal contexts of their discoverers. It has often been claimed that the time is right for a new scientific discovery because of development of a particular field; dissatisfaction with previous theories; appearance of new methods, concepts or technology; widespread awareness among scientists of opportunities for advancing understanding in a given field; and a chance observation that precipitates the development of a new theory. These influences affect the personal situation of the discoverer of a new theory, and the discovery of the new theory in turn affects the discoverer.

In the case of the homocysteine theory of arteriosclerosis, the observation of the relation between homocysteine and vascular disease, the development of the theory and its publication had some remarkable effects on my career and personal situation. As a person with a solid educational background in chemistry, biochemistry, biology and medicine; an interest in understanding the relation between biochemistry and disease; and the experience of training in several superb scientific laboratories under the guidance of outstanding scientists, my situation at the time I discovered the homocysteine theory was promising. I had recently completed my residency training in pathology, a discipline of medicine that had only begun to respond to the revolutionary developments in molecular biology, cell biology and biochemistry that occurred in the 1950s and 1960s.

My position was one of high visibility in pathology and medicine: Associate Pathologist at the Massachusetts General Hospital and Assistant Professor of Pathology at Harvard Medical School. I truly believed that my discovery of the homocysteine theory could be developed and applied to patients with arteriosclerosis effectively and expeditiously. The facilities for medical research and the atmosphere where I worked were stimulating and conducive to basically oriented scientific research on a significant problem in contemporary medicine. However, for a variety of reasons, my promising career became sidetracked and shunted in another direction by forces beyond my control. In reviewing what happened to my career, the events that occurred, the apparent reasons for the changes in my opportunities and the final outcome from a vantage point of 20 years, several conclusions are of interest in regard to the development and fate of the homocysteine theory.

Beginning in 1968 with the observation of arteriosclerosis in children with different genetic diseases causing homocystinuria and continuing with the publication of experiments with animals, cell cultures, physiological and biochemical preparations from 1969 to 1976, my research associates, students and colleagues were active in determining the elements of the homocysteine theory of arteriosclerosis. Because of my background and interests, this research was concentrated on the basic biochemical, pathophysiological and cellular effects of homocysteine on arterial cells and tissues. Only one unsuccessful attempt was made to measure blood homocysteine levels in patients with arteriosclerosis. Furthermore, the abnormal processing of homocysteine thiolactone by cancer cells and the discovery of a series of new homocysteine compounds that affect cancer growth in animals were under active study in 1976, occupying the laboratory efforts of my associates.

In 1976 I was contacted by two neurophysiologists from Massachusetts Institute of Technology, Stephen A. Raymond and Edward R. Gruberg. They had heard a seminar by Dr. Moses Suzman, who described the development of the homocysteine theory, and had read all of my published articles on the subject. They became fascinated with the subject and decided to write a book for the general reader to explain the theory and its ramifications. The result of their efforts was a fascinating book *Beyond Cholesterol: Vitamin B6, Arteriosclerosis and Your Heart,* published in 1981.[12] Besides reviewing my discovery of the homocysteine theory, they interviewed prominent medical scientists in the homocystinuria and arteriosclerosis fields. In the book they described the nature of arteriosclerosis, the cholesterol hypothesis, evidence for the homocysteine theory, risk factors for arteriosclerosis, the recommended dietary allowance for vitamin B6, dietary composition of methionine and vitamin B6 and other implications of the theory. Prior to publication of the book, an article based on the book was published in *Atlantic Monthly.*[13]

These publications were remarkable in several ways. The authors were not experts in the field of arteriosclerosis. They were not physicians, but they were highly educated and experienced medical scientists in another field, neurophysiology. Yet they were able to capture the essence of the disease, to describe the development and implications of the homocysteine theory, and to contrast the new theory with the traditional cholesterol hypothesis. They admirably reviewed the evidence for the theory that was available in the late 1970s, described the background of the discovery and development of the theory, and made a cogent, well-reasoned presentation of its implications. The article and book were minor successes, generating comment in the media, generally favorable reviews, and realizing several printings.

Partly as the result of *Beyond Cholesterol,* the media paid more attention to the homocysteine theory. An interview was published in *Prevention* magazine in which I explained the use of the homocysteine theory in preventing arteriosclerosis.[14] An article was published in *Time* magazine introducing the homocysteine theory and contrasting it with the recent observation of arteriosclerosis induced in chickens by the herpes virus, as alternatives to the cholesterol approach.[15] In the article in *Time,* an expert in the cholesterol field was quoted as saying that "taking vitamin B6 . . . [for arteriosclerosis is] . . . crazy."

In addition to the book and subsequent articles, a number of newspapers, some reputable and some of the tabloid variety, reported on the publicity surrounding the homocysteine theory. A leading proponent of the cholesterol/fat approach denounced the theory in a newspaper interview as "errant nonsense" and suggested that failure to prescribe cholesterol-lowering drugs for arteriosclerosis amounted to "malpractice" or worse. Even Canadian television interviewed me regarding the controversy.

The chairman of the department at the hospital where I worked retired in 1975, and the new chairman informed me that I would need to find a position elsewhere. In explanation I was told by the hospital director that I had "failed to prove my theory." Harvard had decided against renewing my appointment or promoting me to a tenured position. I had held an appointment as assistant professor of pathology at Harvard Medical School for eight years. My 28-year association with Harvard as an undergraduate, medical student, intern, resident, research fellow, instructor, assistant professor and associate pathologist came to an end in December of 1978.

Although I had declined several inquiries about positions in other medical centers during the period when I was developing the homocysteine theory, I was now ready to accept a new position that would enable me to continue my career as a medical scientist. I was surprised to find, however, that my attempts to secure such a position were repeatedly frustrated during a two year period by unexplained obstacles. After this substantial threat to my survival as a medical scientist, assistance from a colleague and indirect pressure on my former employer finally resulted in my appointment as pathologist at the Veterans Affairs Medical Center in Providence, Rhode Island in 1981. This position, which I still occupy today, has a primary responsibility for the practice of anatomic and clinical pathology in the care of U.S. veterans. In the past 16 years, I have continued to investigate the importance of homocysteine in arteriosclerosis, cancer and aging as best as I can with the limited facilities that are available to me. My position in Providence has enabled me to develop my own individual approach to understanding the homocysteine theory, which I will describe more fully in Chapter 6.

Watson's Rules for Success in Science

In an article published by one of my former mentors, James D. Watson, on the occasion of the 40th anniversary of the discovery of the DNA double helix, he outlined the strategies for his success in science.[16] Watson's rules for success certainly applied to his career as a revolutionary molecular biologist. His rules also apply to my own experience in advancing the homocysteine theory of arteriosclerosis.

Watson's first rule is to learn from superb scientists who are winners in the intense competition in the world of science. He was able to learn about the new field of molecular biology from Salvatore Luria, an outstanding scientist in the genetics of microbiology and bacteriophage. He decided to explore his interest in DNA structure during a postdoctoral fellowship at Cambridge University in England, where he made his famous discovery with Francis Crick.

Watson's second rule is to take risks by exploring a new unrecognized approach to a significant scientific problem. In taking this risk, Watson said, a scientist has to be prepared to "get into deep trouble" because colleagues and rivals will tell you that you are "very likely to be unqualified to succeed." He added that this risk taking often leads to criticism because "your very willingness to take on a very big goal will offend some people who will think that you are . . . crazy."

Watson's third rule is to have scientific allies "who will

save you when you find yourself in deep [trouble]." Watson's mentor Luria saved him when he offended one of his thesis advisors, and Max Perutz and John Kendrew saved him when his American fellowship stipend was cut off for tackling the DNA structure problem. These allies at Cambridge University supported Watson and Crick's work on DNA in its early stages, allowing successful resolution of the problem.

Watson's fourth rule is to "never do anything that bores you." You must persist with a scientific problem that is exciting and appealing to you. As Louis Pasteur said, the scientist's most precious asset is his enthusiasm for investigating a problem that interests him. Because the scientist who takes risks is likely to encounter criticism and ridicule, it is necessary to turn to experts who have knowledge in other fields for advice and to "constantly expose your ideas to informed criticism."

My own risk in advancing a new theory of the cause of arteriosclerosis was that I would offend the generations of scientists who had devoted their careers to propounding the cholesterol hypothesis. Although I had experience in superb research laboratories concerned with cholesterol biosynthesis, steroid hormones, molecular biology of protein synthesis and transfer RNA, molecular and microbial genetics, and methionine and homocysteine metabolism, I had never worked directly on the problem of arteriosclerosis. I was able to take a fresh look at the fundamental causes of this disease because I had not participated in this area of research during my years of fellowship training. I was able to apply my knowledge and background in protein synthesis, cholesterol and hormone biochemistry, molecular genetics and experimental pathology in new ways that had not been considered by previous investigators in the arteriosclerosis field.

After the first eight years of research on the homocysteine theory, I found myself in 1976 in deep trouble. My career development grant from the National Institutes of Health had expired, and the new department chairman, the hospital director and Harvard Medical School were not convinced that my approach was promising. After my involuntary termination from a promising career two years later, I found myself unable to continue my research into the homocysteine theory, and unable to investigate my new discoveries about abnormal homocysteine metabolism in cancer cells. Thereby I found myself fulfilling Watson's rule about getting into trouble over ambitious scientific ideas.

The longtime friend and colleague in medical science who helped me to salvage my research career was William Sunderman Jr. of the University of Connecticut. He recommended me for my current postion at the V.A. Medical Center in Providence. Within the first two years in that position, I was able to complete and publish my first monograph on the homocysteine theory.[5] With help and collaboration from a new colleague in Providence, Michael Vezeridis, I was able to resume laboratory research on my synthetic homocysteine compounds that antagonize carcinogenesis and inhibit the growth of malignant cells in culture and in animals, as I describe in Chapter 6. By learning from outstanding scientists in different fields, taking a risk to explore a new approach to a very large scientific and medical problem, turning to scientific allies who could help me out of career troubles and persisting in my enthusiasm for investigating an exciting scientific observation, I had fulfilled Watson's rules for success in science.

A revolution occurred in molecular biology following the discovery of the DNA double helix. Likewise, there promises to be a revolution in the understanding of degenerative diseases of aging as a result of observations on how homocysteine controls the growth, aging, and death of body cells. The observation of changes in homocysteine with aging are an extraordinary sequel to an event in my career that occurred before I began my studies on homocysteine. In the course of an interview, I was asked about how a biomedical scientist could investigate the fundamental nature of aging at a cellular and molecular level. My response to the question was inadequate and uninformed because I was at an early stage in my career and had not considered aging as a promising field of study. Although I was later granted an American Cancer Society Faculty Research Award, I was intrigued by the question and disappointed with my lack of knowledge in the field of aging at the time.

If there is to be a revolution in understanding the role of homocysteine in the aging process, two basic conditions must be fulfilled. First, there needs to be a plausible theoretical framework for understanding how changes in homocysteine processing could explain the basic phenomena observed in aging. Second, there must be experimental validation of the theoretical formulation of changes in homocysteine with aging and with the degenerative diseases of aging, including arteriosclerosis and cancer. If these conditions are fulfilled, a fifth rule could be added to Watson's rules for success. The rule is that one's scientific success can be judged by the creative advances a new scientific theory inspires in the younger generation of scientists who follow in one's field of study.

THE NEW STATUS OF THE HOMOCYSTEINE THEORY

Although the homocysteine theory is no longer new, it has yet to be widely accepted among medical investigators and practitioners. A paradigm shift has not yet occurred in the arteriosclerosis field. The homocysteine theory is currently undergoing reexamination by increasing numbers of medical investigators worldwide. Some consider the homocysteine approach increasingly interesting, promising and productive because of its power to explain otherwise inexplicable facts.

The principal reason for the new status of the homocysteine theory as a hot new area for medical research on arteriosclerosis is that a reliable test for blood homocysteine levels has begun to be applied to human studies. While studies with experimental animals, cell cultures, and biochemical pathways are of theoretical interest to medical experts and investigators, only with successful human studies[9,10] do the results begin to convince the skeptics. Surveys using the test for blood homocysteine on populations at risk and groups of patients with arteriosclerotic disease have now fulfilled the major predictions of the homocysteine theory.[17] As explained in Chapter 3, these human studies have shown that elevated blood homocysteine, hyperhomocysteinemia, is a major independent risk factor for the development of arteriosclerosis.

The status of the homocysteine theory has now reached a critical stage. Large-scale testing of the theory in populations at high risk of arteriosclerosis is urgently needed to demonstrate its effectiveness in preventing and treating the disease. Such a successful demonstration may well fulfill the prediction made in an article published in *Science* this year, "heart attack: gone with the century."[18] By showing that nutritional measures, supplemental vitamins, and other nontoxic strategies to control elevated blood homocysteine levels reduce the risk of vascular disease, a dramatically lower risk of heart attack and stroke and increased longevity will be demonstrated in a successful study of this type will constitute final proof of the validity of the approach. It is time that some of the funding which has been lavished for decades on the cholesterol/fat hypothesis with equivocal, disappointing or inconclusive results should now be directed to planning and concluding long-term prospective trials of the homocysteine theory.

Over the past half-decade there has commenced a worldwide interest in planning a prospective trial of the homocysteine theory. As yet, these efforts have been only desultory and incipient. The past record of disappointing results in the large-scale intervention trials aimed at controlling arteriosclerosis by lowering of cholesterol levels is a warning that poorly conceived or inadequately executed trials may fail to accomplish ambitious objectives.

In the development of a prospective trial to test the homocysteine theory of arteriosclerosis, several principles must be followed. Since arteriosclerosis develops slowly over a period of decades, the trial must be of sufficient duration to demonstrate a difference between treated and control groups in slowing progression of the disease. Prevention by dietary modification should emphasize limitation of methionine consumption and augmentation of natural sources of vitamins B6, folic acid and B12. Prevention and treatment with supplemental vitamins must be at sufficient doses to insure control of blood homocysteine levels. Other factors affecting homocysteine levels, such as age, gender, family history, thyroid function, kidney function, blood pressure, diabetes, drugs, hormones and toxins must be controlled and compared between those in treated and control groups. Batteries of clinical tests are needed to document changes in blood homocysteine, levels of vitamins B6, folic acid and B12, LDL, HDL and tests of major organ function. Finally, documentation of the clinical complications of arteriosclerosis, such as heart attack, stroke, gangrene and embolism needs to be established by reliable criteria.

The interpretation of results of a prospective trial to test the homocysteine theory needs to focus on changes in disease incidence, the relation to nutritional status and dietary consumption, the results of laboratory testing and clinical studies, and the importance of genetic and toxic factors. Modern molecular methods to detect hidden genetic defects affecting both homocysteine and lipoproteins will add to the decisiveness of the results. Successful conclusion of such prospective trials in the future will demonstrate beyond doubt that an optimal diet with or without supplemental vitamins over a sufficient period of time will substantially reduce heart attack, stroke, kidney failure and arteriosclerotic gangrene as killer diseases.

The First International Conference on Homocysteine Metabolism from Basic Science to Clinical Medicine held in Ireland in 1995, gathered over 300 medical scientists working in the homocysteine field.[19] Over 120 separate scientific studies from different countries were presented to demonstrate increased acceptance among the medical community of the homocysteine approach to control vascular disease and other medical conditions, including birth defects, cancer and kidney failure.

Studies on the intake of folic acid to prevent spina bifida and other serious neurological birth defects have prompted the U.S. Food and Drug Administration to require the addition of this vitamin to all enriched foods, including flour, pasta, cereals and rice by 1998. The action of folic acid not only prevents neural tube birth defects but also prevents elevation of blood homocysteine in mothers during the first trimester of pregnancy.[20] Sufficient folic acid in enriched foods will help to insure that all pregnant women will consume 400 mcg of the vitamin per day from the moment of conception and throughout their pregnancies. An additional anticipated benefit will be the prevention of up to 50,000 deaths from heart disease per year attributable to elevation of blood homocysteine.[21]

REFERENCES

1. Thomas S. Kuhn, *The Structure of Scientific Revolutions* (Chicago: University of Chicago Press, 1962).
2. Thomas B. Newman and Stephen B. Hulley, "Carcinogenicity of lipid-lowering drugs." *Journal of the American Medical Association* 275:55–60, 1996.
3. Richard A. Willis, Karl Folkers, J. Lan Tucker, Chun-Qu Ye, Li-Jun Xia and Hiroo Tamagawa, "Lovastatin decreases coenzyme Q levels in rats." *Proceedings of the National Academy of Sciences USA* 87:8928–8930, 1990.
4. Kilmer S. McCully and Robert B. Wilson, "Homocysteine theory of arteriosclerosis." *Atherosclerosis* 22:215–227, 1975.
5. Kilmer S. McCully, "The homocysteine theory of arteriosclerosis: Development and current status." In: Antonio M. Gotto, Jr. and Rodolfo Paoletti, editors, *Atherosclerosis Reviews,* volume 11 (New York: Raven Press, 1983), pp. 157–246.
6. Kilmer S. McCully, "Chemical pathology of homocysteine. I. Atherogenesis." *Annals of Clinical and Laboratory Science* 23:477–493, 1993.
7. Phyllis Frosst, Henk J. Blom, R. Milos, Philippe Goyette,

O.A. Shephard, Rowena G. Matthews, Godfried J.H. Boers, Martin den Heijer, Leo A.J. Kluijtmans, Lambert P. W.J. van den Heuvel and Rima Rozen, "A candidate genetic risk factor for vascular disease: A common mutation in methylenetetrahydrofolate reductase." *Nature Genetics* 10:111–113, 1995.

8. "Vitamin status of cardiac patients." *Nutrition Reviews* 25:116–118, 1967.
9. Jacob Selhub, Paul F. Jacques, Peter W.F. Wilson, David Rush and Irwin H. Rosenberg, "Vitamin status and intake as primary determinants of homocysteinemia in an elderly population." *Journal of the American Medical Association* 270:2693–2698, 1993.
10. Killian Robinson, Ellen L. Mayer, Dave P. Miller, Ralph Green, Frederick van Leute, Anjan Gupta, Kandice Kottke-Marchant, Susan R. Savon, Jacob Selhub, Steven E. Nissen, Michael Kutner, Eric J. Topol and Donald W. Jacobsen, "Hyperhomocysteinemia and low pyridoxal phosphate. Common and independent reversible risk factors for coronary artery disease." *Circulation* 92:2825–2830, 1995.
11. Kilmer S. McCully, "Atherosclerosis, serum cholesterol and the homocysteine theory: A retrospective study of 194 consecutive autopsies." *American Journal of the Medical Sciences* 299:217–221, 1990.
12. Edward R. Gruberg and Stephen A. Raymond, *Beyond Cholesterol. Vitamin B6, Arteriosclerosis and your Heart* (New York: St. Martin's Press, 1981).
13. Edward R. Gruberg and Stephen A. Raymond, "Beyond cholesterol. A new theory on arteriosclerosis." *Atlantic Monthly* 243:59–65, 1979.
14. Jane Kinderlehrer, "B6—maybe the answer to heart disease." *Prevention* 31:138–145, 1979.
15. "Diet debate. Is cholesterol the culprit?" *Time* August 6, 1979, p. 61.
16. James D. Watson, "Succeeding in science: some rules of thumb." *Science* 261:1812–1813, 1993.
17. Kilmer S. McCully, "Homocysteine and vascular disease." *Nature Medicine* 2:386–398, 1996.

18. Michael S. Brown and Joseph L. Goldstein, "Heart attacks: Gone with the century?" *Science* 272:629, 1996.
19. International Conference on Homocysteine Metabolism from Basic Science to Clinical Medicine. *Irish Journal of Medical Science* 164 Suppl 15:1–36, 1995.
20. Johan B. Ubbink, "Is an elevated circulating maternal homocysteine concentration a risk factor for neural tube defects?" *Nutrition Reviews* 53:173–175, 1995.
21. Carol J. Boushey, Shirley A.A. Beresford, Gilbert S. Omenn and Arno G. Motulsky, "A quantitative assessment of plasma homocysteine as a risk factor for vascular disease. Probable benefits of increasing folic acid intakes." *Journal of the American Medical Association* 274:1049–1057, 1995.

CHAPTER 5

Homocysteine and Individual Risk

Lifelong Prevention of Arteriosclerosis

As explained in previous chapters, the role of homocysteine in human arteriosclerosis has been clarified by clinical and epidemiological studies over the past two decades. Experimental and laboratory studies have documented homocysteine's role in the genesis of plaques, progression of arterial narrowing, and complications of thrombosis of arteries to the vital organs. In human populations the control of blood homocysteine levels by known risk factors for arteriosclerosis, including diet, genetic background, gender, toxic factors, hormones, drugs, exercise, aging and lifestyle, have been explored sufficiently to suggest, for individuals at risk, lifelong strategies for the prevention of arteriosclerosis.[1]

The importance of a new theory about a given disease is judged by the ability of individuals at risk to prevent or cure that disease by practical application of the theory. Consider these examples: (1) John Snow's theory, which linked cholera to contaminated water in 18th-century London, was put to a practical test when he demonstrated that removing the pump handle of a suspected contaminated well prevented cholera in the people using water from the contaminated well. (2) Louis Pasteur's theory, which linked immunity to rabies with exposure to killed rabies virus from the dried spinal cords of infected rabbits, was dramatically applied to individuals at risk for the disease. A child doomed to die of rabies because of rabid wolf bites was saved by Pasteur's attenuated rabies virus vaccine treatments. (3) The devastating effects of scurvy, beri-beri and pellagra were definitively dealt with when scientists identified key vitamins in foods—ascorbic acid, thiamine and niacin—that would prevent or cure these nutritional deficiency diseases. In all of these cases, an individual at risk could avoid the effects of a devastating infectious or nutritional disease by applying the theory explaining the origin of disease.

One of the most appealing features of the homocysteine theory is its simplicity and ease of application to the prevention of arteriosclerosis. Although the scientific details of the homocysteine theory are complex in many respects, any lay person can understand the basic principles of the theory, which attributes increased risk of vascular disease to increased blood levels of homocysteine, i.e., the higher the homocysteine level, the greater the risk. A person at risk needs to understand that homocysteine is derived from methionine, a normal amino acid building block of all proteins in the diet. This derivative of a normal amino acid can damage the artery walls if allowed to accumulate excessively in the body's blood and tissues. The other basic concept that is important to understand is that the level of homocysteine in the blood is controlled by the action of three B vitamins—B6, B12 and folic acid—within the body. By consuming an optimal diet containing an abundance of these vitamins over a period of months and years, an individual at risk can achieve a lifelong measure of protection against development of arteriosclerosis.

When confronting the possibility of developing a disease of aging such as arteriosclerosis, it is important to realize that some risk factors can be modified or improved, but other factors cannot be changed. It is also important to understand which factors can be changed, how this will reduce the risk of disease, and why other risk factors—especially age, gender and genetic background—can be minimized but not removed by control of diet and lifestyle.

The most valuable single study of the influence of risk factors on homocysteine levels is the Hordaland study from Norway.[2] In this study a cross-section of a population at risk was studied. A total of 7,591 normal men and 8,585 normal women, aged 40 to 67, with no history of serious disease was studied. Blood homocysteine levels were higher in men than women (10.8 vs. 9.1 micromoles per liter), and the levels increased with age in both sexes (12.3 and 11.0 micromoles per liter, respectively, at ages 65 to 67). The level of blood homocysteine increased significantly with the number of cigarettes smoked per day for both men and women in all age groups. The combined effect of age, gender and smoking was prominent, resulting in a homocysteine level that was 4.8 micromoles per liter higher in older male smokers, aged 65 to 67 (13.2) than in younger women nonsmokers, aged 40 to 42 (8.4). Moderate exercise produced somewhat lower homocysteine levels in both men and women compared with inactive subjects, but the effect was in the range of 1 micromole per liter lower for active vs. sedentary subjects. The results of dietary intake of fruits and vegetables and added vitamin supplements were also found to affect blood homocysteine levels, producing differences of 0.8 and 1.4

micromoles per liter in the fruit and vegetable eaters and supplement users, respectively.

The results of the Hordaland study and many other smaller epidemiological studies confirm that the risk of complications of arteriosclerosis, especially heart attack, stroke and generalized vascular disease, can be decreased by controlling the risk factors of diet, smoking and exercise that contribute to elevation of blood homocysteine. Several studies have also suggested that risk of disease is correlated with blood homocysteine levels even in the normal range. This finding means that careful attention to all of the controllable factors affecting blood homocysteine will promise protection from disease. If the blood homocysteine level can be kept in the 8 to 10 micromole per liter range, a significant measure of protection against the development and progression of arteriosclerosis is assured.

As mentioned before, certain important factors influencing risk of arteriosclerosis by elevation of blood homocysteine levels cannot be changed. These include age, genetic background and gender. However, beneficial dietary and lifestyle improvements can significantly lengthen life and improve health until the onset of senescence. As Chapter 6 discusses, the processes that control aging and senescence are only partially understood by medical science. Nevertheless, current knowledge of aging is helpful in increasing those trends toward longer life expectancy that are apparent in major developed countries. This knowledge includes the principles of the homocysteine theory. Experts in gerontology (the science of aging) anticipate that healthful years can indeed be added to the present life expectancies of 73 to 76 years for men and 77 to 84 years for women. The total achievable life span is not currently known precisely, but evolution and genetic control of the aging process appear to limit human life span to a maximum of about 100 to 120 years.

The influence of genetic background on risk of arteriosclerosis, like the influence of aging, is only partially understood. Although genetic inheritance cannot be changed, hereditary effects on the processing of homocysteine can be controlled in some instances by increasing the quantity of vitamins B6, B12 and folic acid needed to control blood homocysteine level. In this way dietary and nutritional strategy can help overcome the deleterious effects of heredity on the risk of arteriosclerosis. This concept is well-established in other areas of nutritional knowledge, and it has long been known that individuals require different amounts of vitamins and minerals for optimal health according to their genetic makeup.[3] If a parent carries a defective gene for controlling homocysteine, his or her children can be tested for the presence of this gene by new techniques of molecular biology. If the children are found to have the unfavorable gene, this knowledge can be used to increase the quantities of B vitamins in the diet or by supplements to control blood homocysteine levels.

Besides age and genetic background, the only other major risk factor for arteriosclerosis that cannot be changed is gender. For many years men have been known to develop coronary heart disease and other manifestations of arteriosclerosis at an earlier age than women in susceptible populations. In fact, women enjoy a measure of protection against arteriosclerosis until after menopause, when their risk rapidly approaches that of men. This protection is attributed to the production of estrogen and other hormones by the ovary during the reproductive years.

In many epidemiological studies the level of blood homocysteine has been found to be lower in women than in men of the same age. Generally, the level of homocysteine is about 2 micromoles per liter less for women than for men. After the menopause, homocysteine levels increase about 2 micromoles per liter in women. At age 65 to 67 the homocysteine level for women reaches 10.5, and the corresponding level for men of the same age is 12.5 micromoles per liter. The persistently higher level of blood homocysteine for men in all age groups may be related to testosterone production by the testis, increased muscle mass and other factors that have not been studied in detail. The effect of contraceptive hormones, replacement estrogen therapy and antiestrogen drugs to modify risk of arteriosclerosis are discussed in a subsequent section of this chapter.

Arteriosclerosis is a disease which begins in childhood and adolescence, develops gradually and insidiously without symptoms during the early adult years, and first strikes, often suddenly, in men in the 40s, 50s and 60s. The onset in women is generally delayed until their 50s and 60s. Because of the silent, gradual and prolonged onset of arteriosclerosis, the most successful strategy for prevention must start in childhood and continue in adolescence and adulthood, providing the elder years with little risk of developing heart attack, angina pectoris, stroke, kidney failure or peripheral vascular disease. This lifelong strategy requires control of known modifiable risk factors, especially consumption of an optimal diet; moderate physical activity and avoidance of tobacco, drug and alcohol abuse. The best way to carry out this preventive strategy is outlined and discussed in succeeding sections of this chapter.

For those adults who find themselves developing symptoms, signs and effects of arteriosclerosis because of poor nutrition, substance abuse, sedentary lifestyle or deleterious genetic background, the homocysteine theory offers guidance concerning those measures which may improve one's chances for prevention or regression of established disease. Once the disease has become established and symptomatic, however, intensive preventive measures need to be combined with medical and surgical therapy in some cases to improve life expectancy and quality of living. These measures are best coordinated with physicians and surgeons who specialize in the treatment of established vascular disease. The nutritional preventive strategies specified by the homocysteine theory can contribute in a major way to successful control of established arteriosclerosis.

DIETARY PREVENTION OF ARTERIOSCLEROSIS

In its simplest form, an optimal diet to prevent arteriosclerosis consists of abundant fresh vegetables and fruits, whole grains and legumes, limited quantities of fresh meat and dairy products, a minimum of highly processed and packaged foods, and strictly limited consumption of fats and sugars. This diet will provide sufficient vitamins B6, B12 and folic acid to prevent excessive accumulation of homocysteine in the blood and other tissues of the body.

Unfortunately, it is all too common for children, young adults and the elderly to consume a diet containing few if any vegetables and fruits, large quantities of meat and dairy products with an emphasis on highly processed, preserved and packaged foods which contain excessive fats and sugars. The typical American diet of fast convenient foods is the major cause for the high risk of arteriosclesis and its complications of coronary heart disease, stroke, kidney failure and generalized vascular disease in the U.S. This pattern of food consumption is unfortunately highly profitable to the food industry, which relentlessly promotes and advertises poor eating habits.

Since the discovery of vitamins in the early 20th century, nutritionists have studied in great detail the quantity of each vitamin that is needed to prevent deficiency disease. These studies have led to the concept of the RDA (recommended dietary allowance) and the RDI (recommended dietary intake) of virtually all known constituents of foods, including vitamins, minerals, trace elements, protein, fat and carbohydrate. The RDA for each nutrient is decided by a panel of expert nutritional scientists and medical scientists who are convened by the National Research Council in Washington D.C., sponsored by the National Academy of Sciences, the Institute of Medicine, and the National Academy of Engineering.[4] After evaluating all available scientific studies of each food constituent, the panel decides "the levels of intake of essential nutrients considered, in the judgment of the Committee on Dietary Allowances of the Food and Nutrition Board on the basis of available scientific knowledge, to be adequate to meet the known nutritional needs of practically all healthy persons."

The concept of the RDA is that a sufficient quantity of a vitamin or other nutrient in the diet will maintain health and prevent deficiency disease. In regard to the homocysteine theory of arteriosclerosis, there has been until recently little available information about the quantities of vitamins B6, B12 and folic acid needed to prevent elevation of homocysteine in the blood. In an exhaustive review of human vitamin B6 requirements in 1978 by a conference sponsored by the National Research Council, for example, there was no consideration of the possibility that inadequate or marginal vitamin B6 intake could be related to elevation of blood homocysteine and susceptibility to arteriosclerosis.[5] Thus the RDA for vitamin B6 of 2.2 mg per day for adult men, 2.0 mg per day for adult women and 2.6 mg per day for pregnant or lactating women was established without considering the evidence that chronic vitamin B6 deficiency causes arteriosclerosis by elevation of blood homocysteine.

Folic Acid and Vitamin B6

In the case of folic acid, the RDA for adult men and women was set at 400 micrograms (mcg) per day in 1980. In 1989, however, the RDA for folic acid was *lowered* to 200 mcg per day, primarily because large segments of the U.S. population failed to consume the established RDA of 400 mcg. Because of persuasive evidence that dietary deficiency of folic acid in pregnant women leads to birth defects in newborn infants, especially neural tube defects such as spina bifida and anencephaly, the Food and Drug Administration has recently ruled that sufficient folic acid be added to enriched foods, starting in 1998, to assure a minimum intake of 400 mcg of folic acid per day for pregnant women. Folic acid will be added to rice, grains, pasta, bread and other enriched foods that are consumed by wide segments of the population.

Since publication of the lowered RDA for folic acid (200 mcg) in 1989,[4] an important study of 1,160 elderly subjects in the Framingham Heart Study, aged 67 to 96, has concluded that blood levels of homocysteine become elevated if the dietary folic acid intake is less than 250 mcg per day.[6] Folic acid intakes in the 250 to 400 mcg range were associated with slight elevation of blood homocysteine in the range of 11 to 12 micromoles per liter, and intakes greater than 400 mcg per day were associated with blood homocysteine levels of 10 to 11 micromoles per liter. This discovery demonstrates that the RDA for folic acid of 200 mcg is insufficient to prevent significant elevation of blood homocysteine in the elderly. In a follow-up study of 1,041 subjects from the same population, the degree of thickening of the wall of the carotid artery to the brain by arteriosclerosis was shown to be correlated with the level of blood homocysteine.[7] Blood homocysteine levels in the range of 10 to 18 micromoles per liter in men and levels of 13 to 18 in women were correlated with carotid arteriosclerosis.

In a study of 304 patients with coronary arteriosclerosis and 231 control subjects, elevated blood homocysteine levels of greater than 14 micromoles per liter were found in 50 percent of the patients.[8] In the analysis, risk of coronary arteriosclerosis was found to correlate with blood homocysteine levels even in the presumed normal range of 8 to 12 micromoles per liter. Low levels of vitamin B6 in the blood were found in 10 percent of the patients, significantly correlating with elevation of blood homocysteine compared to control subjects. A similar correlation was found with vitamin B6 intake and blood levels of vitamin B6 in the elderly Framingham Heart Study subjects.[6] Low folic acid and vitamin B6 intakes and low blood levels of these vitamins were found to correlate with elevation of blood homocysteine in a study of 130 patients with heart attack, compared to 118 control subjects.[9]

In summary, the results of these and other studies show that the amounts of dietary folic acid and vitamin B6 that are required to prevent abnormal elevation of blood homocysteine are 350 to 400 mcg per day of folic acid and

3 to 3.5 mg per day of vitamin B6. This figure for sufficiency of vitamin B6 agrees well with the estimate that an intake corresponding to 4 to 4.3 milligrams per day of vitamin B6 in humans is needed to prevent arteriosclerosis in pyridoxine-deficient monkeys.[10] This amount of B6 is almost twice the current RDA for this vitamin.[4]

Vitamin B12

In the case of vitamin B12, the RDA is only 3 mcg per day for adults.[4] Unlike folic acid and vitamin B6, which are widely distributed in foods of animal and plant origin, vitamin B12 is formed only by bacteria, fungi and algae. Yeast, plants and animals cannot make vitamin B12 for themselves and are dependent upon microorganisms for this essential vitamin. In the human diet vitamin B12 is supplied primarily by foods of animal origin (meats and dairy products) where the vitamin is accumulated by the action and growth of microorganisms. This extremely low quantity of vitamin B12 is absorbed in the human stomach and intestine by the action of a protein made in the stomach called intrinsic factor. This factor complexes with vitamin B12 in the stomach, and the complex is absorbed in the end portion of the small intestine. Additional protein factors in the blood (transcobalamin I and II) are required for transport of vitamin B12 to the liver and other organs. Most normal adults who eat foods of animal origin consume about 5 to 8 mcg per day of vitamin B12, more than an adequate intake to meet the established RDA for this vitamin.

In the elderly and in ulcer disease, the absorption of vitamin B12 may be impaired by inflammation of the stomach. In the nutritional deficiency disease pernicious anemia, there is a total failure of absorption of vitamin

B12 because of deficiency of the intrinsic factor required for absorption. Such total vitamin B12 deficiency may cause severe or fatal anemia and neurological damage to the spinal cord if untreated by injections of vitamin B12. Strict vegetarians may develop pernicious anemia after 20 to 30 years because of failure to consume meat and dairy products that supply vitamin B12. It is only in subjects with low levels of vitamin B12 in the blood due to absorptive problems that the blood homocysteine becomes elevated, generally in the 13 to 15 micromoles per liter range.[6] In fact, elevation of blood homocysteine is now widely used by hematologists as an indicator of inadequate vitamin B12 absorption or inadequate dietary folic acid intake.

Protein

Homocysteine is derived only from methionine, one of the 20 amino acids of all proteins, as explained in Chapter 3. Because all proteins contain methionine, dietary deficiency of methionine is not found in well-nourished populations. In populations with inadequate dietary protein consumption, however, the failure of normal growth and development in children is partly attributable to inadequate intake of the amino acids of proteins, including methionine. Excessive dietary intake of methionine is toxic in experimental animals, and the toxicity is partly counteracted by increased vitamin B6, which helps to convert excess homocysteine from methionine into cystathionine, the safe form for excretion. The RDA for protein is 63 grams per day for adult men and 50 grams per day for adult women.

Foods of animal origin, such as meat, eggs, milk and cheese, generally contain more protein than most plant foods. In addition, the protein of animal foods contains two to three times as much methionine as the protein of plant foods. Because of this fact, human populations that are mainly vegetarian consume less methionine than those that consume meat and dairy products. Most plant foods contain larger amounts of vitamins B6 and folic acid to help prevent excessive conversion of methionine to homocysteine, compared to animal foods. If a human population consumes primarily proteins of animal origin, the diet must also contain abundant amounts of vitamin B6 and folic acid to prevent excessive conversion of methionine to homocysteine. Unfortunately, processing, cooking and storing foods causes major losses of these vitamins, leading to marginal dietary intakes and the eventual elevation of blood homocysteine levels. Although a recent study found no correlation between dietary methionine intake and levels of blood homocysteine, the study population did not contain identified vegetarians for comparison with subjects consuming abundant animal foods.[9]

The U.S. population currently consumes 14 to 18 percent of food calories in the form of protein.[4] Approximately 65 percent of the protein is from animal sources such as meat and dairy products; 16 to 20 percent of protein is from grain products such as bread, cereals and pasta; and 15 to 20 percent is from vegetable protein such as legumes and soy products. A diet that contains only one-third animal protein and two-thirds vegetable protein yields 60 to 85 percent of the amount of methionine in meat and eggs. These figures show that consumption of a predominantly vegetarian diet supplies somewhat less methionine than a diet containing a predominance of meat, dairy and egg protein. Accordingly, an optimal diet for prevention of arteriosclerosis would emphasize an adequate dietary intake of vitamins B6 and folic acid (see Table 1, page 158) to prevent excessive conversion of the methionine of either animal or vegetable protein to homocysteine.

The importance of vitamin B6 and folic acid in controlling the blood homocysteine level was dramatically demonstrated with an experimental study of severe deficiencies of these vitamins in animals.[11] Deficiency of folic acid causes an elevation of blood homocysteine in fasting animals, yet an oral dose of methionine by stomach tube has no effect on the blood homocysteine level. In contrast, deficiency of vitamin B6 causes no elevation of blood homocysteine in the fasting state, but an oral dose of methionine causes a dramatic rise in blood homocysteine within one hour, lasting about five hours. These results suggest that chronic deficiency of folic acid in a human population causes elevation of blood homocysteine in the fasting state, and chronic vitamin B6 deficiency causes high elevation of blood homocysteine in the several hours following a meal containing abundant methionine from dietary proteins.

An important biochemical theory was advanced to explain these observations in experimental animals and in human subjects.[12] According to this theory, the methionine derivative, adenosyl methionine, synthesized in the liver from methionine administered to rats or from the methionine of dietary protein in man, decreases the conversion of homocysteine to methionine by the enzyme dependent upon vitamins B12 and folic acid and increases the conversion of homocysteine to cystathionine by the enzyme dependent upon vitamin B6. If methionine is in excess, increased adenosyl methionine is produced in the liver. When only folic acid is deficient, increased adenosyl methionine produced from excess methionine does not decrease the enzymatic conversion of homocysteine to methionine, and the homocysteine level in blood remains elevated and unchanged. When only vitamin B6 is deficient, increased adenosyl methionine produced from excess methionine does not increase the enzymatic conversion of homocysteine to cystathionine, and the homocysteine level in blood becomes highly elevated. After several hours, the excess homocysteine is converted back to methionine by the enzyme that is dependent upon folic acid and vitamin B12.

Carbohydrates and Fats

The other major components of the diet—fats and carbohydrates—are also important in determining dietary consumption of vitamin B6 and folic acid. Both of these vitamins are soluble in water and insoluble in fats. As a result, the more dietary fat that is consumed, the less vitamin B6 and folic acid will be available for absorption. In a diet that contains 40 to 50 percent of calories as fat, for example, the remaining components of the diet, foods with carbohydrates and protein, must supply all of the requirement for vitamin B6 and folic acid. In a diet that contains very little fat, in the range of 10 to 20 percent of calories, the foods containing 80 to 90 percent of calories as carbohydrate and protein are better able to supply the vitamin B6 and folic acid requirements. In general, the greater the fat content of the diet, the greater the risk of marginal deficiencies of vitamin B6 and folic acid. The lower the fat content of the diet, the lower is the risk of marginal deficiencies of these vitamins.

Carbohydrates are supplied in the diet in two principle forms, complex starches and simple sugars. Starches are consumed as vegetables, whole grains and legumes—foods that contain appreciable amounts of vitamin B6 and folic acid. Foods of animal origin also contain carbohydrates in somewhat lower amounts than foods of plant origin.

Fresh meats, liver and eggs contain abundant amounts of vitamin B12 and appreciable amounts of vitamin B6 and folic acid if the foods are not excessively processed, heated or preserved.

In contrast to starches, sugars are frequently consumed in prepared, cooked or baked foods that contain cane or beet sugar, corn syrup or fruit sugars. These sugars are highly processed carbohydrates that contain no vitamins or minerals. The higher the sugar content of the diet, the less these sugar-rich foods are able to supply vitamin B6 and folic acid. In a diet that contains abundant sugar from candies, cakes, ice cream or frozen yogurt, the required intake of vitamins B6, B12 and folic acid is completely dependent upon other constituents of the diet. Consumption of a diet with 25 to 30 percent of calories as sugar and 40 to 50 percent of calories as fats, therefore, forces the body to obtain its dietary requirement for B vitamins from the remaining 20 to 35 percent of food calories. Thus failure to consume adequate whole grains and vegetables plus a diet rich in sugars and fats leads to marginal or frankly deficient intakes of vitamin B6 and folic acid.

Processed Foods

Food processing, preservation and storage lead to significant losses of vitamin B6 and folic acid, which are destroyed by milling, heating, chemical additives, radiation and storage. The losses of these vitamins, compared to fresh, raw ingredients, ranges from a low of 10 to 15 percent by freezing foods, to as much as an 85 to 90 percent loss by refining rice or wheat to prepare white rice, rice flour or white flour. If a diet contains processed ingredients, along with a high content of sugars and fats, the deficiencies of vitamin B6 and folic acid may become marginal to serious over a period of months and years and can lead to elevation of blood homocysteine, arterial damage and arteriosclerosis.

Besides arteriosclerosis, another common complication of a diet with abundant sugars, fats and processed foods is obesity. The control centers for appetite in the brain produce eating behavior sufficient to supply the body with adequate vitamins and minerals for survival. If the diet is seriously deficient in multiple nutrient factors because of high sugar and fat content, the brain requires consumption of larger quantities of food to obtain these nutrients. The tendency then is to overconsume calories from sugars and fats, leading to obesity. In susceptible individuals, this dietary pattern also increases the risk of developing diabetes, which also seriously increases the pace of arterial damage and development of arteriosclerosis.

Fiber

Fiber is the indigestible starch-like roughage of plant foods. Fiber may either be soluble, e.g., fruit pectins, or insoluble, e.g., vegetable lignins and celluloses. In either case, the fiber component remains in the stomach, intestine and colon during digestion of food. Because fiber is not digested or absorbed into the bloodstream, it contributes no calories and has no nutritional value. Fiber fills the stomach, producing satiety, decreases the absorption of fats and sugars and increases the intestinal contents, promoting regular elimination. The fiber of plant foods is rich in vitamins and minerals which are lost during refining and processing. Numerous medical and epidemiological studies have shown an inverse relation between consumption of dietary fiber and many major diseases of developed societies, including arteriosclerosis.[13] For these reasons, an optimal diet for preventing arteriosclerosis contains abundant fiber from plant foods.[14]

Vitamin E and Other Antioxidants

Another vitamin, tocopherol or vitamin E, has also been found helpful in preventing arteriosclerosis and coronary heart disease. Numerous studies have shown that dietary intake of vitamin E either in fresh vegetables and whole grains or in supplements decreases risk of coronary disease by as much as 50 percent,[15,16] Recent studies affirm the importance of vitamin E in prevention and control of arteriosclerosis, which was first advocated by the Shute Clinic in Canada in the 1950s. Attempts to prove the beneficial effects of beta-carotene supplements have not yet been successful. However, vitamin C, bioflavonoids and other antioxidant compounds are under study for possible beneficial preventive effects in controlling arteriosclerosis. In one study, men with arteriosclerosis who had survived myocardial infarction were shown to have lower blood homocysteine, cholesterol, LDL and triglycerides following treatment with troxerutin, a bioflavonoid, in combination with vitamin B6, folic acid, vitamin B12, choline and riboflavin.[17]

Minerals

For many years it has been known that susceptibility to arteriosclerosis and coronary disease are inversely related to hardness of the water supply.[18] In particular, magnesium, calcium, bicarbonate, sulfate and fluoride were found to confer protection against coronary heart disease when present in the drinking water. Magnesium is an important factor in aiding the enzymatic digestion and utilization of foods by organs of the body. Magnesium is essential for the action of the enzymes that process proteins and the amino acids methionine and homocysteine. Zinc is also an important factor in numerous functions of the body, including expression of DNA and the aging process. All of these mineral elements are seriously depleted when whole grains are refined into white flour and white rice, amounting to losses of 50 to 90 percent.

Other trace minerals such as chromium, copper, manganese, fluoride, selenium and molybdenum are required in small quantities for optimal health. Consumption of whole grains, fresh meats and seafoods and fresh vegetables will assure an adequate intake of these elements. Insufficient intake of iodine causes hypothyroidism because of decreased formation of thyroid hormone. Severe iodine deficiency causes goiter, elevation of blood homocysteine levels,[19] increased blood cholesterol and lipoproteins and thus increased susceptibility to coronary heart disease. Adequate intake of iodine is assured by occasional consumption of seafood and the use of iodized salt.

Iron must be consumed in adequate quantities to prevent anemia and to promote healthy growth and development. Recent studies have suggested that excessive iron intake may predispose to increased risk of arteriosclerosis. Iron and homocysteine are known factors which cause damage to fats and proteins when LDL reacts with oxygen radicals in developing arteriosclerotic plaques. In experimental animals, the feeding of excess homocysteine causes increased uptake and storage of iron in the liver and other tissues. The possible role of excess dietary iron in the promotion of arteriosclerosis in human populations is currently under investigation by medical scientists.

Other Dietary Factors

Certain other trace compounds in the diet are known to be capable of converting homocysteine to methionine in the body by biochemical reactions. These nutrients, especially betaine, dimethyl thetin, and S-methylmethionine, are present in foods such as beets, garlic and onions. Consumption of these nutrients may prove to be of importance in counteracting hyperhomocysteinemia.[20] Other sulfur compounds in garlic and onions, such as alliin, may also be found in future studies to be helpful in preventing high blood homocysteine levels.

An interesting protective effect of dietary fish intake against arteriosclerosis was discovered in Greenland Eskimos, whose traditional diet contains large amounts of cholesterol and fats from whale blubber. The active nutrient in fish that confers this protection is omega-3 unsaturated fish oil. The effect of fish oil is to lower blood homocysteine levels in men with high blood fats.[21] Unsaturated plant oils, such as corn oil, also prevent elevation of blood homocysteine and prevent arteriosclerosis in experimental animals.[22] Unsaturated fish and plant oils also act in the body to prevent the damaging effects of oxygen radicals on cells and tissues. Fish is also an abundant source of vitamin B6, which controls elevated blood homocysteine.

As discussed in Chapter 2, oxycholesterols, the products of reaction of highly purified cholesterol with oxygen, rapidly cause arteriosclerotic plaques in monkeys and rabbits. On the other hand, highly purified cholesterol, protected from the oxygen of air, causes no change in the arteries when fed or injected into experimental animals. The highly damaging oxycholesterols are found in foods in which cholesterol is subjected to heating and exposure to the oxygen of air during food processing, cooking and preservation.[23] Examples of foods that contain these oxycholesterols are dried egg yolk, dried milk powder and foods fried in heated oils. The oxycholesterols of these foods are absorbed into the blood during digestion where they become concentrated in the low-density lipoprotein (LDL) fraction of the plasma. When lipoproteins are taken up by arterial wall cells, the cholesterol oxides that are released cause damage to artery wall cells and tissues, promoting arteriosclerotic plaque development. These oxycholesterol compounds are present in human arteriosclerotic plaques. Another source of these oxycholesterols results from the modification of LDLs by oxygen radicals that occurs in arterial wall cells. The homocysteine that is released from aggregates of LDL within arterial wall cells also promotes formation of oxycholesterols by affecting the way oxygen is used in these cells, causing accumulation of reactive oxygen radicals.[1]

AN OPTIMAL DIET FOR HEALTH

The most important prerequisites for a healthful diet are quality, freshness, variety and proper nutritional balance. Most adults know which foods are to be avoided. However, in today's busy world, the average person is in a hurry, impatient with the need to shop for and prepare meals, and eager to minimize expense. Yet, the investment of time and money in good nutrition will yield significant lifelong benefits to health and longevity. Health is a precious commodity at any age. Maintaining good health through a high-quality diet will greatly enhance the enjoyment and fulfillment of life.

First and foremost, an optimal diet will feature food

that is fresh or minimally processed and composed of the finest ingredients. The modern agricultural and transportation systems of contemporary America offer a wonderful year-round selection and variety of these foods. The most nutritious fruits and vegetables are those that are selected, cooked and consumed as quickly after harvesting as possible. Everyone knows that homegrown or local fruits and vegetables have the most flavor; they are also the richest in vitamins, minerals and other essential ingredients. In the seasons when local produce is unavailable, an amazing selection of fresh fruits and vegetables is shipped to most areas of America by truck, rail or air.

How does one face cleaning, cooking and preparing all that fresh produce? One way to approach this task is to view food preparation as a form of relaxation after a busy day at work. With practice, an experienced home cook can prepare a nutritious dinner in 45 to 60 minutes. Peeling two or three varieties of fresh vegetables and steaming them takes about 15 to 20 minutes. A pan of brown rice, cracked wheat, beans or lentils can be simmering on the stove for 15 to 45 minutes while the preparation of vegetables and salad is in progress. A fresh salad every day can be assembled in 5 to 10 minutes and dressed with fresh lemon juice or vinegar and olive oil. Depending upon the season, the salad may consist of different varieties of lettuce and other dark leafy greens, cucumbers, tomatoes, onions, carrots, celery, peppers, fennel, small amounts of avocado or other raw vegetables. A small portion of fish, chicken or meat may be added as a source of protein several times a week.

A properly prepared, home-cooked dinner will provide a minimum of three to six servings of fresh vegetables, salad and fruits per day. One to three fruits at breakfast and a vegetable and a fruit at lunch will bring the total to

6 to 10 servings of these foods every day. Day after day, week after week, month after month, consistent consumption of 6 to 10 servings of fresh vegetables and fruits will provide the vitamins, minerals, fiber, antioxidants and other nutrients that are needed to process the proteins, starches and fats in the rest of the diet.

As previously noted, vitamin B6, folic acid, and vitamin B12 are the three vitamins that are necessary for preventing a buildup of homocysteine, when proteins are broken down in the body. Vitamin B6 is abundant in many fresh vegetables, whole grains and fruits as well as in meats and fish. Folic acid, abundant in leafy dark green vegetables and whole grains, is also abundant in liver. Vitamin B12 is required in extremely low amounts and is available only in foods of animal origin such as meat, eggs, fish and dairy products. In Table 1 the amounts of these three vitamins are listed for a variety of foods.

Table 1

SOURCES OF VITAMIN B6, FOLIC ACID AND VITAMIN B12 IN FOODS

FOOD	VITAMIN B6	FOLIC ACID	VITAMIN B12
	(mg)	*(mcg)*	*(mcg)*
Almonds, 20 medium	.03	14	0
Apple, medium	.02	5	0
Asparagus, fresh, 8 spears	.09	38	0
Asparagus, canned, 8 spears	.036	10	0
Avocado, half	.15	18	0
Banana, medium	.51	20	0
Beans, navy	.56	40	0
Beans, green snap	.08	24	0
Beans, lima	.58	37	0
Beef, lean	.52	8	1.7
Beet, medium	.03	27	0
Bread, whole wheat, 2 slices	.11	32	0
Bread, white, 2 slices	.024	21	0

FOOD	VITAMIN B6	FOLIC ACID	VITAMIN B12
	(mg)	*(mcg)*	*(mcg)*
Broccoli, 1 large stalk	.27	76	0
Brussel sprouts, 10 medium	.32	17	0
Cabbage, 1 cup	.22	42	0
Carrot, large	.15	18	0
Cantaloupe, ¼	.10	50	0
Cauliflower, 1 cup	.32	76	0
Celery, ½ cup	.04	7	0
Cheese, cheddar	.05	11	0.6
Cheese, cottage	.04	12	1
Cheese, Camembert	.09		0.5
Cherries, 10 large	.06	3	0
Chicken, dark meat	.39	14	0.5
Chicken, white meat	.82	18	0.5
Corn, 1 medium ear	.16	19	0
Cucumber, medium	.03	3	0
Egg, whole, large	.06	11	1
Eggs, white only, 3 medium	.01	1	0.5
Eggs, yolk only, 2 medium	.16	12	3
Grapes, 12 medium	.05	2	0
Grapefruit, half	.07	12	0
Kale, 4 large leaves	.33	49	0
Lamb, lean	.33	6	2.5
Lemon, 1 small	.01	1	0
Lentils, ½ cup	.60	23	0
Lettuce, 4 large leaves	.06	24	0
Liver, beef	1.00	174	9.6
Milk, cow, cup	.07	4	0.7
Milk, human, cup	.02	9	0.7
Molasses, 1 Tbs.	.06	3	0
Oatmeal, ½ cup	.06	22	0
Onions, 2 medium	.08	10	0
Orange, 1 medium	.07	29	0
Oysters, 6 raw	.05	48	18
Peas, ½ cup	.13	18	0
Peach, 1 medium	.02	2	0
Pepper, green, large	.16	2	0

FOOD	VITAMIN B6	FOLIC ACID	VITAMIN B12
	(mg)	*(mcg)*	*(mcg)*
Plum, 1 medium	.04	2	0
Pork	.54	14	3.2
Potato, 1 large	.30	31	0
Rice, brown, 1 cup	.83	36	0
Rice, white, 1 cup	.26	9	0
Salmon, fresh fillet	.84	20	19
Spinach, 4 large leaves	.28	33	0
Squash, acorn, ⅓	.15	14	0
Squash, summer, large	.08	11	0
Strawberries, 6 medium	.04	4	0
Sweet potato, 1 medium	.22	19	0
Tomato, 2 medium	.1	6	0
Tuna, fresh fillet	1.08	7	16
Tuna, canned	.51	7	10
Wheat flour, whole, 1 oz.	.1	11	0
Wheat flour, white, 1 oz.	.02	2	0
Yeast, baker's, one small cake	.2	130	0
Estimated daily intake, adult[5,26]	1.1–1.3	194–357	9
Estimated daily intake, elderly[6]	1.3–1.6	174–220	4.5
Optimal daily intake	3–3.5	350–400	5–15

The values for each vitamin are determined by microbiological growth assays, taken from the U.S. Department of Agriculture data hand books[24,25] and the National Research Council Reports.[5,25]

The most important sources of calories in freshly prepared meals are the complex carbohydrates found in whole grains, breads, pastas, beans, peas and other legumes. Potatoes, yams, squashes, turnips and other root vegetables are also a good source of carbohydrate calories. The skins of these vegetables provide some of the vitamins, minerals and antioxidant nutrients of these foods.

Vegetables are best prepared and cooked by baking or steaming with a minimum of heat and peeling only if necessary. Avoid boiling these foods in large amounts of water. Vitamin B6 and folic acid are very sensitive to loss through heating.

Brown rice, bulgar wheat, barley and other grains, including whole grain breads and pastas, provide a good balance of carbohydrate calories, moderate protein, low fat, and abundant vitamins and minerals. The most nutritious bread is prepared from whole grain flours, such as multigrain bread or whole wheat bread made from stone-ground flour. Homemade bread from these flours can be prepared once or twice per month on the weekend with a mixer or a bread machine. Extra loaves can be frozen for later use. Some bakery or health food store breads of this type are often as nutritious as the home-baked variety.

Fresh meats, fish, eggs, butter, milk, cream and cheese are at the top of the U.S. Department of Agriculture food pyramid, which means that these components of a healthful diet should be used sparingly and in small quantities to provide flavor and interest rather than to provide a major source of calories. Two to four ounces of meat, poultry, fish or eggs provide more than adequate animal protein in a single day. By reducing the quantity of animal foods, the number of calories from animal fat is minimized. In addition, animal foods need not be consumed every day. For those who wish to avoid meat, a serving of several ounces of eggs, milk or cheese several times per week will provide adequate vitamin B12 to prevent anemia and a buildup of homocysteine in the blood. Vegans who consume no animal products of any kind need to supplement their diets with 0.1 mg vitamin B12 per day (or 1 mg intramuscular injection per month) to prevent vitamin B12 deficiency.

To summarize, an optimal diet for health consists of 6 to 10 servings of raw, lightly cooked or steamed fresh vegetables or fruits; 2 to 3 servings of starchy vegetables, whole-grain bread, cereal or pasta; and one small serving of meat, poultry, fish, eggs, milk or cheese. Flavor and interest are provided by herbs, spices, vegetable or fruit sauces, with small quantities of a vegetable oil such as olive oil, corn oil or canola oil. Faithful adherence to such a beneficial diet will add satisfying, healthy years to your life by helping to prevent heart disease, cancer and other diseases of aging.

Notably absent from this healthful diet are pastries, pies, cakes, heavy fried foods, rich meat sauces, candies, sugary desserts, sugared cereals, sugared soft drinks and other similar temptations. Avoiding totally or greatly minimizing calories from these prepared, baked or cooked foods with high fat or high sugar content will constitute a major improvement in the diet at any age. Not only will this strategy help to prevent weight gain, but it will also shift the diet to foods with fewer calories and beneficial balanced nutrients.

Selecting the Best Processed Foods

The purposes of food processing are to increase flavor, palatability and storage potential. Some common examples of food processing are the preparation of flour from whole grains, the extraction of sugar from sugar beets, sugar cane or corn, and the separation of fats and oils, such as butter from milk and vegetable oils from olives or grains. Separating the protein, carbohydrates and fats of whole foods enhances their flavor, palatability and storage life. However, major losses of vitamins, minerals and fiber occur in all of these examples of food processing. In the case of the refining of wheat into white flour, followed by chemical bleaching, the losses of vitamins, minerals, essential oils and fiber are as much as 90 percent, compared to whole-grain wheat. In the case of extraction of sugar, the final product is chemically pure sucrose, containing none of the vitamins, minerals, essential oils or fiber present in whole beets, sugar cane or corn. Separation of olive oil from olives removes virtually all of the water-soluble vitamins, minerals and fiber that are present in whole olives. Cold-pressed olive oil, on the other hand, does contain antioxidant nutrients that have been found to be beneficial.

The selection of minimally processed, unbleached high quality flour is essential for preparation of the most nourishing bread or pasta. Unbleached, nonbromated, enriched white flour from durum wheat is the best for making pasta. Stone-ground whole wheat flour is best for making whole wheat bread. Multigrain breads are made from flours of this type, milled from different grains. Stone-ground, whole corn meal is best for making corn bread, tortillas, or cornmeal pancakes. During the past two decades, food manufacturers have introduced numerous excellent flours of the minimally processed type.

If the preparation of fresh, home-baked breads and pasta is not possible, many excellent products are now available from food manufacturers and bakeries. Whole wheat or multigrain breads of excellent quality are available from local bakeries or from large-scale food manufacturers. Heavy white breads made from minimally processed or stone-ground flour are preferable to the light, cottony breads made from highly processed white flour.

Hot or cold cereals provide a serving of whole grain food for breakfast. In colder months, a bowl of cooked whole wheat cereal or oatmeal, topped with fruit and a small quantity of whole milk or light cream is a tasty, satisfying, healthful breakfast. Whole grain dry cereals without added sugar are an excellent substitute in the warmer months. Highly enriched cereals are satisfactory, provided that bran, fiber and other components of minimally processed grains are present. Highly sugared cereals should be avoided entirely.

Brown rice is a major cereal grain that supplies protein, fiber, carbohydrate, vitamins and minerals in a healthful combination. Cooking brown rice takes longer (45 minutes) than polished white rice, but the rewards are improved flavor and better nutritional value. Other cooked cereals, such as bulgar cracked wheat, millet, barley, rye or quinoa, are a convenient, tasty, highly beneficial source of whole grains. The more highly refined, processed and purified the cereal derivative, the less desirable from the nutritional point of view.

Canning, Freezing, Drying and Storing Foods

Traditional methods of food preservation and storage can offer satisfactory alternatives to fresh vegetables, fruits, whole grains, legumes, meat and dairy foods. However, in each instance the traditionally preserved foods are inferior to fresh foods with regard to nutritional quality and value. The protective coating devised by nature for fresh foods is preferable to an artificial package prepared by a manufacturer. For example, peeling an orange or grapefruit and eating the fruit or squeezing the juice is preferable to buying a canned or frozen orange or grapefruit juice. Using a fresh egg in cooking is preferable to using powdered or dried eggs.

In the case of dried egg yolks, food processing adds a dangerous ingredient that potentially damages arteries. Cholesterol is a normal constituent of all animal foods.

Cholesterol is protected in the body against the oxygen of air by an elaborate combination of antioxidant vitamins, minerals and enzymes. Highly purified cholesterol that is protected against the oxygen of air causes no damage to the arteries of animals. When the cholesterol of animal foods is exposed to the oxygen of air by food processing, as in spray drying, highly damaging cholesterol oxides are formed. Powdered egg yolks, widely used in the manufacture of prepared foods, are known to contain these highly damaging cholesterol oxides. Eggs, as fresh as possible, are a safe alternative to dried egg yolks. Fresh eggs can be safely stored in the refrigerator for one to two weeks because of the highly effective antioxidant systems that they contain. However, eggshells slowly admit oxygen, and, after several weeks, these antioxidants are overcome, and cholesterol oxides begin to form. The fresher the egg, the lower the risk of containing these dangerous cholesterol oxides.

Canning as a process for preserving foods was invented in the early 19th century to support the troops of Napoleon's armies. Any military quartermaster knows that "an army travels on its stomach." Canning offered a mobile and convenient source of nourishment that lasts for months, regardless of the season of the year. Do canned foods contribute to arteriosclerosis and coronary heart disease? In the canning process, food is cooked and heated to a high temperature. The cans are sealed hot to exclude as much air as possible. Two of the vitamins that are the most sensitive to this form of food preservation are vitamin B6 and folic acid. Canning is known to decrease the vitamin content of foods by as much as 35 percent. As a result, larger quantities of canned foods must be consumed to equal the amount of vitamins present in fresh foods.

Freezing as a method of food preservation became available in the 1920s and 1930s, when refrigerators and freezers were manufactured on a large scale for commercial and home use. To prevent deterioration of frozen foods, particularly vegetables and fruits, the food is first blanched. This process involves the rapid heating of food in water for a short period of time at the boiling point. The heat inactivates the food's enzymes that otherwise would cause slow deterioration of the food while frozen. Unfortunately, this heating step also destroys approximately 10–15 percent of the vitamins that are sensitive to heat. Two of the most sensitive vitamins to destruction by heat are vitamin B6 and folic acid. Again somewhat larger amounts of frozen vegetables or fruits must be consumed to provide the quantity of these vitamins supplied by fresh foods.

The radiation of foods with X-rays or gamma rays has been advocated to increase the shelf life of a variety of foods. Radiation of this type floods the food with activated oxygen and free radicals. These reactive chemicals in irradiated foods combine with cholesterol to produce dangerous cholesterol oxides. Three of the most sensitive vitamins to the effects of this type of radiation are vitamin B6, folic acid and vitamin B12. Radiation of food with gamma rays is likely to increase the risk of arteriosclerosis because the process causes oxidation of cholesterol and essential fats and also destroys the vitamins that are needed to prevent a dangerous buildup of homocysteine in the blood.

Many preserved foods processed by a variety of methods have a long shelf life and need little or no refrigeration. This is because the essential vitamins and other trace nutrients of these foods are intentionally depleted so that bacteria or insects cannot use the food for growth, preventing rapid spoilage of the food.

However, a more insidious form of food poisoning is caused by the damage to foods by destruction of vitamin B6, folic acid and vitamin B12 through heat, exposure to oxygen or slow bacterial growth. Foods depleted of these vitamins in this way may hasten arterial damage by allowing a buildup of blood homocysteine. It is best to prepare only enough food for one meal and to discard any small amounts of leftover food. Larger quantities of left-over food can be adequately preserved by covering and promptly refrigerating or freezing. Such leftover food should be consumed within a day or two.

LIFESTYLE FACTORS AND HOMOCYSTEINE LEVELS

Smoking

The most important controllable lifestyle factor, besides an optimal diet, is cessation of cigarette smoking. The Hordaland study from Norway clearly documents that nonsmokers have a lower level of blood homocysteine than smokers, in the range of 1 to 2 micromoles per liter.[2] A possible explanation is that the carbon monoxide of cigarette smoke combines chemically with a form of vitamin B6, causing inactivation of the vitamin and impairing the ability of the body to dispose of excess homocysteine by conversion to cystathionine. Since cigarette smoke contains over 600 different toxic substances besides carbon monoxide, other factors may also contribute to heart disease risk associated with smoking. An example may be the free radical compounds produced by burning tars that can modify lipoproteins in the wall of the artery, hastening plaque development.

The addictive properties of the nicotine in cigarette smoke have received attention from pharmacologists and medical scientists employed by the tobacco industry, government, universities and the private sector. The results of these studies have shown that nicotine addiction is at least as powerful and as difficult to overcome as the addictions to heroin or cocaine. Recent medical studies have also shown that nicotine affects brain function in a way similar to other addictive drugs. An individual's ability to overcome nicotine addiction and to cease smoking varies with several factors, including psychological dependency, nutrition, state of health, age and gender, among others. Almost every person who tries to overcome nicotine addiction and dependency needs help during the withdrawal phase. Nicotine patches, gum, hypnotic suggestion, group therapy, hot baths and other strategies may help to overcome withdrawal symptoms.

The best strategy for avoiding the great health risks of smoking is preventing the beginnings of nicotine addiction in childhood. However, because of peer pressure, availability of cigarettes, the stress of adolescence and many other causes, children and adolescents are highly vulnerable to this form of substance abuse. Parents may have difficulty preventing nicotine addiction in their children because of the difficulty of controlling these complex behavioral factors. By accepting the rebellious nature of developing adolescents, by setting an example of nonsmoking, by material inducements and other inventive methods, parents should help their children to escape this destructive habit.

Drugs and Toxins

Over the past several decades, a wide variety of drugs, solvents and other toxic substances has been found to cause elevation of blood homocystine levels.[27] Chemotherapeutic drugs for cancer such as methotrexate, antiepileptic drugs such as phenytoin and antihypertensive drugs such as hydrochlorothiazide have been found to increase blood homocysteine levels. Many of these drugs are known to antagonize the action of folic acid or vitamin B6 in the body, causing abnormalities in the control of blood homocysteine. The need of the individual for the therapeutic benefits of these drugs needs to be weighed against the risk of elevated blood homocysteine in hastening the onset and complications of arteriosclerosis. In the case of azaribine, a potent chemotherapeutic drug that was used for treatment of refractory psoriasis, the observation of heart attack, stroke and thrombosis of peripheral blood vessels associated with elevation of blood homocysteine led the U.S. Food and Drug Administration in 1976 to withdraw the drug from general use.[28]

A striking example of a toxic chemical in the workplace, carbon disulfide, was uncovered during an investigation of increased risk of myocardial infarction among viscose rayon production workers.[29] The high risk of arteriosclerosis and heart attack in these workers was attributed to antagonism of vitamin B6, leading to increased blood homocysteine levels.[30] Another commonly used anesthetic gas, nitrous oxide, also known as "laughing gas," has been found to increase the blood homocysteine level by interfering with the ability of vitamin B12 to convert homocysteine to methionine.[27] Because of the relatively brief periods of exposure to nitrous oxide in patients, the added risk of arteriosclerosis is probably minimal. However, the potential hazard of exposure to nitrous oxide among anesthetists or industrial workers and the resulting elevated blood homocysteine over a period of years should be studied.

Exercise

The importance of exercise in preventing arteriosclerosis and coronary heart disease was popularized by the eminent American cardiologist, Paul Dudley White, during the 1950s and 1960s. He inspired a generation of medical scientists and practitioners to examine the effect of a sedentary lifestyle on the progression of arteriosclerosis. In meeting with Dr. White at his office in Boston two years before his death, I was privileged to explain to him how I had discovered the causal link between elevation of blood homocysteine and vascular disease. His response was, "This is a red-letter day in my understanding of heart disease!" He understood very well that lack of exercise was predominantly a contributory factor in susceptibility to coronary heart disease and that complex genetic, dietary and toxic factors are the most important in causation.

In the past two decades the importance of moderate exercise in delaying the onset of arteriosclerosis and benefitting longevity has become widely studied and popularized. Exercise programs have been found to increase levels of high density lipoprotein (HDL) in the blood, contributing to a favorable decrease in the ratio of total cholesterol to HDL. Studies of runners, athletes and marathoners compared to those with sedentary lifestyles have shown a significant but limited reduction of blood homocysteine amounting to 1 to 2 micromoles per liter that is attributed to exercise.[2] Nevertheless, in individuals who have developed arteriosclerosis and coronary heart disease because of their nutritional, genetic or lifestyle history, vigorous exercise may precipitate heart attack, even in a well-conditioned athlete. By chance, I met and conversed briefly with Jim Fixx, a proponent of exercise and conditioning to prevent coronary heart disease, only two days before he died of a heart attack while jogging. He had evidently ignored early signs of heart disease in himself and failed to seek proper medical and surgical therapy.

Stress

While a considerable effort by medical scientists has attempted to relate stress and type A personality to coronary disease susceptibility, a causal role for these factors has not definitely been established. Psychological stress reduction techniques have been claimed to be beneficial in this regard. However, the opposite point of view, that susceptibility to arteriosclerosis from nutritional, genetic or toxic factors may account for a stress-prone personality, has not received adequate investigation. The effects of homocysteine on brain function are incompletely understood, but neurophysiologists have clearly demonstrated that homocysteic acid, the fully oxidized form of homocysteine, is a very potent exciter of brain function. Animals treated with high doses of homocysteine thiolactone develop seizures, and some children with homocystinuria have increased risk of convulsions. A recent limited study showed that patients with fibromyalgia/chronic fatigue syndrome have highly elevated levels of homocysteine in cerebrospinal fluid.[31] These studies suggest that increased levels of homocysteine and related compounds in the brain may modify behavior to produce stressful personality traits or neuropsychiatric disorders.[32]

Alcohol Use

Recent studies have shown that people who chronically abuse alcohol have elevated blood homocysteine levels.[33] Chronic excessive alcohol intake frequently leads to serious depletion of body stores of folic acid. The severity of folic acid deficiency may be reflected in anemia and prominent abnormalities of the bone marrow in the production of red blood cells, platelets and white cells. Deficiency of folic acid predisposes to an elevation of blood homocysteine because of the failure of conversion of homocysteine to methionine, as explained in Chapter 3. Alcohol also has prominent toxic effects on the function of the liver, leading to the accumulation of fat and cirrhosis of the liver. Although occasional patients with severe liver disease have been observed to have a degree of protection against arteriosclerosis, there are numerous examples of severe arteriosclerosis with stroke, coronary heart disease, kidney failure and peripheral vascular disease developing in chronic alcoholics. The idea that alcohol can somehow prevent deposition of fat and cholesterol in the walls of arteries because it may "dissolve the fat" is totally erroneous. Alcohol dissolves preferentially in plasma and exerts its toxic effects mainly on liver function. The elevation of blood homocysteine in alcoholics from folic acid deficiency produces arteriosclerosis by effects on arterial wall cells and tissues, and the function of the liver in producing lipoproteins is impaired by the toxicity of alcohol.

Consumption of alcohol in moderate quantities of one to two drinks per day, depending on body weight, has long been known to increase longevity when compared to the life span of abstainers from alcohol. Recently, the so-called "French paradox," the low incidence of arteriosclerosis and coronary heart disease despite high levels of fat and cholesterol in the French diet, has been attributed to the natural antioxidant pigments and bioflavonoids of red wine.[34] It is said that Thomas Jefferson advocated consumption of wine rather than spirits, saying, "I think it is a great error to consider a heavy tax on wines as a tax on luxury; on the contrary, it is a tax on the health of all our citizens." Another possible explanation for the "French paradox" is the consumption of abundant fresh vegetables and fruits in the French diet and the popularity of fois gras and liver paté in French cuisine. Liver is a rich source of vitamin B6, folic acid and vitamin B12, which all prevent elevation of blood homocysteine.

Analysis of patterns of coffee and tea consumption in the Hordaland homocysteine study[2] concluded that heavy consumption of filtered, boiled or instant coffee, more than nine cups per day, was associated with a 13 to 16 percent increase in blood homocysteine levels.[35] No effect was seen from decaffeinated coffee, and there was a suggestion of a lowering effect on blood homocysteine levels with tea consumption.

Genetic Background, Sex Hormones and Aging

Analysis of the familial incidence of early-onset arteriosclerosis has estimated that genetic background is of importance in approximately one-third of cases of coronary heart disease.[36,37] An important cause of this familial predisposition to coronary heart disease is an abnormal inherited form of methylenetetrahydrofolate reductase that is sensitive to heating. This thermolabile reductase has been estimated to affect as many as five percent of the general population in the homozygous form[38] and as many as 38 percent of a French Canadian population in the heterozygous form.[39] An individual from a family that carries this mutation requires more folic acid in the diet or from supplements to prevent elevation of blood homocysteine, compared with an individual without this genetic defect.[37] Therefore, an individual with this genetic background would be advised to consume a lifelong supplement of at least 1,000 mcg per day of folic acid to insure that plasma homocysteine is kept at a low level, preventing early-onset arteriosclerosis and coronary heart disease.

The parents of children with the most common form of homocystinuria have been studied intensively by medical scientists for evidence of increased risk of arteriosclerosis. Since homozygous homocystinuria caused by this genetic defect (when both parents carry the gene) has an incidence of about 1 per 60,000 to 1 per 200,000 in various populations, the expected incidence of heterozygous cystathionine synthase deficiency (when one parent carries the gene) is estimated to be about 1 per 100 to 1 per 200 in the general population. In studying patients with early-onset arteriosclerosis and elevated blood homocysteine levels, medical scientists have suggested that in 25–30 percent of these cases one parent carries the gene for cystathionine synthase deficiency. These findings are based on the results of the methionine loading test, which measures the degree of elevation of blood homocysteine following an oral dose of methionine. The results were confirmed in some cases by enzyme analysis of cells cultured from the skin of these patients. In studying heterozygous cystathionine synthase deficiency by techniques of molecular biology, however, no correlation could be found between this genetic defect and susceptibility to arteriosclerosis. At the present time, therefore, the evidence that this genetic defect can predispose to arteriosclerosis and coronary heart disease is inconclusive.

As explained in Chapter 3, about 50 percent of cases of homozygous homocystinuria caused by cystathionine synthase deficiency respond to large doses of supplemental vitamin B6. A survey of 629 of these cases concluded that the risk of developing thrombosis was decreased by vitamin B6 therapy.[40] Certainly any individual with a family history of homocystinuria, either in ancestors or in descendants, would be well-advised to consume a lifelong supplement of 10 to 25 mg per day of vitamin B6. Supplemental vitamin B6 may help to limit the elevation of homocysteine in the blood to normal postprandial levels following a protein meal containing methionine. Further studies by medical scientists are in progress to evaluate the advisability of vitamin B6 supplements in families that carry hidden genetic defects for homocystinuria.

Other genetic defects that are involved in controlling plasma levels of homocysteine may be uncovered by future scientific investigation. The cases of homocystinuria caused by methyl transferase deficiency are quite rare, and there is no current information regarding whether vitamin B12 or folic acid supplements are beneficial in heterozygous members of families that carry this genetic defect.

Chapter 2 explains that genetic defects in lipoprotein and cholesterol processing by the liver and other cells of the body predispose to early-onset arteriosclerosis. In the disease hypercholesterolemia the extreme elevations of low density lipoprotein (LDL) and total cholesterol in the plasma are caused by a genetic defect in the receptor which transports LDL into cells. The extreme elevation of blood cholesterol in these cases damages the walls of arteries because the arterial lining cells are continuously exposed to increased quantities of lipoprotein that contains homocysteine. Reducing homocysteine levels in these individuals by combined supplemental therapy with vitamin B6, folic acid and vitamin B12 may theoretically be beneficial because this approach reduces the homocysteine content of lipoproteins. However, no medical studies of this approach have yet been reported in persons with familial hypercholesterolemia. The genetic defects involving lipoproteins underlying other familial predispositions to arteriosclerosis, such as combined familial dyslipidemia or syndrome X with hypertension, diabetes and central obesity, are less well understood by medical scientists. The possible effects of vitamin supplements on these diseases have not been studied.

A family history of arteriosclerosis and heart disease implies a major contribution of genetic factors in causation. A study comparing identical with fraternal adult male twins concluded that the homocysteine level is genetically influenced, although the levels were in the normal range for both groups.[41] Other nongenetically determined factors that influence susceptibility to arteriosclerosis are lifestyle factors in families. Dietary practices, smoking history, exercise habits and other risk factors may be greatly influenced by family tradition. Families who eat a vegetarian or Mediterranean-style diet, engage in athletic activities and do not smoke are more likely to produce heart-healthy offspring than those who smoke, avoid exercise and consume a high-fat, high-sugar diet with an abundance of snack and processed foods.

Numerous medical conditions that may be determined genetically to some degree have a major effect on the risk of arteriosclerosis and coronary heart disease. These conditions include diabetes mellitus, hypertension, high levels of blood cholesterol or lipoprotein(a) and decreased thyroid function. Effective, intensive medical therapy is usually required to control these medical conditions, favorably decreasing risk of vascular disease to some extent. Despite control of diabetes by diet, drugs or insulin, however, vascular disease complications frequently shorten the life span of individuals with diabetes. No specific influence of early diabetes has yet been found to control blood homocysteine level, but the kidney failure that is frequently found in diabetics significantly elevates homocysteine levels and hastens the progression of vascular disease. Hypertension is correlated with elevated blood homocysteine in a number of studies, including the Hordaland study,[2] but the effect of controlling hypertension on homocysteine levels has not been determined. High homocysteine levels have been suggested to exacerbate the narrowing of small blood vessels that is commonly found in diabetes and hypertension.[42]

Sex Hormones

Women enjoy a measure of protection against arteriosclerosis during the reproductive years with a much lower incidence of coronary heart disease than men of the same age. This protective effect is ascribed to secretion of the female sex hormones estrogen and progestin by the ovary. Following menopause, however, the risk of arteriosclerosis and coronary heart disease in women rapidly increases, reaching rates comparable with those of men in their late 50s, 60s and 70s in susceptible populations. Because the ovary ceases to secrete female sex hormones after menopause, the level of homocysteine in plasma increases from 8 to 10 micromoles per liter in premenopausal women to 9 to 12 micromoles per liter in postmenopausal women.[2]

The use of supplemental estrogens in postmenopausal women reduces the risk of coronary heart disease by as much as 50 percent[43] and decreases blood homocysteine levels significantly.[44]

The association of high-dose estrogen and progestins for oral contraception with thrombosis and arteriosclerosis was related to the antivitamin B6 effects of oral contraceptives, causing elevation of blood homocysteine.[45] Subsequent studies have confirmed that oral contraceptives cause episodic elevation of blood homocysteine[46] and cause damage to the lining cells of arteries, called endothelial cells.[47] Low-dose oral contraceptives that are in current use have a lower but still significantly elevated risk of thrombosis compared with the older high-dose preparations. Women using oral contraceptives may benefit from moderate doses of supplemental vitamin B6 of 10 to 50 mg per day to decrease the edema, psychological effects and risk of thrombosis that may occur.

A chemotherapeutic antiestrogen drug, tamoxifen, is currently widely used in the treatment of breast cancer and certain other forms of cancer. Long-term treatment of breast cancer patients with tamoxifen was found to reduce the risk of cardiovascular mortality. The reduced risk of cardiovascular mortality was related to the lower levels of blood homocysteine produced by tamoxifen therapy.[48]

Since normally secreted estrogens and progestins of the ovary have a protective effect against vascular disease, does the secretion of testosterone by the testis in men exacerbate arteriosclerosis? It is known that men have a greater percentage of body muscle mass and muscle protein than women and that their dietary requirement for protein is greater. Very little attention has been paid by medical scientists to the effect of testosterone and synthetic androgenic steroid hormones on blood homocysteine levels. Synthetic androgenic steroids appear to hasten the onset of vascular disease and heart attack, but it is unknown whether this risk is attributable to elevated blood homocysteine levels.

Subtle or overt deficiency of thyroid gland function has long been known to predispose to arteriosclerosis and coronary heart disease. In some cases, the level of blood cholesterol and LDL is increased in hypothyroidism. Studies of blood homocysteine in hypothyroidism have also shown elevated levels of homocysteine, explaining increased risk of vascular disease.[19,49,50] Treatment of hypothyroidism with thyroid hormone may decrease vascular disease risk over a period of years.

High Cholesterol

Individuals with significantly elevated levels of total blood cholesterol and LDL have an increased risk of developing vascular disease. The treatment of this condition with diet, drugs, hormones and exercise is fraught with difficulty because of the resistance to lowering of blood cholesterol through intensive medical therapy. The recent limited success of statin drugs in reducing cholesterol levels and vascular disease risk is tempered by the unpleasant side effects, expense and potential toxicity of these drugs on muscles and the optic lens and from demonstrated carcinogenic effects in animals. The effect of dietary supplements of vitamin B6, folic acid and vitamin B12 in lowering blood homocysteine, cholesterol and LDL was demonstrated in a small number of patients with elevated cholesterol levels,[17] but the effect on vascular disease risk has not been determined. Theoretically, a significant decrease in the homocysteine content of LDL by this strategy should be beneficial because the strategy also decreases formation of LDL aggregates containing homocysteine.

In individuals with advanced arteriosclerosis and symptoms of coronary, cerebrovascular or peripheral vascular disease, a variety of advanced surgical techniques are available for excising, expanding, grafting or bypassing segments of arteries that are severely narrowed by arteriosclerosis. Angioplasty, endarterectomy or bypass grafts relieve symptoms and improve longevity in many cases, but a frequent complication of these procedures is a recurrence of the narrowing of arteries or formation of new arteriosclerotic plaques in the treated arterial segments. The potential effect of delaying or preventing these complications of surgical therapy by intensive dietary treatment and supplemental vitamin B6, folic acid and vitamin B12 is under study in some medical centers, but the results of this strategy remain to be determined.

Aging

Elevation of blood homocysteine levels is correlated with aging in men and women, and aging is a strong risk factor for development of arteriosclerosis. The fundamental nature of the aging process is incompletely understood, as explained further in Chapter 6. Nevertheless, it is well-established that decreased dietary intake, decreased blood levels and effects on blood homocysteine of vitamin B6, folic acid and vitamin B12 are correlated with aging.[6,51] Because of decreased caloric intake of nutrients and difficulties with absorption and mastication in the elderly, supplemental vitamins and minerals, including the B vitamins that control homocysteine levels, are advisable. The suggested intake of moderate quantities (10 mg of vitamin B6, 1.0 mg of folic acid, and 0.1 mg of vitamin B12 per day) of these supplemental vitamins may help to delay or ameliorate the rise in blood homocysteine levels that occurs in aging.[1]

Prevention of Arteriosclerosis

Many clinical studies and surveys over the past decade have clearly shown the effectiveness of dietary improvements and supplemental vitamin B6, folic acid and vitamin B12 in lowering blood levels of homocysteine. In a study from South Africa, for example, these supplemental vitamins were found to decrease elevated blood homocysteine levels by over 50 percent.[52] After discontinuing these vitamin supplements for four months, blood homocysteine levels again rose. A second period of vitamin supplementation was effective in lowering blood homocysteine over a six week trial, while a diet with fewer processed foods that contained adequate levels of the B vitamins was less effective in lowering blood homocysteine. In the Hordaland study from Norway, consumption of B vitamin supplements had a more consistent and stronger effect in lowering blood homocysteine than consumption of vegetables and fruits.[2]

The effectiveness of vitamin supplementation and dietary modification on lowering blood homocysteine is well established, but the reduction of cardiovascular disease and other complications of arteriosclerosis by lowering homocysteine levels is in the early stages of study. In a comparison of 750 vascular cases with 800 controls, a multicenter European study concluded that consumption of vitamin B6, folic acid or vitamin B12 reduced the risk of vascular disease by approximately two thirds.[53] A retrospective study of over 3,000 cases out of a total population of 24,000 during a five-year period of vitamin B6 therapy (50 to 200 mg per day) for carpal tunnel syndrome and related disorders reduced the risk of acute heart attack and angina pectoris by almost three-fourths.[54] In persons taking vitamin B6 supplements for more than one year, there was also an apparent increase in longevity.

Although current studies are suggestive of a preventive effect of dietary modification and vitamin supplementation on arteriosclerosis and its complications, final proof will only be conclusively obtained from a long-term prospective prevention trial. In such a trial, large numbers of subjects would be assigned randomly to groups with and without control of blood homocysteine levels by diet, vitamin supplementation or drug therapy. All of the known risk factors for arteriosclerosis would be closely monitored and analyzed statistically for effects on homocysteine levels and occurrence of vascular disease. After a trial period of five to ten years, a significant reduction of the number of cardiovascular and other complications of arteriosclerosis in the group with low blood homocysteine, produced by diet, vitamin supplementation or high dose vitamin therapy, compared with groups with high blood homocysteine levels, would constitute final proof of the effectiveness of this approach. Although a number of studies of this type are currently in the planning stage, no large-scale trial has yet been funded.

For almost three decades the mortality rate for coronary heart disease and other forms of arteriosclerosis has been declining steadily in the United States, as discussed in Chapter 2. An analysis of consumption of synthetic vitamin B6 in the U.S. food supply concluded that the decline in vascular disease since 1968 is correlated with consumption of significant quantities of synthetic vitamin B6.[55] The incidence of coronary heart disease in Finland had been among the highest in the world for several decades, but during the past decade the incidence has declined significantly, and surveys have shown low homocysteine and lipoprotein(a) levels among cases and controls.[56] Whether the low levels of homocysteine and the declining incidence of arteriosclerosis in Finland are attributable to the consumption of B vitamins has not been clarified. The recent decision of the U.S. Food and Drug Administration to add supplements of folic acid to grains, cereals, rice, pasta, bread and other enriched foods commencing in 1998 promises to continue the decline in vascular disease in the U.S.[1] This strategy, when implemented, is estimated to prevent as many as 50,000 deaths from coronary heart disease annually in the U.S.[57]

Some of the anticipated benefits to the individual from control of vascular disease through application of the homocysteine theory of arteriosclerosis are total freedom from or delayed onset of heart attack, stroke and peripheral vascular disease. As a result, further increases in life expectancy and improved health in the elderly are expected. Improved dietary practices and control of lifestyle factors may also have beneficial effects on the risk of other degenerative diseases and conditions associated with aging, including cancer, degenerative osteoarthritis, rheumatoid arthritis and other autoimmune diseases, obesity, hypertension and diabetes. Although the total human life span may not be increased by these measures, the anticipated benefit is an improved state of gradual and healthful aging.

REFERENCES

1. Kilmer S. McCully, "Homocysteine and Vascular Disease." *Nature Medicine* 2:386–389, 1996.
2. Ottar Nygard, Stein Emil Vollset, Helga Refsum, Inger Stensvold, Aage Tverdal, Jan Erik Nordrehaug, Per Magne Ueland and Gunner Kvale, "Total plasma homocysteine and cardiovascular risk profile. The Hordaland homocysteine study." *Journal of the American Medical Association* 274:1526–1533, 1995.
3. Roger J. Williams, *The Wonderful World within You: Your Internal Nutritional Environment* (New York: Bantam Books, 1977).
4. National Research Council Food and Nutrition Board, *Recommended Dietary Allowances,* Tenth Edition (Washington DC: National Academy of Sciences, 1989).
5. National Research Council Food and Nutrition Board, *Human Vitamin B6 Requirements* (Washington DC: National Academy of Sciences, 1978).
6. Jacob Selhub, Paul F. Jacques, Peter W.F. Wilson, David Rush and Irwin H. Rosenberg, "Vitamin status and intake as primary determinants of homocysteinemia in an elderly population." *Journal of the American Medical Association* 270:2693–2698, 1993.
7. Jacob Selhub, Paul F. Jacques, Andrew G. Bostom, Ralph B. D'Agostino, Peter W.F. Wilson, Albert J. Belanger, Daniel H. O'Leary, Philip A. Wolf, Ernst J. Schaeffer and Irwin H. Rosenberg, "Association between plasma homocysteine concentrations and extracranial carotid artery stenosis." *New England Journal of Medicine* 332:286–291, 1995.
8. Killian Robinson, Ellen L. Mayer, Dave P. Miller, Ralph Green, Frederick van Lente, Anjan Gupta, Kandice Kottke-Marchant, Susan R. Savon, Jacob Selhub, Steven E. Nissen, Michael Kuttner, Eric J. Topol and Donald W. Jacobsen, "Hyperhomocysteinemia and low pyridoxal phosphate. Common and independent reversible risk factors for coronary artery disease." *Circulation* 92:2825–2830, 1995.

9. Petra Verhoef, Meir J. Stampfer, Julie E. Buring, J. Michael Gaziano, Robert H. Allen, Sally P. Stabler, Robert D. Reynolds, Frans J. Kok, Charles H. Hennekens and Walter C. Willett, "Homocysteine metabolism and risk of myocardial infarction: Relation with vitamins B6, B12 and folate." *American Journal of Epidemiology* 143:845–859, 1996.
10. James F. Rinehart and Louis D. Greenberg, "Vitamin-B6 deficiency in the rhesus monkey. With particular reference to the occurrence of atherosclerosis, dental caries, and hepatic cirrhosis." *American Journal of Clinical Nutrition* 4:318–328, 1956.
11. Joshua W. Miller, Marie R. Nadeau, Donald Smith and Jacob Selhub, "Vitamin-B6 deficiency vs. folate deficiency: Comparison of responses to methionine loading in rats." *American Journal of Clinical Nutrition* 59:1033–1039, 1994.
12. Jacob Selhub and Joshua W. Miller, "The pathogenesis of homocysteinemia: Interruption of the coordinate regulation by S-adenosylmethionine of the remethylation and transsulfuration of methionine." *American Journal of Clinical Nutrition* 55:131–138, 1992.
13. L.S. deVilliers and Willem J. Serfontein, *Your Heart. The Unrefined Facts* (Bloemfontein: HAUM, 1989).
14. Eric B. Rimm, Alberto Ascherio, Edward Giovannucci, Donna Spiegelman, Meir J. Stampfer and Walter C. Willett, "Vegetable, fruit and cereal fiber intake and risk of coronary heart disease among men." *Journal of the American Medical Association* 275:447–451, 1996.
15. Meir J. Stampfer, Charles H. Hennekens, JoAnn E. Manson, Graham A. Colditz, Bernard Rosner and Walter C. Willett, "Vitamin E consumption and the risk of coronary heart disease in women." *New England Journal of Medicine* 328: 1444–1449, 1993.
16. Eric B. Rimm, Meir J. Stampfer, Alberto Ascherio, Edward Giovannucci, Graham A. Colditz and Walter C. Willett, "Vitamin E consumption and the risk of coronary heart disease in men." *New England Journal of Medicine* 328:1450–1456, 1993.
17. Andrzej J. Olszewski, Wictor B. Szostak, Magdalena Bial-

kowska, Stefan Rudnicki and Kilmer S. McCully, "Reduction of plasma lipid and homocysteine levels by pyridoxine, folate, cobalamin, choline, riboflavin, and troxerutin in atherosclerosis." *Atherosclerosis* 75:1–6, 1989.

18. Henry A. Schroeder, "Relation between mortality from cardiovascular disease and treated water supplies." *Journal of the American Medical Association* 172:1902–1908, 1960.
19. Yves Ingenbleek, Denis Barclay and Henri Dirren, "Nutritional significance of alterations in serum amino acid patterns in goitrous patients." *American Journal of Clinical Nutrition* 43:310–319, 1986.
20. Kilmer S. McCully, "Homocysteine and vascular disease: Role of folate, choline and lipoproteins in homocysteine metabolism." In: Bernard F. Suhaj and Steven H. Zeisel, Eds. *Proceedings of the 7th International Congress on Phospholipids* (Chicago: Americal Oil Chemists Society Press, 1997), *In Press.*
21. Andrzej J. Olszewski and Kilmer S. McCully, "Fish oil decreases serum homocysteine in hyperlipemic men." *Coronary Artery Disease* 4:53–60, 1993.
22. Kilmer S. McCully, Andrzej J. Olszewski and Michael P. Vezeridis, "Homocysteine and lipid metabolism in atherogenesis: Effect of the homocysteine thiolactonyl derivatives, thioretinaco and thioretinamide." *Atherosclerosis* 83:197–206, 1990.
23. Shi-Kaung Peng and Robert J. Morin, *Biological Effects of Cholesterol Oxides* (Boca Raton: Chemical Rubber Company Press, 1992).
24. Martha Louise Orr, *Pantothenic Acid, Vitamin B6 and Vitamin B12 in Foods. Home Economics Research Report No. 36* (Washington DC: U.S. Government Printing Office, 1969).
25. Edward W. Toepfer, Elizabeth Gates Zook, Martha Louise Orr and L.R. Richardson, *Folic Acid Content of Foods. Home Economics Research Report No. 29* (Washington DC: U.S. Government Printing Office, 1951).
26. National Research Council Food and Nutrition Board, *Folic Acid. Biochemistry and Physiology in Relation to the Human*

Nutrition Requirement (Washington DC: National Academy of Sciences, 1977).
27. Per Magne Ueland and Helga Refsum, "Plasma homocysteine, a risk factor for vascular disease: Plasma levels in health, disease, and drug therapy." *Journal of Laboratory and Clinical Medicine* 114:473–501, 1989.
28. Jerome L. Shupack, Anthony J. Greico, Allen M. Epstein, Claude Sansaricq and Selma E. Snyderman, "Azaribine, homocystinemia, and thrombosis." *Archives of Dermatology* 113:1301–1302, 1977.
29. S. Hernberg, T. Partanen, C.H. Nordman and P. Sumari, "Coronary heart disease among workers exposed to carbon disulfide." *British Journal of Industrial Medicine* 27:313–325, 1970.
30. Edward J. Calabrese, "Environmental validation of the homocysteine theory of arteriosclerosis." *Medical Hypotheses* 15:361–367, 1984.
31. B. Regland, M. Andersson, J. Bagby, L-E. Dyrehag, L. Abrahamsson and C-G. Gottfries, "Homocysteinosis in the central nervous system in patients with fibromyalgia/chronic fatigue syndrome." *Irish Journal of Medical Science* 164 Suppl 15:65A, 1995.
32. C.R. Santhosh-Kumar, K.L. Hassell, J.C. Deutsch and J.F. Kolhouse, "Are neuropsychiatric manifestations of folate, cobalamin, and pyridoxine deficiency mediated through imbalances in excitatory sulfur amino acids?" *Medical Hypotheses* 43:239–244, 1994.
33. Bjorn Hultberg, M. Bergland, A. Andersson and A. Frank, "Elevated plasma homocysteine in alcoholics." *Alcoholism: Clinical and Experimental Research* 17:687–689, 1993.
34. David M. Goldberg, "Does wine work?" *Clinical Chemistry* 41:14–16, 1995.
35. Ottar Nygard, Helga Refsum, Per Magne Ueland, Inger Stensvold, Jan Erik Nordrehaug, Gunnar Kvale and Stein Emil Vollset, "Coffe consumption and plasma homocysteine: The Hordaland homocysteien study." *American Journal of Clinical Nutrition* 65:136–143, 1997.
36. Jacques J. Genest, Jr., Judith R. McNamara, Barbara Upson,

Deeb N. Salem, Jose M. Ordovas, Ernst J. Schaefer and M. Rene Malinow, "Prevalence of familial hyperhomocyst(e)inemia in men with premature coronary artery disease." *Arteriosclerosis and Thrombosis* 11:1129–1136, 1991.

37. Paul N. Hopkins, Lily L. Wu, Steven C. Hunt, Brent C. James, G. Michael Vincent and Roger R. Williams, "Higher plasma homocyst(e)ine and increased susceptibility to adverse effects of low folate in early familial coronary artery disease." *Arteriosclerosis, Thrombosis and Vascular Biology* 15:1314–1320, 1995.
38. Soo-Sang Kang, Edward L. Passen, Neal Ruggie, Paul W.K. Wong and Hyunchoo Sora, "Thermolabile defect of methylenetetrahydrofolate reductase in coronary artery disease." *Circulation* 88:1463–1469, 1993.
39. Phyllis Frosst, Henk J. Blom, R. Milos, Philippe Goyette, C.A. Shephard, Rowena G. Matthews, Godfried J.H. Boers, Martin den Heijer, Leo A.J. Kluijtmans, Lambert P.W.J. van den Heuvel and Rima Rozen, "A candidate genetic risk factor for vascular disease: a common mutation in methylenetetrahydrofolate reductase." *Nature Genetics* 10:111–113, 1995.
40. S. Harvey Mudd, Fleming Skovby, Harvey L. Levy, Karen D. Pettigrew, Bridget Wilcken, Reed E. Pyeritz, G. Andria, Godfried H.J. Boers, Irvin L. Bromberg, Roberto Cerone, Brian Fowler, Hans Grobe, Hildgund Schmidt and Leslie Schweitzer, "The natural history of homocystinuria due to cystathionine beta synthase deficiency." *American Journal of Human Genetics* 37:1–31, 1985.
41. Terry Reed, M. Rene Malinow, Joe C. Christian and Barbara Upson, "Estimates of heritability of plasma homocyst(e)ine levels in aging adult male twins." *Clinical Genetics* 39:425–428, 1991.
42. Atsushi Araki, Yoshiasu Sato and Hideki Ito, "Plasma homocysteine concentrations in Japanese patients with noninsulin-dependent diabetes mellitus: Effect of parenteral methylcobalamin treatment." *Atherosclerosis* 103:149–157, 1993.
43. Meir J. Stampfer, Graham A. Colditz and Walter C. Willett,

"Postmenopausal estrogen therapy and cardiovascular disease." *New England Journal of Medicine* 325:756–762, 1991.
44. M.J. van der Mooren, A.J. Wonters, Henk J. Blom, L.A. Schellekens, Tom K.A.B. Estes and R. Rolland, "Homocysteine concentrations may decrease during postmenopausal hormone replacement therapy." *Irish Journal of Medical Science* 164 Suppl 15:81A, 1995.
45. Kilmer S. McCully, "Homocysteine, atherosclerosis and thrombosis: Implications for oral contraceptive users." *American Journal of Clinical Nutrition* 28:542–549, 1975.
46. Regine P.M. Steegers-Theunissen, Godfried H.J. Boers, Eric A.P. Steegers, Frans J.M. Trijbels, Chris M.G. Thomas and Tom K.A.B. Eskes, "Effects of sub-50 oral contraceptives on homocysteine metabolism: A preliminary study." *Contraception* 45:129–139, 1992.
47. Josef Hladovec, J. Koutsky, I. Prerovsky, V. Dvorak and A. Novotny, "Oral contraceptives, methionine and endothelial lesions." *Vasa* 12:117–120, 1983.
48. G. Anker, P.E. Lonning, Per Magne Ueland, Helga Refsum and E.A. Lien, "Plasma levels of the atherogenic amino acid homocysteine in post-menopausal women with breast cancer treated with tamoxifen." *International Journal of Cancer* 60:365–368, 1995.
49. B. Nedrebo, U.B. Ericsson, Per Magne Ueland, Helga Refsum and E.A. Lien, "Plasma levels of the atherogenic amino acid homocysteine in hyper- and hypothyroid patients." *Irish Journal of Medical Science* 164 Suppl 15:47A, 1995.
50. F. Parrot-Roulaud, C. Cochet, B. Catargi, F. Leprat and J.L. Latapie, "Hypothyroidism and hyperhomocysteinemia." *Irish Journal of Medical Science* 164 Suppl 15:56A, 1995.
51. Kilmer S. McCully, "Chemical pathology of homocysteine. III Cellular function and aging." *Annals of Clinical and Laboratory Science* 24:134–152, 1994.
52. Johan B. Ubbink, Annatjie van der Merwe, W.J. Hayward Vermaak and Rhena Delport, "Hyperhomocysteinemia and the response to vitamin supplementation." *The Clinical Investigator* 71:993–998, 1993.

53. R. Meleady, L. Daly and Ian Graham, "Homocysteine—do vitamin supplements protect against vascular disease?" *Irish Journal of Medical Science* 164 Suppl 15:51A, 1995.
54. John M. Ellis and Kilmer S. McCully, "Prevention of myocardial infarction by vitamin B6." *Research Communications in Molecular Pathology and Pharmacology* 89: 208–220, 1995.
55. Kilmer S. McCully, "The homocysteine theory of arteriosclerosis: Development and current status." In: Antonio M. Gotto, Jr. and Rodolfo Paoletti, editors, *Atherosclerosis Reviews,* volume 11 (New York: Raven Press, 1983), pp. 157–246.
56. G. Alfthan, J. Pekkanen, M. Jauhiainen, J. Pitkaniemi, M. Karvonen, J. Tuomilheto, J.T. Salonen and C. Ehnholm, "Relation of serum homocysteine and lipoprotein(a) concentrations to atherosclerotic disease in a prospective Finnish population-based study." *Atherosclerosis* 106:9–19, 1994.
57. Carol J. Boushey, Shirley A.A. Beresford, Gilbert S. Omenn and Arno G. Motulsky, "A quantitative assessment of plasma homocysteine as a risk factor for vascular disease. Probable benefits of increasing folic acid intakes." *Journal of the American Medical Association* 274:1049–1057, 1995.

CHAPTER 6

The Homocysteine Revolution: Medicine for the New Millennium

The Homocysteine Revolution

The medical discovery of the causative role of homocysteine in vascular disease and the hypothesis implicating homocysteine in the pathogenesis of arteriosclerosis were new and startling when first proposed in 1969.[1] In the succeeding years a new pathway of medical research was uncovered that relates homocysteine to arteriosclerosis, cancer, aging, normal growth and development and the degenerative diseases of aging. This pathway was taken by the author, his colleagues and students and by increasing numbers of other independent medical investigators. This "trail of research" was inspired by and expanded upon past discoveries by Vincent DuVigneaud and other pioneers in knowledge about homocysteine and related sulfur amino acids.[2]

What began as a chance observation in children with rare inherited diseases of homocysteine metabolism now promises to unlock mysteries that have long puzzled medical scientists. In 1969 it was difficult to predict the extent to which a seemingly unimportant byproduct of protein breakdown, homocysteine, could unite understanding of how vital nutrients, including vitamins A, C, B12, B2, folic acid, E and B6 function within cells and tissues to control the basic processes of life itself. These processes include cellular respiration, cell and tissue growth, cell removal and replacement, maintenance of connective tissues, expression of genetic information, reproduction and embryonic development. Over three decades of medical research on homocysteine have yielded a true revolution in the understanding of the role of this amino acid in living cells and tissues, in aging, and in the degenerative diseases of cancer and arteriosclerosis.

During the past decade and especially since 1990 a large number of human studies, both epidemiological and clinical, have confirmed the validity of the homocysteine approach to arteriosclerosis. A veritable avalanche of new data has supported its basic tenets, as explained in previous chapters. This work by increasing numbers of international medical investigators has begun to rewrite the current concepts of the cause of arteriosclerosis in human populations. The simplicity of the homocysteine theory has provided a convincing explanation for the decline in coronary heart disease mortality in the U.S. since the mid-1960s and led to important new proposals for the control of the disease in the population. Assuring adequacy of dietary intakes of vitamin B6 and folic acid is now understood as a promising strategy for prevention of vascular disease through control of elevated blood homocysteine levels in the population at risk.[3] Dietary intake of vitamin B12 is adequate for the population, except for a very few strict vegetarians who consume no animal products at all. The decision of the U.S. Food and Drug Administration to add folic acid to enriched foods beginning in 1998 is a milestone in the long journey toward substantial reduction of arteriosclerosis in the U.S. population. A goal for the future is for the F.D.A. also to require addition of vitamin B6 to enriched foods to replace the quantity of the vitamin lost in food processing and preservation. Not only will the addition of these two vital nutrients to the food supply continue the decline in arteriosclerosis, it will improve the general health and promote increased life expectancy in the population.

The important studies of the relation of risk factors for arteriosclerosis to homocysteine levels in susceptible populations, as exemplified by the Hordaland Homocysteine Study,[4] give guidance for prevention of the disease in those at risk, as explained in Chapter 5. These studies explain the supreme importance of lifelong consumption of an optimal diet combined with cessation of smoking, adequate exercise and other simple measures. Any person can assure adequate dietary intake of vitamins, minerals, fiber, antioxidants and other beneficial nutrients to prevent or delay the onset of elevated blood homocysteine levels. This strategy for prevention of arteriosclerosis is revolutionary because it shifts the emphasis toward consumption of beneficial nutrients and places the consumption of sugars and fats in a new context. These highly processed foodstuffs are a rich source of calories, but a poor source of the vitamins and other nutrients which prevent induction of arteriosclerosis by homocysteine. This approach is revolutionary because it emphasizes that depletion of essential nutrients is the key factor in understanding the origin of the disease. Until recently the traditional view has been to incriminate consumption of cholesterol, fats and sugars because of supposed damage to arterial cells and tissues by these foods. Today, we can view arteriosclerosis as a deficiency disease, rather than a disease of excess.

A wide range of discoveries by medical scientists over

the past three decades in basic biochemistry, cell physiology and oncology has shown how the homocysteine revolution is illuminating understanding of cancer and the aging process as well as arteriosclerosis. These exciting discoveries are in the early stages of development because their application to human studies is as yet very limited. Nevertheless, a theoretical basis for understanding, based upon experiments with the cells and tissues of animals, must be developed prior to initiating human studies.

This final chapter is written for the reader who has some acquaintance with the concepts and terminology of biochemistry and basic medical science. It gives a general description of how experiments with cells and tissues led to the synthesis of *thioretinamide* and *thioretinaco,* substances of great importance to cellular biochemistry and physiology. These new compounds were discovered by organic synthesis from homocysteine in its reactive thiolactone form, from vitamin A in its retinoic acid form, and from vitamin B12 in its cobalamin form. The functions of thioretinamide and thioretinaco are the focal points in understanding how homocysteine participates in controlling cell division, cell function, and the biochemical processes of living cells and tissues. These substances orchestrate the functions of many vitamins and other trace substances, including folic acid, flavins, ascorbic acid, retinoic acid, cobalamin, pyridoxine and ubiquinol in the vital processes of living cells. Understanding how thioretinamide and thioretinaco may be altered in the aging process and how their functions change in degenerative diseases of aging, such as arteriosclerosis, cancer, arthritis and autoimmune diseases, can lead to revolutionary new approaches to controlling these diseases in human populations.

Biochemistry and Physiology of Homocysteine

A century ago the brilliant medical investigator Sir Archibald E. Garrod began his studies of a rare inherited disease, alcaptonuria, which led to the concept of a genetic "error of metabolism."[5] In his lectures and monograph entitled *Inborn Errors of Metabolism,* Garrod developed the idea that a mutation in a single essential gene could cause an inherited disease because of formation of an abnormal enzyme in all cells of the body.[6] An enzyme is a protein which facilitates a specific chemical reaction within the body's cells and tissues. The chemical reactions and transformations of constituents of food within the body are known as metabolic processes or metabolism. Garrod's brilliant and productive concept has led to the elucidation and treatment of thousands of genetic diseases during the past century, as described in detail in the classic text *The Metabolic Basis of Inherited Disease*.[7]

In the case of homocystinuria, Garrod's concept was shown to be correct by the demonstration that cells cultured from the skin of children with this inherited disease contain an abnormal enzyme, cystathionine synthase, that fails to convert homocysteine into cystathionine normally.[8] By studying these abnormal cells from a patient with homocystinuria, perhaps some clue could be observed that would explain why these children develop arteriosclerosis at an early age. The lack of the enzyme cystathionine synthase in these cultured cells might lead to an abnormality of metabolism that could explain features of this inherited disease.

As described in Chapter 3, the growth of cells in culture from patients with homocystinuria revealed that the cells produce an aggregated matrix substance called proteoglycan that has reduced solubility compared to the finely fibrillar proteoglycan produced by normal cells in culture.[9] Labelling experiments with radioactive sulfate ions showed that this aggregated matrix proteoglycan is more heavily sulfated than the proteoglycans of normal cells.[10] The molecular basis for this aggregated proteoglycan matrix was suggested to be conversion of the normal helical structure of protein to an unfolded random coil that binds more sulfate because of displacement of potassium ions by homocysteine thiolactone cation from the surface of the protein.[11] Because of the chemical properties of homocysteine thiolactone cation, this conversion of fibrillar helical proteins to aggregated unfolded proteins of decreased solubility may have wide implications in the solubility of different types of proteins. Future studies may show that not only proteoglycans but also lipoproteins, nucleoproteins and membrane proteins may be converted to a less soluble aggregated form because homocysteine thiolactone cation and increased numbers of sulfate ions bind to the surface of these proteins. Because of the decreased solubility of aggregated proteoglycan matrix produced by cultured cells lacking cystathionine synthase activity, the accumulation of sulfated proteoglycans in the arteriosclerotic plaques of children with homocystinuria is attributed to the change in proteoglycan conformation induced by homocysteine.[10,11]

A second important lesson taught by study of cultured cells from children with homocystinuria is that a previously unknown pathway for activation of sulfate was discovered by using homocysteine thiolactone labelled with radioactive sulfur in the culture medium of these cells.[10] The classic pathway for formation of bound sulfate was discovered in the 1950s by Philip Robbins and the famous biochemist Fritz Lipmann.[12] In this pathway, free sulfate ions, derived by metabolism from cysteine, react with ATP (adenosine triphosphate) to form PAPS (phosphoadenosine phosphosulfate), which transfers bound sulfate groups to proteoglycan matrix. In the experiments with cultured cells that are deficient in cystathionine synthase, this classic pathway could not explain the rapid and complete conversion of homocysteine to sulfate because their enzyme abnormality prevents homocysteine from conversion to cystathionine, cysteine and sulfate.

Subsequent experiments suggested that the new pathway for PAPS formation in cystathionine-synthase-deficient cells involves the participation of thioretinamide, a compound synthesized from homocysteine thiolactone and retinoic acid (vitamin A acid) by organic synthesis.[13] In this scheme thioretinamide reacts with superoxide, a reactive oxygen radical, to form sulfite and retinoic acid, and sulfite is converted to sulfate by the enzyme sulfite oxidase for activation by ATP to form PAPS.[14] This scheme explains the previously discovered participation of vitamin A (retinoic acid) in the formation of PAPS and bound sulfate.[15]

The third important lesson taught by study of cultured cystathionine-synthase-deficient cells is that the pattern of growth in the culture dish is abnormal, resembling the growth of malignant cells in culture.[9,10] When malignant cells are cultured they grow abnormally, piling up in multiple layers, whereas normal cells form a beautiful layer, one cell thick, covering the surface of the culture dish. The cystathionine-synthase-deficient cells grow in multiple layers, like cancer cells, forming a distinctive pattern with sparse areas alternating with piled up areas. When additional vitamin B6 is added to the cell culture medium, growth of the cells is stimulated and the proteoglycan matrix becomes partially fibrillar in addition to the aggregated form. If homocysteine thiolactone is added to the culture medium, the cells degenerate, detaching from the surface of the culture dish. Added vitamin B6 in the culture medium prevents the toxic effect of homocysteine on the cultured cells, because enough pyridoxal phosphate, the coenzyme form of the vitamin, is produced to activate traces of the abnormal cystathionine synthase enzyme, converting excess homocysteine to cystathionine.

These observations on growth disturbances in cystathionine synthase-deficient cells are important for two reasons. First, the smooth muscle cells of developing arteriosclerotic plaques multiply and form piled-up layers within the artery wall because of disturbed control of cellular growth. Second, the observations on abnormal cellular growth led to studies of homocysteine thiolactone in malignant cells and to the discovery of thioretinaco, as described in the next section of this chapter.

Vitamin C, also known as ascorbic acid, was first isolated, crystallized and characterized chemically by the brilliant biochemist Albert Szent-Györgyi in the 1930s. The human vitamin deficiency disease caused by lack of vitamin C in the diet is called scurvy, a fatal illness that develops about two to four months after deprivation of fruits and vegetables. A characteristic abnormality of the blood vessels in scurvy is bleeding, especially from the gums and into the skin. Investigation of experimental scurvy in guinea pigs caused by feeding a vitamin C-deficient diet shows that the sulfated proteoglycans of blood vessel walls become attenuated and thinned. As a result the blood vessels begin to leak because of lack of cohesiveness of the artery walls and because of abnormalities of the platelets, the specialized blood-cell particles that are needed for blood clotting. In addition, the animals abruptly stop growing because the matrix of the cartilage in the growth centers of the bones fails to bind sulfate when deprived of vitamin C.

Homocysteine reacts more rapidly with ascorbic acid than its chemical relative, cysteine, in biochemical experiments. Furthermore, ascorbic acid levels within cells are known to change characteristically during cell division. In some ways the abnormalities of the blood vessels and platelets in scurvy are opposed to the arteriosclerosis and increased reactivity of platelets found in children with homocystinuria. In addition, the cell cultures from children with homocystinuria reveal a new pathway for conversion of the sulfur atom of homocysteine thiolactone to sulfate. By studying the biochemistry of homocysteine in scurvy, therefore, the function of ascorbic acid in the reaction of homocysteine with oxygen could be investigated.

Experiments with normal guinea pigs and those deprived of vitamin C in their diet showed that experimental scurvy impairs the reaction of homocysteine with oxygen.[16] After radioactively labelled homocysteine thiolactone was injected into the guinea pigs, the livers of the scorbutic guinea pigs were found to accumulate the unoxidized form of homocysteine, but in the livers of normal guinea pigs, the homocysteine thiolactone reacted with oxygen to form homocysteic acid and sulfate. By synthesis of labelled homocysteic acid by reaction of homocysteine with hydrogen peroxide, it was further found that normal liver converts the sulfur atom of homocysteine to PAPS, phosphoadenosine phosphosulfate, as shown by isolation of the labelled sulfating coenzyme.

The results of these biochemical experiments showed that vitamin C is necessary for the reaction of homocysteine with oxygen to form the active form of sulfate, phosphoadenosine phosphosulfate. Subsequent work with thioretinamide showed that a form of vitamin A, retinoic acid, is needed for the biochemical reaction of homocysteine with oxygen.[14,15] The importance of retinoic acid in the formation of adenosine triphosphate (ATP) was shown in cultured cells.[17] These experiments, therefore, united homocysteine with formation of ATP and PAPS, combined with participation of vitamins A and C. ATP is an important form of chemical energy within cells formed by reaction of oxygen with hydrogen from the carbon atoms of foods, a process known as oxidative phosphorylation. These experiments showed that homocysteine is intimately involved with the basic processes of living cells by which food is burned with oxygen to produce chemical energy in the form of ATP.

In the growth and development of bone and cartilage in young animals, the process of adding sulfate to cartilage matrix is under the control of growth hormone secreted by the pituitary gland. In young animals growth hormone causes release of a protein factor known as insulin-like growth factor, which increases the binding of sulfate to the matrix of cartilage. This explains why some children with homocystinuria have accelerated growth, causing them to develop increased stature, long arms, legs, fingers and toes. Homocysteine acts in cartilage to increase binding of sulfate, mimicking the action of insulin-like growth factor.[18]

In experiments with rats from which the pituitary gland had been removed surgically, homocysteic acid, the form of homocysteine containing three extra oxygen atoms, stimulates the growth of the animals, as measured by tail growth or by cartilage growth.[19] In order to achieve growth, the animals were also treated with thyroxine, the thyroid hormone that is required for normal growth and development. In the plasma of the growing rats, insulin-like growth factor was demonstrated by increased binding of sulfate when incubated with fragments of pig cartilage. The homocysteic acid and thyroxine treatments were promoting the growth of these animals in the absence of pituitary growth hormone by stimulating the release of insulin-like growth factor from the liver.

Earlier experiments had shown that feeding or injecting homocysteic acid into normal rabbits or guinea pigs increased the growth rate of these animals, producing giant rabbits in one experiment.[20] To this day pathologists who were present in the 1970s when the experiments were done remember the extraordinary appearance of these apparently normal but giant rabbits. In experiments with cultured cartilage cells from chick embryos, homocysteic acid was found to increase binding of sulfate to cartilage, an action that mimics the effect of insulin-like growth factor on cartilage.[21] In several patients with untreated homocystinuria with accelerated growth, increased secretion of growth hormone was demonstrated.[22] Taken together, the physiological experiments and other observations on the action of growth hormone and insulin-like growth factor show that homocysteine plays a vital role in the control of normal growth.

The experiments with cell cultures from children with homocystinuria showed that the abnormal aggregated proteoglycan matrix produced by these cells binds more sulfate than the proteoglycan of normal cells, an effect that is reminiscent of the effect of insulin-like growth factor on cartilage matrix.[9,10] The experiments concerning reaction of homocysteine thiolactone with low-density lipoprotein showed that the thiolated lipoprotein had become aggregated, smaller, more dense and moved more rapidly in an electric field.[23] Additional observations on the properties of malignant cells showed that overproduction of homocysteine thiolactone by cultured cancer cells causes binding of homocysteine to proteins, membranes, nucleoproteins and proteoglycans, producing aggregation, condensation, stickiness and other abnormalities.[24] These effects of homocysteine thiolactone on proteoglycans of cystathionine-deficient cells, aggregated lipoproteins, membrane proteins, nucleoproteins and other constituents of malignant cells are explained by its effect on secondary structure and by binding of sulfate to the charged form of homocysteine thiolactone adhering to the surface of these macromolecules.[11]

HOMOCYSTEINE AND CANCER

Since the discovery of the double helix of DNA in 1953 by Francis Crick and James Watson,[25] the general opinion of most medical investigators has been that alteration of the genes of DNA by the action of carcinogenic chemicals, radiation, oncogenic viruses or other carcinogenic factors is responsible for induction of the malignant state of cellular growth in cancer. In the first half of the 20th century, in contrast, the favorite opinion regarding induction of cancer among medical scientists was the altered respiration theory championed by Otto Warburg.[26] According to this theory, carcinogenic factors act by alteration of the process by which cells combine oxygen with electrons from the carbon atoms of food to produce carbon dioxide, water and chemical energy in the form of ATP.

Over the years there has been no apparent way to reconcile these two major theories of the cause of cancer. In the 1950s and early 1960s Albert Szent-Gyorgi extracted undefined substances from normal tissues that retard the growth of malignant cells in animals by altering the way electrons are processed within living cells.[27] He believed that a substance he termed "retine" is lost from normal cells when they become malignant. If he had been able to establish the chemical identity of this substance, his findings may have been able to unite the genetic and respiration theories of the origin of cancer.

Closely related to the genetic theory of carcinogenesis is the participation of growth-regulating and growth-controlling factors called oncogenes. Over 100 genetic factors have been found to control protein and polypeptide gene products that become activated or deactivated in malignant cells. An example is the P53 oncogene which has been found to become altered during carcinogenesis so that its gene product is unable to restrain the growth of normal cells. This oncogene has been found to be involved frequently in cases of colon, lung and ovarian cancer, among others, allowing growth of these malignancies. Another example is the oncogene involved in breast cancer, BRCA-1, which is altered in familial cases of breast cancer.

When these many oncogenes become altered by genetic, dietary, chemical or environmental factors, there is interference with the normal control of the process of cell division, allowing unrestrained growth of a particular type of cell within the body. Oncogenes also become altered or activated in other non-malignant types of cellular growth, for example, in regeneration of liver cells in animals. The oncogene theory does not explain at a detailed molecular level how relaxation of the control of cellular growth allows the unrestrained nature of malignancy to develop and to become autonomous, allowing spread and growth of cancer cells throughout the body.

Experiments with cultured malignant cells, inspired by the resemblance of the growth pattern of cells from children with homocystinuria to the growth pattern of cancer cells in culture, resulted in the discovery that the sulfur atom of homocysteine thiolactone fails to react with oxygen to form sulfate in these cells.[24] This finding suggested that normal cells in culture are able to convert homocysteine thiolactone to sulfate because they contain a hypothetical homocysteine thiolactonyl derivative which allows this chemical reaction to proceed. In cancer cells, on the other hand, homocysteine thiolactone accumulates within the cells and reacts with proteins and other cellular constituents, including proteoglycans, nucleoproteins and membrane proteins, to cause aggregation of and alteration in solubility and function of a wide range of cell components. In later experiments, free homocysteine thiolactone was demonstrated in human tumors[28] and in cultured cancer cells.[29]

The result of accumulation of excess homocysteine thiolactone within cancer cells causes widespread abnormalities of cellular function according to present concepts. The reaction of homocysteine thiolactone with membrane proteins causes diffuse abnormalities of membrane structure, termed simplification of cellular membranes. The reaction of homocysteine thiolactone with nucleoproteins causes altered formation of specialized proteins of different cell types, for example liver, muscle or nerve cells, leading to decreased or abnormal expression of these characteristic proteins. Aggregation and decreased solubility of nucleoproteins from reaction with homocysteine thiolactone causes abnormalities in chromosome structure, chromosome numbers and appearance of nuclear chromatin, producing the abnormalities that pathologists use to recognize cancer cells under the microscope. Reaction of homocysteine thiolactone with nucleoproteins of oncogenes leads to increased or decreased expression of growth factors and growth inhibitors, causing increased cellular growth. Reaction of homocysteine thiolactone with proteoglycans and proteins of cell membranes alters the appearance of these marker substances to the immune system of the body, leading to recognition of cancer cells as significantly altered immunologically.

The chemical nature of the hypothetical homocysteine thiolactone derivative that is lost from normal cells during their transformation to cancer cells was investigated by chemical synthesis of model homocysteine compounds and by testing the ability of these new compounds to inhibit growth of cancer cells in animals.[14] In this way some insight was gained into the chemical characteristics of this hypothetical regulator of homocysteine thiolactone formation within normal cells. If the chemical model compound was able to modify this process in cancer cells by slowing their growth, then the chemical nature of the hypothetical substance within normal cells could be deduced, and the substance could be made in the laboratory by organic chemical synthesis.

The first approach to the problem was to mimic the reaction of homocysteine thiolactone with oxygen since this reaction was found to be blocked in cancer cells.[24] When homocysteine thiolactone hydrochloride was mixed with perchloric acid, a strong oxidizing substance, a new compound was found to crystallize from the solvent solution, and the chemical structure was demonstrated to be homocysteine thiolactone perchlorate by X-ray analysis of the crystals.[30] When injected into animals with transplanted malignant tumors, the substance caused the tumors to swell and degenerate, stimulating their growth.

When homocysteine thiolactone was mixed with the fatty acids oleic acid or arachidonic acid, new compounds were formed that control the growth of malignant tumors, either increasing or decreasing their growth rate.[31] This finding extended the significance of the effect of homocysteine thiolactone perchlorate since all of these substances require for their anticancer activity the property of solubility in organic solvents or fats. The interpretation is that these anticancer compounds are very likely to be bound to cellular membranes at the site of their action since most fats within cells are present in cellular membranes.

Another interesting compound formed from homocysteine thiolactone and vitamin B6, homocysteine thiolactone pyridoxal enamine, was found to decrease tumor growth if the substance was injected for two weeks prior to transplantation of the malignant tumor. This result was interpreted to indicate that the enamine compound decreased the availability of homocysteine by formation of cystathionine, slowing tumor growth. This interpretation agrees with the results of previous studies by other scientists showing that methionine, the precursor of homocysteine, is needed to prevent induction of malignant tumors.

The more detailed chemical nature of the hypothetical regulator of homocysteine formation in cells was studied by formation of new compounds with maleic anhydride and maleimide, substances that are known to mimic the effects of radiation on normal cells. Although the maleic acid and maleimide derivatives of homocysteine thiolactone inhibit the growth of malignant tumors in animals, they are moderately toxic and require administration with liposomes, a form of artificial cell membrane, for optimal anticancer activity.[32]

In yet another model compound, homocysteine thiolactone was modified by reaction with a reactive oxygen-containing reagent, oxalyl chloride. The resulting oily substance, oxalyl homocysteine thiolactone, is soluble in organic solvents and fats. However, this new compound had no effect on growth of malignant tumors in animals unless it was first combined with rhodium trichloride.[33] Rhodium is a metal from the transition group which includes cobalt, an essential constituent of vitamin B12. This complex of rhodium trichloride and oxalyl homocysteine thiolactone dissolves in fats and has a strong inhibitory effect on growth of malignant tumors in animals. However, the complex is moderately toxic and even caused the development of a new malignant tumor in one of the animals.

Taken together, the results of all of these experiments with model compounds showed that the hypothetical regulator of homocysteine formation in cells is likely to be soluble in or bound to the fats of cell membranes and to contain oxygen atoms and unsaturated carbon atoms that modify the reactivity of homocysteine thiolactone and a transition metal atom, quite possibly the cobalt atom of vitamin B12.

Vitamin A is known to modify or prevent the growth of some malignant tumors in man and animals. Vitamin A is also known to be involved in formation of PAPS and bound sulfate, as described previously in this chapter.[15] Furthermore, vitamin A in the form of retinoic acid had been found to be involved in ATP synthesis in cultured cells, potentially linking homocysteine to the process of cellular respiration by which oxygen reacts with electrons from carbon atoms of food to produce chemical energy for the cells. How could vitamin A be involved as the regulator of both homocysteine thiolactone formation and cellular respiration in normal cells?

In experiments with the free-base form of homocysteine thiolactone, a way was found to make a chemical compound with retinoic acid, the acid form of vitamin A.[13] This new compound, called thioretinamide, was found to slow the growth of malignant tumors in animals and to prevent tumor formation in animals that had been given a chemical carcinogen, urethane. The compound, thioretinamide, like vitamin A, is soluble in fats and organic solvents and has some degree of toxicity when given in large amounts to animals. The results of these experiments supported the findings on the previously studied model compounds of homocysteine thiolactone, but how could thioretinamide interact with a transition metal, such as the cobalt atom of vitamin B12, to form a regulator of homocysteine formation in normal cells? Could such a substance slow the growth of malignant tumors and also affect the process of cellular respiration in normal cells?

Vitamin B12 is formed in nature only by microorganisms and yet is required in vanishingly small amounts for all living organisms. The recommended dietary allowance for vitamin B12 is 3 mcg per day for adult women and men. Vitamin B12 forms a beautiful, clear red solution and is sensitive to light, easily breaking down in the presence of strong light sources or radiant energy. Experiments with thioretinamide, the compound of homocysteine thiolactone and retinoic acid, showed that vitamin B12 makes a complex in which two molecules of thioretinamide are bound to the cobalt atom of vitamin B12.[34] When isolated from chemical synthesis, this complex, termed thioretinaco, is deep red-brown in solution and has a rich, fruity odor reminiscent of aged red wine.

Thioretinaco, the complex of thioretinamide and vitamin B12, becomes bound to cellular membranes, inhibits growth of malignant tumors in animals and prevents growth of tumors in animals given the chemical carcinogen urethane. It was exciting to find that thioretinaco is nontoxic when injected into normal tissues but strongly inhibits growth of human cancer cells in athymic, immunologically compromised mice when injected into the growing tumors.[35]

An extremely interesting effect of thioretinaco on normal mice is that injections of the compound cause the animals to become hyperactive, to consume excess food, to excrete excess urine and feces and yet fail to gain weight normally. Thioretinaco speeds up the processes of food consumption, waste excretion and activity so that weight gain is prevented in the animals. When the thioretinaco injections are stopped, the animals calm down, eat less food, excrete less and resume normal weight gain.

In considering the chemical structure of thioretinaco, it is apparent that the complex is bound to the membranes of mitochondria and endoplasmic reticulum within cell cytoplasm. Mitochondria are the power plants of cells which make chemical energy in the form of ATP by burning the electrons of the carbon atoms of food with oxygen that is transported to cells by the hemoglobin of red blood cells. Endoplasmic reticulum consists of layers in membranes within the cytoplasm of cells, where chemical formation of a wide variety of cellular constituents is accomplished and where toxic chemicals and carcinogens react with oxygen to become activated and excreted from cells. Thioretinaco is bound to these membranes, oriented in such a fashion that the sulfur atoms of the two thioretinamide groups reach the inner membrane surface and the phosphate group of cobalamin reaches the outer membrane surface.[14] Thioretinaco is anchored to the membrane by binding of its thioretinamide groups to the fats, cholesterol and phospholipids of the core of the membrane. In this way the many proteins of the membrane can interact with the cobalt atom of the vitamin B12 (cobalamin) group and the sulfur atoms of the thioretinamide groups of thioretinaco.

A breakthrough in understanding occurred when it was discovered that ozone, a highly reactive triple form of oxygen, can bridge the two sulfur atoms of thioretinaco, forming a cluster of five oxygen atoms that are bound to the active site.[14] Because of the positions of the oxygen and sulfur atoms of this thioretinaco ozonide oxygen complex, the active site is capable of binding ATP by two of its phosphate groups. When ATP is formed by reaction of ADP and phosphate on the F_1F_0 complex of inner mitochondrial membranes, the binding to the thioretinaco ozonide oxygen active site pulls the ATP off of the F_1F_0 complex and releases it into the inner compartment of the mitochondrion. This interaction causes electrons to flow from the proteins of the membrane into the ubiquinone (coenzyme Q10) of the membrane. The electrons are attracted to the thioretinaco ozonide oxygen complex through the thioretinamide and corrin (vitamin B12-like) groups, where they are added to the bound oxygen to form oxygen radicals.

Vitamin C stabilizes the oxygen radicals by forming monodehydroascorbate, a stable radical form of the vitamin. These bound oxygen radicals cause hydrogen ions (protons) to flow through the F_1F_0 complex, where they form water from the bound oxygen through several intermediate forms. During this process six molecules of ATP are formed for each oxygen molecule that is converted to two water molecules. The net result of this process is that chemical energy in the form of ATP is formed by the coupled reduction of oxygen to water. In summary, this complex process occurring in mitochondria allows the electrons from the carbon atoms of food molecules to combine with oxygen to produce chemical energy in the form of ATP for use in powering the vital functions of living cells.

Working independently, scientists in Russia discovered that a chemically modified form of vitamin B12 could interrupt the process of oxidative phosphorylation, preventing the orderly reaction of electrons and protons with oxygen and formation of ATP in mitochondria.[36] This analogue of vitamin B12 presumably interferes with the thioretinaco ozonide oxygen active site by competing with and short-circuiting its function in producing ATP. Other supporting evidence comes from the observation that an ozonized form of ADP reacts with phosphate to form ATP in a chemical system.[37] Over 30 years ago scientists in Germany and Wisconsin discovered that oxidized sulfur compounds, including homocysteine thiolactone and methionine, are active in producing ATP from ADP and phosphate in a chemical system.[38,39] Finally, scientists in India found that rats consuming a high-fat, high-cholesterol diet had decreased ability to form ATP in their livers, and treatment of the rats with vitamin B12 restored normal oxidative phosphorylation.[40] Very recently scientists in Germany found that homocysteine in rats causes abnormalities of mitochondria similar to those found in the livers of children with homocystinuria during the earliest stages of damage to arterial walls in arteriosclerosis.[41] All of these scientific studies support the crucial role of homocysteine in the function of mitochondria and point to the importance of these effects in the early stages of arteriosclerosis.

This biochemical theory of cellular respiration, explaining how cells burn the electrons from food with oxygen to produce chemical energy, has profound implications both for the induction of cancer by carcinogenic agents and for the induction of arteriosclerosis by the effects of increased homocysteine. In the case of cancer, the loss of thioretinaco from the membranes of cancer cells allows a buildup of reactive oxygen radicals within cancer cells. These reactive oxygen radicals interact with DNA, causing the chromosomal damage and gene mutations that are found in malignant cells. Reactive oxygen radicals also damage proteins, fats and other components of cancer cells. Experiments with transformed cells and cancer cells showed that methionine could partially restore the normal processing of oxygen and carbon within these cells.[42] This effect may be due to partial restoration of residual thioretinaco formed from increased methionine within these malignant cells.

The French embryologist L. Rapkine, working in the early 20th century, was able to deduce the extreme importance of normal oxygen processing in the development of embryonic cells during cell division. He discovered that during mitosis, the distribution of chromosomes to daughter cells during cell division, reactive oxygen radicals are greatly increased within dividing cells until the two new daughter cells are reconstituted.[43] This finding means that the normal process of oxidative phosphorylation is temporarily interrupted during cell division. A new complex of homocysteine thiolactone and cobalamin, named thioco, was found to promote cell division in normal and malignant cells, whereas thioretinaco prevents cell division.[44] Thus during cell division thioretinaco is temporarily converted to thioco, allowing the accumulation of oxygen radicals that Rapkine discovered, because of conversion of thioretinaco to thioretinamide and the cobalamin component of thioco.[45] In this way the normal process of cell division is regulated by alternation between a complex which processes electrons, thioretinaco ozonide, and a form of homocysteine thiolactone and cobalamin (thioco) which allows accumulation of oxygen radicals during cell division.

This experimental and theoretical explanation of the function of the homocysteine derivatives thioretinamide, thioretinaco and thioco in cellular growth and in processing of oxygen within cells allows new interpretations of the induction of cancer. What began as an observation of abnormal metabolism of homocysteine thiolactone in cancer cells[24] now constitutes a coherent theory that explains how carcinogenic agents induce cancer by depletion and inactivation of these newly discovered homocysteine compounds from the membranes of cells.[14]

Some examples of carcinogenic agents which lead to depletion of thioretinaco from membranes of malignant cells, according to this theory, are dietary methionine deficiency and the carcinogenic chemical ethionine, both of which interfere with normal processing of methionine within target cells [14] Cultured malignant cells characteristically have low levels of adenosyl methionine and elevated levels of adenosyl homocysteine within their cytoplasm. The DNA of malignant cells is characteristically depleted of methyl groups in cancer cells, an effect that is attributed to lowered levels of adenosyl methionine. Finally, the demonstration that homocysteine thiolactone is carcinogenic when painted on the skin of mice[46] or injected into animals given a chemical carcinogen[34] supports the theoretical formulation of induction of cancer by loss of thioretinaco and conversion to thioco in cellular membranes.

In summary, the discoveries of the role of homocysteine thiolactone, thioretinamide, thioretinaco and thioco in malignant cells offer a new way to unite the respiration, genetic and oncogene theories of the induction of cancer. The loss of thioretinaco ozonide from cell membranes leads to the abnormal respiration of mitochondria in malignant cells, with secondary accumulation of reactive oxygen radicals. The loss of thioretinaco also allows excessive synthesis of homocysteine thiolactone from methionine, causing aggregation and altered activation of nucleoproteins, abnormalities of cellular membranes, altered immunological recognition and increased growth potential through increased activation of oncogenes and increased formation of thioco.

HOMOCYSTEINE AND AGING

Except for children and young adults who frequently have illusions of eternal youth and immortality, most adults are very concerned about the nature of the aging process, how aging increases risk of disease, and how aging leads to deterioration of functions of the organs of the body. In many respects, the aging of one's body is as mysterious a process as the processes of birth, development, reproduction and death. Comparison of the bodies of newborns or young children with young adults focuses attention on aspects of development, maturation and reproduction. Comparison of the bodies of young adults with persons of advanced age calls attention to the profound and dramatic changes, with aging, in the appearance and function of the skin, eyes, ears, brain, heart, bones, muscles, kidneys and every other organ of the body.

Can the fundamental nature of the aging process be understood from the point of view of the many biochemical and physiological changes associated with aging? What are the current theories of aging which can explain the striking changes in appearance and function of all organs and tissues of the body? What inborn processes limit life span? Can these processes be accelerated or retarded? What is healthful aging and how can understanding of the functions of homocysteine, methionine, thioretinaco and adenosyl methionine contribute to promotion of healthful aging? Is it possible to slow the aging process and achieve healthful enjoyment of advanced years?

The miracle of living organisms, including human beings, is that the living cells and tissues of the body are surrounded by oxygen, a highly reactive gas which interacts with the nutrients of ingested food to power the growth, development, maintenance and declining function of all organs of the body. By combining oxygen with the electrons from the carbon atoms and other constituents of food, enough ATP is generated to operate all of the enzymes, membranes, chromosomes and other components of living cells in a continual process of renewal and regeneration of all the body's tissues.

In the aging process, the ability of the cells and tissues of living animals and humans to handle the reactive gas oxygen begins to decline. Less ATP becomes available to run the machinery of the body, and oxygen in the form of reactive oxygen radical forms begins to attack and degrade the vital constituents of cells and tissues. Less oxygen can be utilized by the tissues of aging animals and humans for maintaining the functions of the body's organs. For example, less ATP is available to power contractions of heart and muscles. Because less ATP is available, the function of brain and nerves to coordinate mental activity and muscular movements declines in advanced age. Because of the inability of aging cells and tissues to utilize oxygen efficiently, reactive oxygen radicals gradually accumulate and begin to degrade all cellular constituents by reaction with the fats of membranes, DNA of chromosomes, sugars of carbohydrates and amino acids of proteins. The principal method of extension of life span in experimental animals is life-long caloric restriction in the diet. By limiting the total amount of food that is converted to ATP by burning of hydrogen with oxygen, the generation of reactive oxygen radicals may be curtailed, decreasing damage to cells and tissues, allowing prolonged maximal survival in the range of 10 to 20 percent.

An example of a chemical degradation product of aging

is the pigment called lipofuscin. This pigment gradually accumulates within the cells of aging people through the degradation of the membranes of mitochondria of cell cytoplasm. Lipofuscin is produced by reaction of membrane components with oxygen radicals, forming highly oxidized, polymerized fats and proteins. Because cells cannot dispose of the lipofuscin pigment, it gradually accumulates within many cells of the body during aging. Experimentally, lipofuscin accumulates within the cells of animals deprived of dietary vitamin E, an antioxidant vitamin that retards oxygen radical reactions.

The radiochemical theory of aging based on the gradual reaction of cellular constituents with oxygen radicals was introduced in the 1950s.[47,48] More recently the loss of enzymatic function of proteins because of degradation by oxygen has been discovered in the cells and tissues of aging animals.[49] Many other examples of the reaction of oxygen with cellular constituents during aging attest to the soundness of the radiochemical theory of aging. However, the underlying reason for the loss of ability of senescent tissues to utilize oxygen normally and to prevent accumulation of toxic oxygen radicals is not explained in detail by this theory.

In the previous section, the theory which explains the participation of homocysteine in the process of oxygen utilization and ATP production is explained in detail. Thioretinaco, which is composed of two thioretinamide groups bound to vitamin B12, reacts with ozone and oxygen to provide an active site for burning of the electrons of food with oxygen to produce water and chemical energy in the form of ATP. In the aging process the decline in the ability of cells and tissues to consume oxygen and ATP was suggested to be the gradual loss of thioretinaco from the membranes of mitochondria and microsomes of all cells of the body.[45] According to this theory, because the active site for energy production by oxidative phosphorylation is gradually lost in aging, reactive oxygen radicals produced from incomplete reaction of oxygen with electrons and protons accumulate within cells and escape into the tissues of aging animals.[50] This hypothesis explains why reactive oxygen radicals accumulate in aging tissues, damaging the fats of membranes, the proteins of enzymes and the DNA of chromosomes, causing chemical deterioration of all of the chemical constituents of the body.[47,48]

The normal defenses of cells and tissues against excess oxygen radicals are dependent upon antioxidant nutrients, such as vitamin E and carotenoids like lycopene and carotene of vegetables, glutathione within cell cytoplasm and the enzymes superoxide dismutase and catalase. All of these chemicals and enzymes inactivate and dispose of reactive oxygen radicals by direct chemical or enzymatic effects. In aging this complex protective system is gradually overwhelmed by excess oxygen radicals because of loss of the thioretinaco ozonide active sites from cellular membranes.

Many of the epidemiological studies of arteriosclerosis have shown that human blood levels of homocysteine gradually increase with age.[4] Early studies with animals showed that homocysteine thiolactone accumulates in the livers of older animals.[51] Furthermore, the dimerized and oxidized homocysteine form, homocystine, of predominates in the livers of older animals. The reactive monomeric form of homocysteine which has not reacted with oxygen predominates in the livers of young animals. The decreased ability of aging tissues to prevent gradual accumulation of homocysteine thiolactone and to prevent reaction of homocysteine with oxygen is also related to gradual loss of thioretinaco from cellular membranes, according to this theory.[45,50] Therefore, homocysteine thiolactone gradually accumulates in aging tissues, and blood homocysteine increases because of the increased reaction of homocysteine thiolactone with water and the transport of homocysteine from cells into body fluids.

The master regulator of levels of methionine within cells, adenosyl methionine, gradually declines within the aging brain, liver and other organs as well as in the blood of man and animals.[52–54] Recent studies have shown that adenosyl methionine is lower in the blood of patients with coronary artery disease than in controls.[55] Thioretinaco ozonide was suggested as an alternative process by which methionine reacts with ATP to form adenosyl methionine.[45] As thioretinaco is lost from cellular membranes during aging, the cells and tissues gradually lose their ability to maintain normal levels of adenosyl methionine because of decreased ability of residual thioretinaco ozonide to form this compound from methionine. Adenosyl methionine is the substance which controls the flow of methyl groups (one-carbon fragments) to modify the chemical structures of hormones, DNA and other vital constituents of cells and tissues. The efficiency of this methylation process by adenosyl methionine declines with aging. Some examples of this process are the decreased production of melatonin, epinephrine and other neuroendocrine hormones in aging animals[56] and the decreased methylation of DNA within senescent cells in culture.[57]

As discussed previously, increased blood levels of homocysteine cause vascular damage and arteriosclerosis, and the depletion of thioretinaco ozonide from the membranes of normal cells by carcinogenic agents leads to abnormal cellular growth potential and abnormal utilization of oxygen by malignant cells. During the aging process the gradual loss of thioretinaco ozonide from cellular membranes leads to increased production of homocysteine thiolactone and its complex with vitamin B12, thioco. Dietary imbalance of methionine, folic acid and pyridoxine increases the conversion of methionine to homocysteine during atherogenesis, and the loss of thioretinaco ozonide from cellular membranes during aging increases the reaction of homocysteine thiolactone with low-density lipoprotein, explaining the close correlation of susceptibility to arteriosclerosis with age. Similarly, the loss of thioretinaco ozonide from cellular membranes during the aging process increases susceptibility of cells to malignant transformation by carcinogenic chemicals, radiation or viruses, explaining the close correlation of susceptibility to cancer with age. In a similar way, overproduction of homocysteine during aging may increase susceptibility to arthritis and other autoimmune diseases of aging by interference with the function of immune cells[58] and lead to alteration of antigenic properties of tissues in the autoimmune diseases of aging.[45]

Although the presumed loss of thioretinaco ozonide from cellular membranes explains important aspects of changing oxygen utilization, energy production and degeneration of cellular components with aging, many additional features of senescence and senility need more complete elucidation by medical science. The degeneration of elastic tissue, the coarsening of collagen fibers of skin and the degeneration of cartilage and bone produce some of the most striking changes in appearance and function of the body in aging. Homocysteine may have a role in these aging changes by effects on the structure of elastin and collagen, which are as yet incompletely understood.[45,50]

The very characteristic failure of contractility of heart muscle, leading to congestive heart failure in many aged persons, may be related to loss of oxygen utilization and ATP formation because of loss of thioretinaco ozonide from the membranes of heart cells. This interesting possibility needs careful exploration by medical investigators in the future. A striking feature of some children with homocystinuria is the lightening of hair color that is reversed by vitamin B6 therapy.[59] Homocysteine interferes with normal melanin pigment formation by interaction with copper,[60] and this effect may have relevance to the graying of hair in normal aging. The role of homocysteine in the rare human diseases of accelerated aging, progeria and Werner's syndrome, has not as yet been determined. Recently the defective gene coding for helicase, an enzyme controlling DNA structure, has been described in Werner's syndrome.[61]

Some other theories of aging are the "error catastrophe" theory of cumulative damage to genes and proteins,[62] the DNA-genetic control theory of aging[63] and the neuroendocrine theory of aging.[56] The error catastrophe theory predicts an accumulation of proteins of abnormal structure because of gradual accumulation of genetic damage from interaction of reactive oxygen radicals with DNA, causing erroneous amino acid sequences of proteins. Except for recent evidence of oxidative changes in enzyme structure with aging, presumably caused by reaction of oxygen with proteins,[49] no clear evidence has been found to support the error catastrophe theory.

The DNA-genetic control theory of aging emphasizes the important role of evolution and genetic control of the life span of animals.[63] Evolution has programmed senescence and mortality into the genetic control of life span so that through death senescent parents make ecological space available for their offspring. Recent studies with fruit flies and roundworms have suggested genetic control by genes that significantly prolong life span. The mode of action of the products of these genes controlling aging is suggested by the finding of extension of life span in transgenic fruit flies containing extra genes for superoxide dismutase and catalase.[64] This result generally supports the important role of reactive oxygen radicals in aging.

The neuroendocrine theory of aging generally attributes control of the aging process to declines in the secretion of a variety of hormones, including melatonin, dehydroepiadrosterone, testosterone, estrogen and others. The theory generally presumes that a brain center such as the hypothalamus is responsible for the decreased secretion of multiple hormones during aging. While there is no doubt about the decline in secretion of many hormones during aging, there is little evidence for the primary function of the brain in coordinating the many changes in cells throughout the senescent body through these hormonal changes. Secondary effects of oxygen radicals, DNA with altered expression, or loss of thioretinaco ozonide and increased formation of homocysteine thiolactone, however, may well involve altered brain function and declining production of many hormones under the control of brain centers.

As explained in Chapter 5, the lifelong consumption of an optimal diet for prevention of arteriosclerosis decreases risk of vascular disease by counteracting the elevation of blood homocysteine levels. Although medical science currently has no specific therapy or preventive strategy for extension of maximum life span, decreased risk of arteriosclerosis will contribute in a major way to the achievement of healthful aging and increased life expectancy. Lifelong consumption of an optimal diet will also decrease risk of developing cancer, arthritis and other degenerative diseases of aging. In this way the final decades of human life may be enjoyed with relative freedom from disease, even though total life span may not be lengthened significantly.

MEDICINE FOR THE NEW MILLENNIUM

Medicine in the new millennium will use the medical discovery of the causative role of homocysteine as a starting point in the rational conquest of the diseases of aging. Improved methods will be developed for the complete, rapid, routine measurement of total homocysteine in blood. New methods for the analysis of low-density lipoprotein and homocysteine aggregates will allow closer correlation with the progression of arteriosclerosis. In this way the homocysteine theory of arteriosclerosis will become established in the 21st century as the mainstream path to understanding the cause, prevention and treatment of the most important diseases in the population.

The complex interaction of growth factors, macrophages, endothelial and smooth muscle cells and the signalling substances of immune and inflammatory cells will become understood more clearly in the atherogenic process. For example, the important function of nitric oxide, a reactive radical of one nitrogen and one oxygen atom, in relaxing blood vessels and lowering blood pressure has already been related to reaction with homocysteine to form nitrosohomocysteine.[65] The anesthetic gas nitrous oxide, the less reactive combination of two atoms of nitrogen and one atom of oxygen, interacts with vitamin B12 to decrease formation of methionine, leading to elevated blood levels of homocysteine. The more reactive nitric oxide may be found in future work to interact with thioretinaco ozonide to displace oxygen and decrease production of ATP by oxidative phosphorylation. Thus the reversible relaxing effect of nitric oxide on blood vessels may be related to decreased production of chemical energy in the form of ATP, diminishing the contractility of muscle cells of the arterial wall. Increased understanding of this area of cardiovascular physiology will help medical scientists to understand and to control the effects of hypertension and to develop new approaches to controlling congestive heart failure.

In the future the roles of *Chlamydia pneumoniae,*[66] cytomegalovirus and herpesvirus will be more clearly defined and related to production of polyamines of viruses from adenosyl methionine, and alteration of homocysteine formation by infected arterial wall cells. These developments will enable medical scientists to understand the importance of controlling a wide range of risk factors in prevention of arteriosclerosis.

Since malignant cells are believed to have enhanced growth potential because of the loss of thioretinaco ozonide from cellular membranes, medical scientists may find ways of replacing this substance within malignant cells or preventing its loss from cells that are targeted by carcinogenic chemicals, viruses or radiation. The cytokine interferon is known to prevent the toxic effect of ozone in lung tissue[67] and to decrease the production of reactive oxygen radicals in hepatitis C patients.[68] These discoveries suggest that interferon and other cytokines may be useful in enhancing the anticancer effects of thioretinaco ozonide. The mode of action of interferon may be to affect the membrane binding and orientation of thioretinaco ozonide, preserving and enhancing its function within malignant cells and preventing growth and spread of cancer cells throughout the body.

The closely related substances thioretinaco, thioretinamide and thioco control cell division and cellular growth and function.[45] A better understanding of the role of these substances in organization and function of the membranes of cells will lead to new discoveries in controlling transmission of neural impulses, contractility of heart muscle, blood vessel wall muscle cells and skeletal muscle cells. The deterioration of these functions with aging may be ameliorated by replacement or enhanced function in the membranes of cells of aging animals and man. The homocysteine derivative, homocysteic acid, containing three extra oxygen atoms, is a potent excitor of nerve function. Vitamin B12, vitamin B6 and folic acid may control human psychiatric or neurological abnormalities by affecting the formation of homocysteic acid in the nervous system.[69]

The important role of folic acid in prevention of birth defects, particularly neural tube defects such as spina bifida and anencephaly, has been related to effects of homocysteine on mother and developing fetus.[70] This discovery shows that improved understanding of the control of homocysteine formation may lead to important advances in the prevention of common birth defects by introducing folic acid into the food supply of pregnant women as mandated by the U.S. Food and Drug Administration beginning in 1998. In addition, this discovery points to the importance of homocysteine in the control of normal cell division and cellular function in the developing human fetus.

One of the most debilitating aspects of human aging is the degenerative disease of bones and joints known as osteoarthritis. The only currently effective way of ameliorating the effects of this condition known to medical science is surgical removal of the hip or knee joint and implantation of artificial prosthetic joints. By understanding the effects of aging on the cells and tissues of cartilage and bone, theoretically related to loss of thioretinaco ozonide from cellular membranes, it may be possible for the next generation of medical investigators to develop strategies for prevention of osteoarthritis. At present the most promising way to prevent the disease is lifelong consumption of an optimal diet which provides the cells of bone and cartilage with balanced amounts of methionine, folic acid, vitamin B6 and vitamin B12, preventing elevated homocysteine levels. Although osteoarthritis is not caused by complications of arteriosclerosis, the beneficial effects of an optimal diet may slow progression of both degenerative diseases through similar effects on connective tissues of arteries, bones and joints.

Rheumatoid arthritis is an autoimmune disease that is related to but distinct from osteoarthritis. In rheumatoid arthritis antibodies are formed against components of bone, cartilage and synovia of joints, and the immune cells of the body attack the joints of most parts of the body, causing inflammation, fibrosis and joint destruction. Although this disease can affect children in the juvenile form of rheumatoid arthritis, most sufferers from arthritis are middle-aged or elderly. The finding of immune cells that are modified by homocysteine in this disorder[58] may lead to a new understanding of its cause and prevention. Other autoimmune diseases of aging, including thyroiditis with Grave's disease, pernicious anemia and lupus erythematosus, are diseases that may arise because of alteration of the antigenic properties of the thyroid gland, acid-secreting cells of the stomach and circulating DNA fragments in the blood, respectively. These diseases may be shown by future work to be related to increased homocysteine thiolactone formation secondary to the effects of aging because of loss of thioretinaco from cellular membranes.

The consequences of the homocysteine revolution for medicine in the new millennium will be profound. Through better understanding of the nature of the aging process, the role of diet and other risk factors in the causation of arteriosclerosis, and the importance of thioretinaco and related substances in cancer, better control of the principal degenerative diseases of aging will enable large segments of the population to enjoy healthful aging well into their advanced years. Because of increased longevity and freedom from disease, the elderly population will require less interventional medicine through effective disease prevention. This development will call for major accommodation and changes in the attitudes, actions and philosophy of the medical, pharmaceutical, nutritional and governmental sectors of society.

REFERENCES

1. Kilmer S. McCully, "Vascular pathology of homocysteinemia: Implications for the pathogenesis of arteriosclerosis." *American Journal of Pathology* 56:111–128, 1969.
2. Vincent DuVigneaud, *A Trail of Research in Sulfur Chemistry and Metabolism and Related Fields* (Ithaca, New York: Cornell University Press, 1952).
3. Kilmer S. McCully, "Homocysteine and vascular disease." *Nature Medicine* 2:386–389, 1996.
4. Ottar Nygard, Stein Emil Vollset, Helga Refsum, Inger Stensvold, Aage Tverdal, Jan Erik Nordrehaug, Per Magne Ueland and Gunner Kvale, "Total plasma homocysteine and cardiovascular risk profile. The Hordaland homocysteine study." *Journal of the American Medical Association* 274:1526–1533, 1995.

5. Archibald E. Garrod, "A contribution to the study of alkaptonuria." *Proceedings of the Royal Medical and Surgical Society* 2:130, 1899.
6. Archibald E. Garrod, *Inborn Errors of Metabolism* (London: Oxford University Press, 1923).
7. Charles R. Scriver, Arthur L. Beaudet, William S. Sly, David Valle, John B. Stanbury, James B. Wyngaarden and Donald S. Frederickson, editors, *The Metabolic Basis of Inherited Disease,* 7th Edition (New York: McGraw-Hill, 1995).
8. B.W. Uhlendorf and S. Harvey Mudd, "Cystathionine synthase in tissue culture derived from human skin: Enzyme defect in homocystinuria." *Science* 160:1007–1009, 1968.
9. Kilmer S. McCully, "Importance of homocysteine-induced abnormalities of proteoglycan structure in arteriosclerosis." *American Journal of Pathology* 59:181–193, 1970.
10. Kilmer S. McCully, "Macromolecular basis for homocysteine-induced changes in proteoglycan structure in growth and arteriosclerosis." *American Journal of Pathology* 66:83–95, 1972.
11. Kilmer S. McCully, "Homocysteine and vascular disease: Role of folate, choline and lipoproteins in homocysteine metabolism." In: Bernard H. Szuhaj and Steven H. Zeisel, editors, *Proceedings of the 7th International Congress on Phospholipids* (Champaign, Illinois: American Oil Chemists Society Press, 1997), *In Press.*
12. Philip W. Robbins and Fritz Lipmann, "Identification of enzymatically active sulfate as adenosine 3' phosphate 5' phosphosulfate." *Journal of the American Chemical Society* 78: 2652–2653, 1956.
13. Kilmer S. McCully and Michael P. Vezeridis, "Chemopreventive and antineoplastic activity of N-homocysteine thiolactonyl retinamide." *Carcinogenesis* 8:1559–1562, 1987.
14. Kilmer S. McCully, "Chemical pathology of homocysteine. II. Carcinogenesis and homocysteine thiolactone metabolism." *Annals of Clinical and Laboratory Science* 24:27–59, 1994.
15. P.R. Sundaresen, "Vitamin A and the sulfate-activating enzymes." *Biochimica et Biophysica Acta* 113:95–109, 1966.

16. Kilmer S. McCully, "Homocysteine metabolism in scurvy, growth and arteriosclerosis." *Nature* 231:391–392, 1971.
17. Elie Rapoport, E.W. Schroeder and Paul W. Black, "Retinoic acid-promoted expansion of total cellular ATP pools in 3T3 cells can mediate its stimulatory and growth-inhibitory effects." *Journal of Cellular Physiology* 110:318–322, 1982.
18. J.M. Dehnel and M.J.P. Francis, "Somatomedin (sulphation factor)-like activity of homocystine." *Clinical Science* 43:903–906, 1972.
19. Pierre Clopath, Virginia C. Smith and Kilmer S. McCully, "Growth promotion by homocysteic acid." *Science* 192: 372–374, 1976.
20. Kilmer S. McCully and Robert B. Wilson, "Homocysteine theory of arteriosclerosis." *Atherosclerosis* 22:215–227, 1975.
21. Roberta Ricci e Kilmer S. McCully, "Azione dell'acido omocysteico su culture di condriociti in vitro." *Atti Associati Genetica Italia* 17:25–28, 1972.
22. H.K. Schedewie, C. Lipinski and H. Schmidt, "Elevated growth hormone levels in homocystinuria: Mechanism of tall stature?" *Clinical Research* 25:69A, 1977.
23. Marek Naruszewicz, Ewa Mirkiewicz, Andrzej J. Olszewski and Kilmer S. McCully, "Thiolation of low-density lipoprotein by homocysteine thiolactone causes aggregation and increased interaction with cultured macrophages." *Nutrition, Metabolism and Cardiovascular Diseases* 4:70–77, 1994.
24. Kilmer S. McCully, "Homocysteine thiolactone metabolism in malignant cells." *Cancer Research* 36:3198–3202, 1976.
25. James D. Watson and Francis H.C. Crick, "A structure for deoxyribose nucleic acid." *Nature* 171:737–738, 1953.
26. Otto Warburg, "On the origin of cancer cells." *Science* 123: 309–314, 1956.
27. Albert Szent-Gyorgi, "Cell division and cancer." *Science* 149:34–37, 1965.
28. Kilmer S. McCully and Michael P. Vezeridis, "Homocysteine thiolactone in arteriosclerosis and cancer." *Research Communications in Chemical Pathology and Pharmacology* 59: 107–119, 1988.
29. Heironim Jakubowski and Emanuel Goldman, "Synthesis of

homocysteine thiolactone by methionyl-tRNA synthetase in cultured mammalian cells." *Federation of European Biochemical Societies Letters* 317:237–240, 1993.

30. Kilmer S. McCully, E. Raymond Boyco and Gene B. Carpenter, "Homocysteine thiolactone perchlorate: X-ray crystallography of a lipophilic salt." *Chemical-Biological Interactions* 56:121–124, 1985.
31. Kilmer S. McCully and Peter Clopath, "Homocysteine compounds which influence the growth of a malignant neoplasm." *Chemotherapy* 23:44–49, 1977.
32. Kilmer S. McCully and Michael P. Vezeridis, "Antineoplastic activity of N-maleimide homocysteine thiolactone amide encapsulated within liposomes." *Proceedings of the Society for Experimental Biology and Medicine* 180:57–61, 1985.
33. Kilmer S. McCully and Michael P. Vezeridis, "Antineoplastic activity of a rhodium trichloride complex of oxalyl homocysteine thiolactone." *Cancer Investigation* 5:25–30, 1987.
34. Kilmer S. McCully and Michael P. Vezeridis, "Chemopreventive effect of N-homocysteine thiolactonyl retinamido cobalamin on carcinogenesis by ethyl carbamate in mice." *Proceedings of the Society for Experimental Biology and Medicine* 191:346–351, 1989.
35. Kilmer S. McCully, George N. Tzanakakis and Michael P. Vezeridis, "Inhibition of neoplastic growth by N-homocysteine thiolactonyl retinamido cobalamin." *Research Communications in Chemical Pathology and Pharmacology* 66:117–122, 1989.
36. L.L. Kiseleva, G.N. Novadarova, M.E. Wol'pin and A.D. Vinogradov, "Influence of a cobalt dehydrocorrin complex on mitochondria." *Biokhimiya* 47:1877–1882, 1982.
37. Richard D. Lippman, "A new method that investigates superoxide versus respiration in vitro using bioluminescence and Sepharose-bound adenosine derivatives." *Journal of Biochemical and Biophysical Methods* 6:81–87, 1982.
38. T. Wieland und E. Bauerlein, "N-acetyl homocysteine thiolacton als Vermitter einer oxydativen Synthese von Adenosindiphosphat und Adenosintriphosphat aus Adenosinmonophosphat

und Orthophosphat." *Chemiche Berichte* 100:3869–3876, 1967.

39. D.O. Lambeth and Henry A. Lardy, "The oxidation of thioethers by bromine: A model system for oxidative phosphorylation." *Biochemistry* 8:3395–3402, 1969.
40. T.G. Reddi and M.C. Nath, "Influence of vitamin B12 and glucose cycloacetoacetate hydrolysate on oxidative phosphorylation in liver mitochondria of rats fed an atherogenic diet." *Journal of Vitaminology* 17:101–104, 1971.
41. Dietrich Matthias, Curt-H. Becker, R. Riegler and Paul H. Kindling, "Homocysteine-induced arteriosclerosis-like alternations of the aorta in normotensive and hypertensive rats following application of high doses of methionine." *Atherosclerosis* 122:201–216, 1996.
42. Paula Boerner and Efraim Racker, "Methionine-sensitive glycolysis in transformed cells." *Proceedings of the National Academy of Sciences USA* 82:6750–6754, 1985.
43. L. Rapkine, "L'energetique de developpment de l'oeuf." *Archives of Anatomy and Microscopy* 25:482–488, 1929.
44. Kilmer S. McCully, George N. Tzanakakis and Michael P. Vezeridis, "Effect of the homocysteine thiolactonyl derivatives, thioretinaco, thioretinamide and thioco on growth and lactate production by malignant cells." *Research Communications in Chemical Pathology and Pharmacology* 77: 125–128, 1992.
45. Kilmer S. McCully, "Chemical pathology of homocysteine. III. Cellular function and aging." *Annals of Clinical and Laboratory Science* 24:134–152, 1994.
46. Kilmer S. McCully and Michael P. Vezeridis, "Histopathological effects of homocysteine thiolactone on epithelial and stromal tissues." *Experimental and Molecular Pathology* 51:159–170, 1989.
47. Denham Harman, "Aging: A theory based on free radical and radiation chemistry." *Journal of Gerontology* 11: 298–300, 1956.
48. Deham Harman, "The aging process." *Proceedings of the National Academy of Sciences USA* 78:7124–7128, 1981.

49. Earl R. Stadtman, "Protein oxidation and aging." *Science* 257:1220–1224, 1992.
50. Andrzej J. Olszewski and Kilmer S. McCully, "Homocysteine metabolism and the oxidative modification of proteins and lipids." *Free Radical Biology and Medicine* 14:683–693, 1993.
51. Kilmer S. McCully, "Growth disorders and homocysteine metabolism." *Annals of Clinical and Laboratory Science* 5:147–152, 1975.
52. Ross J. Baldessarini and Irwin J. Kopin, "S-adenosyl methionine in brain and other tissues." *Journal of Neurochemistry* 13:769–777, 1966.
53. Giorgio Stramentinoli, Maria Gualano, Emilia Catto and Sergio Algeri, "Tissue levels of S-adenosylmethionine in aging rats." *Journal of Gerontology* 32:392–394, 1977.
54. C. Bohuon and L. Caillard, "S-adenosyl methionine in human blood." *Clinica Chimica Acta* 33:256, 1971.
55. Franziska M.T. Loehrer, Christian P. Angst, Walter E. Haefeli, Paul P. Jordan, Rudolf Ritz and Brian Fowler, "Low whole-blood S-adenosyl methionine and correlation between 5-methyltetrahydrofolate and homocysteine in coronary artery disease." *Arteriosclerosis, Thrombosis and Vascular Biology* 16:727–733, 1996.
56. Vladimir Dilman and Ward Dean, *The Neuroendocrine Theory of Aging and Degenerative Disease* (Pensacola, Florida: The Center for Bio-Gerontology, 1992).
57. Vincent L. Wilson and Peter A. Jones, "DNA methylation decreases in aging but not in immortal cells." *Science* 220:1055–1057, 1983.
58. Xiao-Ming Gao, Paul Wordsworth, Andrew J. McMichael, Myo M. Kyaw, Martin Seifert, David Rees and Gordon Dougan, "Homocysteine modification of HLA antigens and its immunological consequences." *European Journal of Immunology* 26:1443–1450, 1996.
59. G. Winston Barber and George L. Spaeth, "The successful treatment of homocystinuria with pyridoxine." *Journal of Pediatrics* 75:463–478, 1969.
60. Orit Reish, DeWayne Townsend, Susan A. Berry, Michael

Y. Tsai and Richard A. King, "Tyrosinase inhibition due to interaction of homocyst(e)ine with copper: The mechanism of reversible hyperpigmentation in homocystinuria due to cystathionine beta synthase deficiency." *American Journal of Human Genetics* 57:127–132, 1995.

61. Chang-En Yu, Junko Oshima, Ying-Hui Fu, Ellen M. Wijsman, Fuki Hisana, Reid Alisch, Shellie Matthews, Jan Nakura, Tetsuro Miki, Samir Ouais, George M. Martin, John Mulligan and Gerard D. Schellenberg, "Positional cloning of the Werner's syndrome gene." *Science* 272:258–262, 1996.
62. Leslie E. Orgel, "Ageing of clones of mammalian cells." *Nature* 243:441–445, 1973.
63. Caleb E. Finch, *Longevity, Senescence and the Genome* (Chicago: University of Chicago Press, 1990).
64. William C. Orr and Rajindar S. Sohal, "Extension of life span by overexpression of superoxide dismutase and catalase in *Drosophila melanogaster.*" *Science* 263:1128–1130, 1994.
65. Jonathan S. Stamler and Joseph Loscalzo, "Endothelium-derived relaxing factor modulates the atherothrombotic effects of homocysteine." *Journal of Cardiovascular Pharmacology* 20(Suppl 12):S202–S204, 1992.
66. Cho-chou Kuo, Allan Shor, Lee Ann Campbell, Hideto Fukushi, Dorothy L. Patton and J. Thomas Grayston, "Demonstration of *Chlamydia pneumoniae* in atherosclerotic lesions of coronary arteries." *Journal of Infectious Diseases* 167: 841–849, 1993.
67. Daniel Dziedzic and Harold J. White, "Quantitation of ozone-induced lung lesion density after treatment with an interferon inducer or an anti-interferon antibody." *Toxicology Letters* 39:51–62, 1987.
68. Victoria Higueras, Angel Raya, Jose Manuel Rodrigo, Miguel Angel Serra, Joaquin Roma and Francisca J. Romero, "Interferon decreases serum lipid peroxidation products of hepatitis C patients." *Free Radical Biology and Medicine* 16:131–133, 1994.
69. C.R. Santhosh-Kumar, K.L. Hassell, J.C. Deutsch and J.F. Kolhouse, "Are neuropsychiatric manifestations of folate, cobalamin and pyridoxine deficiency mediated through im-

balance in excitatory sulfur amino acids?" *Medical Hypotheses* 43:239–244, 1994.
70. Johan B. Ubbink, "Is an elevated circulating maternal homocysteine concentration a risk factor for neural tube defects?" *Nutrition Reviews* 53:173–175, 1995.

THE AUTHOR

Kilmer S. McCully, M.D. is a pathologist at the Veterans Affairs Medical Center in Providence, Rhode Island. A graduate of both Harvard College and Harvard Medical School, Dr. McCully is credited with one of the major medical and scientific breakthroughs of this century. He has been the subject of much media attention since the story of his discovery of the homocysteine-heart disease connection was published in the *New York Times* in July 1995. Dr. McCully is the author of many research articles and holds several U.S. patents on anticancer homocysteine compounds. This is his first book.

Index

Index

Index

Index

Index

Index